Our Separate Ways

OUR SEPARATE WAYS

THE STRUGGLE *for the* FUTURE
of the U.S.-ISRAEL ALLIANCE

★ ★ ★ ★ ★

DANA H. ALLIN
STEVEN N. SIMON

PUBLIC AFFAIRS
NEW YORK

IISS An International Institute for Strategic Studies book

PublicAffairs books are available at special discounts for bulk purchases in the U.S. by corporations,
institutions, and other organizations. For more information, please contact the Special Markets
Department at the Perseus Books Group, 2300 Chestnut Street, Suite 200, Philadelphia, PA 19103, call
(800) 810-4145, ext. 5000, or e-mail special.markets@perseusbooks.com.

Book design by Milenda Nan Ok Lee

The Library of Congress has cataloged the printed edition as follows:
Names: Allin, Dana H., 1958– author. | Simon, Steven, author.
Title: Our separate ways : the struggle for the future of the U.S.-Israel alliance / Dana H. Allin and
    Steven N. Simon.
Description: First edition. | New York : PublicAffairs, [2016] | ?2016
Identifiers: LCCN 2016006444 (print) | LCCN 2016006749 (ebook) | ISBN 9781610396417 (hardback) |
    ISBN 9781610396424 (ebook)
Subjects: LCSH: Israel—Foreign relations—United States. | United States—Foreign relations—Israel. |
    BISAC: POLITICAL SCIENCE / International Relations / Diplomacy. | HISTORY / Middle East /
    Israel.
Classification: LCC E183.8.I7 A43 2016 (print) | LCC E183.8.I7 (ebook) | DDC 327.5694073—dc23
LC record available at http://lccn.loc.gov/2016006444

First Edition
10 9 8 7 6 5 4 3 2 1

To David P. Calleo
—D. H. A.

To Julius and Anna Simon: May their memories be for a blessing
—S. N. S

Contents

Introduction

IN MAY 2011—sixteen months before President Obama's reelection, when his prospects were starting to look precarious—the prime minister of Israel arrived at the White House to lecture the president of the United States. As astonished journalists watched and recorded, Benjamin Netanyahu instructed a stone-faced Obama on the Jewish people's many millennia of struggle, and on the impossibility of Israel ever returning to anything like the June 1967 borders that Obama himself had, just the day before, established as the basis for negotiating a just and lasting peace.

White House aides were furious, and they became angrier still as Netanyahu returned in the months and even weeks before the election and appeared to intervene—brazenly, as they saw it—on the side of Republican nominee, Mitt Romney. Among the Republican charges that he seemed to be backing was that a feckless Obama preferred appeasement to confronting Iran's growing nuclear capacity and its threat to Israel's existence. Obama, Romney enjoyed repeating, was inclined to throw "Israel under the bus." In political terms, this seemed a potent and worrying charge.

And yet a strange thing happened. Election night 2012 was over by 11:15 P.M. eastern time. Obama won every swing state but North Carolina with an ease that suggested an emerging Democratic lock on the Electoral College.

The entire episode was dismaying for leaders of the pro-Israel lobby in the United States, one of whom complained to us privately that by ineptly injecting Israel into U.S. partisan politics, the emperor—that is, the supposed power of the Israeli government and its U.S. supporters in Washington—now stood naked. That embarrassment was compounded over the next three years as Netanyahu led his mainly Republican allies in an effort in the U.S.

Congress to kill the nuclear deal with Iran—one of the central achievements of Obama's presidency—and failed again. These missteps were correspondingly satisfying to the Israel lobby's critics, who have long felt that American, and ultimately Israeli, interests require a more "normal" relationship between the two countries, and that this will only be possible once the lobby becomes less powerful.

The satisfaction and the dismay are both understandable. But both sides are missing something important. The U.S.–Israeli alliance is not simply under strain; it is at risk of being fundamentally transformed by long-term trends in both countries that will be impossible to stop and difficult to manage. Powerful demographic and cultural currents in Israel and the United States are driving the two countries apart. On the American side, the commitment of a postwar generation to the ideals of Zionism is fading as that generation moves toward old age. The demographic basis of support for an intimate alliance is also eroding. Four generations of intermarriage have weakened both Jewish identity and the visceral attachment that many Jews have felt since the establishment of the State of Israel in 1948. American Jews are not destined to disappear in any genetic sense, but as a cohesive community dedicated to Israel's security and deeply entangled in its fate, they are dwindling. This will leave behind a tougher core of Jews who are often orthodox in their religious practice and mainly conservative in their political preferences. As we shall see, this will place them outside the political mainstream, even as it concentrates them in fewer and less dispersed communities.

A more general decline in the religious commitment of younger Americans will also have consequences for their commitment to Israel. Conservative Christianity remains powerful and almost exclusively Republican; yet even organized Evangelicalism shows signs of change. The shifting preferences for religious organizations in an age of social media, splintered communities, and demographic change could eventually affect the priorities of younger Evangelicals. They are not the Jerry Falwell—let alone the Billy Graham—generation, packing stadium rallies staged by Christians United for Israel. Some have other worries and other projects closer to the social gospel than to more traditional conservative causes. These newer preoccupations no longer emphasize American support for a strong Israel so that the eschatological prophecies of the Book of Revelation come to pass. When they see news coverage of civilian deaths in Gaza and they ask themselves—what would

Jesus do?—the answer is not self-evident. For now, this is only a nascent trend within a broader hardening of political and social attitudes. Time will tell whether it gets traction as the country as a whole shifts to the left.

The consolidation of a Likud–Republican alliance and the parallel emergence of a structural advantage for the Democratic Party in national elections will bring further trouble to the alliance. As the ardor of Democrats has cooled, their fortunes appear to be riding on the emergence of a bigger and more engaged Latino electorate. These voters are simply less concerned about the Middle East and, to the extent they harbor the religious convictions acquired in their countries of origin, they are less likely to share the concerns of Jewish Americans. The considerable American Jewish disappointment with Israel for its treatment of Palestinians, accurately identified by Peter Beinart, is therefore not even the most important of structural American changes.[1]

Inverse changes are underway in Israel. Today, half of all Israeli preschool children are either ultra-Orthodox or Arab. These are the two fastest growing communities in Israel, and they are also poorly educated. Prospects for the "Global Israel" that liberal Zionist visionaries like Bernard Avishai hope to see supplanting the quest for "Greater Israel" are dimming as the Israeli educational system groans under the weight of burgeoning poorer populations and long-term underfunding.[2] And the political instincts of these students are beginning to reflect their lackluster training and the rhetoric of right-wing politicians. Surveys of Jewish eighteen-year-olds reveal a preference for a strong leader, a disdain for democracy, and a readiness to curb the civil liberties of non-Jews. The ultra-Orthodox Israeli communities that venerate the great ecstatic rabbis of eighteenth-century Poland, Hungary, Moldova, and Romania, and which retain the sartorial splendor of that time and place, now embrace Israelis whose ancestors came from Iraq, Morocco, and Yemen.[3] Meanwhile, right-wing, ultra-Orthodox young men are joining combat units they had long sought to avoid, recasting the character of the Israel Defense Force (IDF). IDF officer candidates are much more likely to identify themselves as religious than they were only a decade ago. And there are political moves to further define the country by its religion. The Israeli Knesset in 2015 debated a bill that would have made Israel "the nation state of the Jewish people" and by definition exclude from a place in the national narrative the large part of its population that is not

Jewish. (The bill was shelved, to the credit of many Israeli lawmakers, but it was supported by Netanyahu, and it could come back.) These changes will produce an Israel that looks increasingly unfamiliar to many Americans.

So the bad blood between the Obama administration and the Netanyahu government is a symptom, not the cause, of serious underlying problems. And those in both countries who imagine that a full separation would be a good thing—relieving their respective states of profound moral and strategic burdens—should think hard. Such a separation would be terribly damaging to the fundamental interests of both Israel and the United States. For Israel the danger should be obvious. Yet many Israelis whom we interviewed for this book believe that the Jewish state has outgrown its relationship with the United States. For these Israelis, Washington is no longer a reliable ally. Israel, they say, has one overriding strategic foe—Iran—but the United States has declined to take it on. What, then, is the point of the partnership? They are also justifiably proud of the military capability they have built since the founding of what is still a young state. In regional terms, the IDF is a true juggernaut. More broadly, they see the United States retreating from the Middle East. In economic terms, Israelis are themselves looking increasingly toward Asia, especially to India and China. They already have significant ties with Russia, due in part to the huge Russian exodus in the waning years of the Soviet Union. Beijing, New Delhi, and Moscow embrace political values and doctrines of noninterference that make them unlikely to hector Israel for mistreating Palestinians. And Israelis are looking to establish ties with Arab states that now look more plausible as the region splits along both sectarian lines and the divide between radicals and conservatives.

In recent years the strategic outlook of Israel and Saudi Arabia often has seemed more in sync than Israel and the United States. Yet we wonder if Israelis have adequately considered the implications of a future in which their partnership with the United States resembles the U.S.–Saudi partnership. As an American security partner, Saudi Arabia is deeply problematic. U.S.–Saudi relations were powerfully shaken by the fact that fifteen of the nineteen 9/11 hijackers were Saudi citizens, and that they all followed a harsh form of Islam with roots in the kingdom's officially sanctioned doctrine. Since then, the American partnership with Saudi Arabia has suffered from Riyadh's unwillingness or inability to clamp down on Saudi private donations to extremist groups; from the longstanding Saudi-funded effort to propagate the Wahhabi interpretation of Islam worldwide in mosques and madrassas where imams financed by the Saudi government preach an ideology that is difficult to distinguish from the ideology of ISIS; from the lackluster Saudi engagement in the fight against ISIS in Iraq and Syria; and, as this book went to press, from public mass beheadings that resembled the ritual executions staged by ISIS.

There are thoughtful Americans who believe that extremism and anarchy in much of the Middle East will require the United States to remain locked in a close strategic partnership with Israel. Israel, according to this argument, will possess military and intelligence capabilities that America will find indispensable in its war against terrorism. Yet we have trouble seeing how Israel's strategic collaboration can really help the United States to preserve its position in the region or mitigate the increasing violence there. In any event, a U.S.–Israeli relationship that became, like the Saudi one, essentially transactional, would be very different from the one we have known for half a century. It is an outcome that we hope can be avoided.

American Zionism

The authors of this book are of that postwar generation of Americans who were viscerally committed to Zionism. Steven Simon grew up in an Orthodox Jewish family, and went to Israel as a civilian war volunteer in 1973. In a U.S. government career that placed him in the State Department and the White House, the security of Israel was a recurring concern. Simon's first experience in government was in the U.S. embassy in Tel Aviv; during the Reagan administration he staffed the U.S. side of the Joint Political-Military Group, which gave operational substance to the strategic alliance. In the Clinton White House, his work on counterterrorism involved close collaboration with his Israeli counterparts. In the Obama White House he served as senior director for the Middle East and North Africa, including Israel. He remains, and expects always to remain, a Zionist.

Dana Allin is not Jewish. But his connection to Zionism, though more distant, is in its own way a profound reflection of the broader American commitment. Both of his grandfathers, liberal social scientists, migrated from Western states to Washington in the 1930s to work in a federal government that was expanding for the mission of Roosevelt's New Deal. Allin grew up in the 1960s in a liberal milieu that was both troubled by Vietnam and optimistic about continued American progress. The values imparted to him included the Jewish values of his parents' and grandparents' close associates; these included admiration for Israel and commitment to its security. At college in the 1970s he had a few friends who were left-wing anti-Zionists, but more were pro-Israel. Going to graduate school in Europe, he started a career of scholarship in American foreign policy and European relations. Israel, it became clear, was an important and sometimes troubling factor in those relations. He has lived in Europe for most of his adult life, and more often than he can remember has found himself arguing the American case for Zionism against more skeptical Europeans.

In our encounters with Israelis, including for this book, we have experienced the understandable irritation, and even resentment, that some of them, including Israeli liberals, feel about Americans who profess foreigners' Zionism and proceed to lecture them about Israeli societal arrangements, the plight of Palestinians, and the solutions to Israel's security dilemmas. We can well imagine that President Obama's repeated lectures about the threat to Israeli democracy from the construction of settlements and the closing window for a two-state solution come across as grating and even patronizing. Americans cannot stand in Israelis' shoes. Yet neither can Americans maintain a self-deprecating silence regarding policies promulgated by an Israel that is still morally entangled in American society and central to American foreign policy. We have tried to write a book that is balanced in tone but also honest about the changes and threats we see to the two countries' shared future. And we worry that many Israelis and Americans are in denial about those changes.

One form of denial would be to note, accurately, that such warnings have been heard many times before. In 2001, for example, American historian Steven T. Rosenthal published a book arguing that Israel's 1982 invasion of Lebanon, the Jonathan Pollard spy case, Israel's fierce crackdown on the Palestinian intifada, and controversies over Israel's restricted recognition of non-Orthodox Jewish conversion had caused deep disenchantment in an American Jewish community that was undergoing its own profound changes in any event.[4] Yet the publication of this book coincided with the al Qaeda attacks of 9/11; in the aftermath, a shared preoccupation with counterterrorism seemed to bind the United States and Israel as tightly together as ever.

Such changes, however, normally take a long time to unfold—and can cause disruption that appears shocking when it occurs. Consider, for example, the disruptions of the Arab Spring that started in early 2011. For many decades, informed analysts had argued that authoritarian Arab regimes were fragile, that their apparatus of patronage and repression could not ultimately withstand the forces of popular discontent. When the convulsions came, they were pretty much as predicted, yet seemed to take everyone by surprise. And so, we would argue, the evidence for underlying transformation to the U.S.-Israeli relationship, which Chapter 7 lays out in detail, should not be ignored simply because much of it is longstanding. You never know how much time you have left, but it is often less than you think.

This book is also about the chasm in American politics. Simon worked in government under two Republican and two Democratic administrations. Allin has always had strong liberal convictions, but as a student of American foreign policy, and in the research for this book, he has been impressed by the consistency of administrations from both parties in combining the pursuit of American interest with a commitment to Israeli security and to shared democratic values. That consistency is now threatened by the ideological rancor of American politics. Estrangement from Israel would poison American political discourse far into the future. The threat to the U.S.-Israeli alliance is also a threat to American harmony. This book charts the changes and recent stresses to the relationship, and explains why further disruption is likely. But the book also reaches hopefully for the design of a grand bargain that would restore not only the balance for a durable future between Israel and America but greater consensus within the domestic politics of both countries.

PART I

The History

1

Israel in the Liberal Imagination

---

*Where is this city that was believed to have God himself
inhabiting therein?*

—ELEAZAR THE GALILEAN, AS RECORDED IN JOSEPHUS,
THE WARS OF THE JEWS, CHAPTER 8

COLD COMES EARLY to the desert. Steven Simon rolled up the windows and unrolled his sleeping bag on the narrow back seat of a VW Beetle. He crawled into it, then reached to the front passenger seat for a battered paperback and a flashlight. He would rise before dawn to ascend on foot to 400 meters above the Dead Sea. Now he opened the account of Josephus, Jewish historian for the Romans, on what happened to the zealots who took refuge in Herod's abandoned fortress on that mountain of Masada.

Simon was 20 years old. He was working that year as a war volunteer at Kibbutz HaHotrim, having arrived as one of the great tank battles in history was raging on the Golan Heights. The year was 1973, a dramatic juncture in U.S.–Israeli relations, for it was America's emergency resupply of the Israel Defense Forces (IDF) that turned the tide on that flaming escarpment. It is difficult to say what would have happened to Israel without the American airlift. But from that year on, U.S. military support would be understood as at least part of the shield protecting Israelis from the fate of the Jewish zealots at Masada, or of the Jews in Nazi Europe.

Simon came to Israel that year as an observant Jew. He would return frequently in subsequent decades as an American diplomat, White House official, and foreign-policy scholar. Americans have long identified with the small Jewish state as an embattled democracy reflecting American values. The steady onslaught of terrorism suffered by Israeli Jews earned the anguish and solidarity of Americans well before 9/11 brought to the United States a similar sense of vulnerability. And there are strong religious affinities, not only between Israelis and American Jews, but more broadly and perhaps more importantly, in the deep devotion of American Evangelical Christians to Israel's cause.

And yet, to put it in the simplest terms, the image of Israelis in many Americans' eyes has gradually evolved: from courageous and humane warrior-kibbutzniks—for whom Simon was working the kibbutz while they fought on two fronts against Syria and Egypt—to religious settlers of occupied territory. This is, of course, an oversimplification; neither image captures the messy reality or the nuances of U.S.–Israeli intimacy. Yet it will be the contention of this book that this evolution of Israel's image is grounded in truth—and could have an enduring impact on the future of the relationship.

Some forty years after Simon's climb of Masada, two other American Jews of his generation published an exchange of emails on the website of *Foreign Policy* magazine. Like Simon, Michael Oren and David Rothkopf had studied during the 1970s at Columbia University, where they were roommates. Soon after graduation, Oren—who would become an academic historian—emigrated to Israel. He took Israeli citizenship in 1979 and gave up his American passport thirty years later in order to accept an appointment as Israel's ambassador to Washington. Rothkopf became a consultant, journalist, and publisher, and he served for some years in the Clinton administration, overlapping there with Simon. Rothkopf's father was a committed Zionist, but the younger Rothkopf did not visit Israel until 2013. That visit was the subject of their exchange. A question that his friend had posed—did Israel meet his expectations?—started "careening around my brain like a stray pinball," and Rothkopf replied with a story of disillusion.[1]

Rothkopf recalled sitting with his family in 1967 "around a radio in our kitchen to get real-time reports of the Six-Day War." He was likewise gripped by the drama of the Yom Kippur War in 1973, and for the same reason: This was "the Israel of David standing up against the Goliaths." It was the region's lone democracy "fighting against tyrants and bullies—the brave few using brains and technology to defeat the brutal millions who wanted them gone." But as he grew into his late twenties, a different image of Israel intruded: the victim now itself a bully, blundering through Lebanon and brutally repressing Palestinian children who were guilty of throwing stones. "[F]rom the massacres in Lebanon through the Intifada, to the contentious and willful construction of settlements that should not be built, Israel has undercut its moral high ground," Rothkopf wrote.

Michael Oren pushed back on some familiar fronts: He accused his friend, like many Americans, of holding Israel to a double and impossibly higher standard; he rejected some of the charges as dishonest propaganda; he accepted the truth of other complaints but insisted they must be understood in the context of Israel's excruciating dilemmas. The most interesting part of Oren's case, however, was in accusing his friend of having swallowed his "Hebrew School fantasy"—an impossibly heroic and idyllic place that never in fact existed. "Israel before 1967," Oren wrote,

> was in fact a far less equitable place than it is today. There were hardly any Sephardi Jews, much less Arabs, Africans, and other minorities in government. And the government was controlled by a single party composed almost exclusively of secular and socialist Eastern European Jews. Most of the Arab population (of Israel!) lived under military rule. The Palestinians didn't really exist and for the same reason that Israel appeared pristine— because the Western press so decided.

In one respect, Oren got the better of the argument, because his appeal was an appeal to realism. "As so many American Jews of our generation," he admonished Rothkopf, "you have this idealized image of pre-1967 Israel. But we're adults now and adults inhabiting an illusion-less world."

In another sense, however, Oren's realism carried its own burden of naïveté, because it avoids a central problem: Can an America without illusions maintain its special relationship with the real Israel—the hard Israel that seems, for whatever reasons, to be getting harder? To answer this question we should first think carefully about the bundle of realities and illusions that have fed Americans' devotion to Israel over a span of almost seven decades. These were Americans from across many spectrums of politics and religion and social class. They included liberals and conservatives—notably neoconservatives—and Christians and Jews.

The distinctive American groups, subcultures, and allies have had distinctive, though hardly exclusive, reasons for supporting or, at times, opposing Israel and its policies. One underrated reason, perhaps, is sheer fascination—for the story of Israel is a great and amazing story. Haunted and inspired by catastrophic exile in the first and second centuries C.E., conceived by improbable visionaries in the nineteenth, modern Israel was finally born out of the central cataclysm of the twentieth. In its first three decades of life Israel fought three existential wars, plus a fourth in which it played a supporting role in the comic-operatic death throes of European colonialism. At the end of those three decades and four wars, Israel signed a peace treaty with its most formidable enemy and thus, with considerable help from the United States, seemed to have secured its existence.

Through these decades, at the higher levels of American politics and government, we can discern two broad currents of argument about the appropriate U.S. relationship with Israel. These two currents have corresponded roughly to questions of strategic interests and moral values. Until at least the administration of George W. Bush, it was a fair rule of historical thumb that Democratic administrations favored Israel on the basis of liberal values: because of their strong identification with Israeli democracy, Israel's Labor-dominated political ethos, and sympathy for the plight of Jews in the Holocaust. This set of attitudes did not depend on a perception of Israel as a strategic partner; in fact, it was adopted despite a broad assessment that U.S. support for Israel was a strategic liability. Republican administrations typically were more attuned to Israel's strategic importance, assessed mainly in positive but also, in at least a couple of cases, negative terms. George W. Bush, as we shall see, was convinced equally of Israel's value as a strategic asset and as a moral companion. Barack Obama has been a dedicated friend of Israel who, like previous presidents, saw its flaws and also has been perhaps more vocal on what he views as the growing gap between Israel's policies and Israel's long-term interests.

The tensions could be resolved, in theory at least, by peace. And peace between Israel and its neighbors is something that the United States under successive administrations has worked hard, albeit not very effectively, to achieve. There was one notable success. The first three decades of Israel's life and war ended with an Egypt–Israel peace agreement brokered by the most scripturally learned and devoutly Christian U.S. president of the post–World War II era. The formal and real end of Egyptian belligerence meant that conventional armies no longer threatened Israel's existence. Tragically, however, the story does not end in 1978. To begin with, and almost immediately, that devout U.S. president Jimmy Carter, preoccupied with his mission of peace and, arguably, ill served by his intelligence agencies, would be surprised by the explosive birth of a new enemy in revolutionary Iran. This revolution had nothing to do with the Arab–Israeli conflict, but in the nearly four decades of enmity that followed between America and the Islamic Republic of

Iran, the latter would come to weigh heavily in Israel's perceived constellation of threats, and in the most recent decade it has also greatly complicated U.S.–Israel relations. Meanwhile, and almost as quickly, Carter felt betrayed by the Israeli government's continued construction of settlements in occupied territory, after he thought he had an agreement from Menachem Begin, the Israeli prime minister, to stop building them. This pattern would become very familiar. And there would also be a Groundhog Day familiarity to the Israeli military operations, including the 1982 invasion of Lebanon, that successive Republican and Democratic administrations both accepted as justified on the basis of Israel's real security predicaments, and criticized as excessive use of force.

September 11, 2001, marked a crucial moment in U.S.–Israeli relations. After the terrorist attacks, U.S. foreign and national security policy went off the rails. The debacle of invading Iraq, then watching it descend into civil war; the nationalist contortion of American society and expansion of its security state, one that, in its most egregious manifestation, tortured suspected terrorists; and the massive human and financial costs of all of this sent America into a dark tunnel from which it is still struggling to emerge.[2] America's engagement in the Middle East has become a factor in the partisan polarization that has been growing steadily worse over the past generation. Israel, for reasons both logical and illogical, has become entangled in the partisan argument.

This development should alarm Israelis and American friends of Israel. It is a central focus of Chapter 2 and it is a major theme of this book. But first, to understand where we might be going, we should consider how we got here.

The Zionist Half Century

"I pray that you will believe me," intoned CBS radio correspondent Edward R. Murrow, accompanying U.S. army troops who liberated the Dachau death camp on April 19, 1945.[3] What Murrow proceeded to describe did indeed defy belief. By this end-stage of the war, the program to exterminate Europe's Jews was not unknown or unreported. But only with allied victory in view could the magnitude and meaning of this extermination begin to be grasped by the general public.

It had special resonance for American Jews, beyond their sorrowful kinship with the victims. As Peter Grose has noted, their place in the scheme of world history had suddenly changed. "Without fully comprehending it, and only by macabre default, American Jewry had become the largest Jewish community in the world."[4] That is one reason why we can think of America's initial support for Jewish statehood as revolving around American Jewish support. To the extent that America's political leaders considered domestic politics in their calculations—and domestic politics were far from the only factor—they were thinking about Jewish votes in big cities.

In understanding this aspect of postwar American politics, however, it is important to avoid two common errors. First, it was hardly the case that only Jews supported Zionism. An enduring secret of the Israel lobby's success was that, in pushing for the United States to support the Jewish state, the lobby almost always was pushing on an open door.[5]

In the first five decades of American diplomatic engagement with the Zionist project—roughly from the 1917 Balfour Declaration to the 1967 Six Day War—the door openers were mostly American liberals. This was in part because leading Zionist Jews were prominent in progressive American politics and thought, in part because liberals (both Democrat and Republican) championed the extension of civil rights and the American covenant to oppressed minorities, and in part because segments of conservatism were still infected with anti-Semitism. Mainly, however, it was because these five decades coincided with a period of progressive ascendency in American politics—starting, arguably, with Theodore Roosevelt's inauguration in 1901, including Woodrow Wilson's presidency,* and cemented in the almost uninterrupted Democratic administrations of Franklin D. Roosevelt, Harry Truman, John F. Kennedy, and Lyndon Baines Johnson.

A second error to avoid is one of imagining that, in the decades leading up to the establishment of Israel, American Jews themselves were uniformly pro-Zionist. Zionism was an exotic and utopian project of European Jews, many of them socialists, who had concluded, with more prescience than they could possibly have imagined, that there was no real future in Europe for the Jewish people. American Jews, though they encountered real and persistent anti-Semitism in the United States, could not plausibly reach this conclusion. The United States, for all its faults, was ultimately as accommo-

---

* Wilson's progressivism was genuine, but he cannot be mentioned without a crucial caveat: On matters of race, he was a southern reactionary, even by contemporary standards. His archrival Theodore Roosevelt, for example, was far more enlightened on matters of civil rights for African Americans. Wilson actually resegregated the federal government, and purged it of many black civil servants.

dating to Jews as it was to most immigrant groups (the main grotesque exception being its racist oppression of African slaves and their descendants[6]). And the Jews who were most successful, yet perhaps still emotionally insecure, in their assimilation, were also most leery of the Zionist idea for what it might say about their place in American society.

In April 1921, when Chaim Weizmann, the great European Zionist and future president of Israel, sailed into New York harbor (accompanied by Albert Einstein), he was received rapturously by throngs of those whom Grose has called the "downtown Jewry"—East European, Yiddish-speaking, and poor—as against the more successful (and more German) uptown bankers and professionals.[7] Weizmann was in the process of winning a battle for control over American Zionism from its erstwhile leader, Louis Brandeis, who five years earlier had been nominated by President Woodrow Wilson, and then confirmed by the Senate (albeit over formidable conservative opposition) as the first Jewish justice on the U.S. Supreme Court. The nature of the Weizmann–Brandeis conflict matters little to the story we are telling here. More important is how these two men brought together the European and American strands of Zionism, and also brought together the two strands of American Jewry—uptown and downtown—in support of the Zionist project.

Brandeis was a leader and archetype of those American progressives at the turn of the twentieth century who would endow that American century with much of its liberal mindset. And Brandeis' Jewishness was fundamental to his progressivism. He was born just before the Civil War, the son of Prague Jews who had emigrated to Louisville, Kentucky, after the collapse of the 1848 revolution. Brandeis was raised in a house without religion, where Judaism was a matter of ethical consciousness and identity. "My people were not so narrow as to allow their religious belief to overshadow their interests in the broader aspects of humanity," he would write.[8] Brandeis' embrace and then leadership of Zionism grew naturally from this progressivism because it was about protecting and improving the conditions of Jews suffering poverty and persecution in the great eastern Pale of Settlement, and in Palestine itself. As John Judis has observed, a certain obliviousness to the consequences for Palestine's Arabs was not surprising: The Zionist project should also improve *their* condition, which was assumed, with some evidence, to be miserable.[9] Even so famous a champion of Arab self-determination as T. E. Lawrence, a friend of Weizmann, joined Churchill in believing that Jewish immigration to Palestine would bring skills and capital to improve the Arab condition. "I look upon the Jews," Lawrence explained, "as the natural importers of Western leaven so necessary for countries in the Near East."[10] Progressivism and imperialism could go together, a proposition for which TR himself was the great advocate and exemplar. As Judis also observes, the Brandeis era was a more innocent time for thinking about the precedent of American pioneers. Jews in Palestine would be like Puritans in Massachusetts, or homesteaders in Kansas, without too much worry regarding the natives.

Among Brandeis's many contributions to progressive thought was his intellectual battle with the accusation of dual loyalty. "Let no American imagine that Zionism is inconsistent with Patriotism," Brandeis insisted in a 1915 speech to a conference of reform rabbis. "Multiple loyalties are objectionable only if they are inconsistent."[11] Brandeis was influential in persuading American Jews of this compatibility, just as he was influential in persuading at least two presidents that a restored Jewish homeland in Palestine was compatible with America's national interest. The first of these was Wilson himself; Brandeis's friendship with him, and easy access to the White House during Wilson's presidency, played some role in tilting the United States toward endorsement of at least a vague concept of Zionism.

But here too came the stirrings of American opposition, centered in the professional diplomatic corps and broader foreign-policy establishment that worried, and still worries today, about the costs paid by the United States for too-close identification with the Zionist project. The recurring anxiety of these diplomats concerned the electoral calculations and enthusiasms of American politicians unmoored from sober consideration of the national interest.

Wilson, the first such unmoored politician, threw American support behind Britain's November 1917 Balfour Declaration. "His Majesty's Government view with favor the establishment in Palestine of a national home for the Jewish people." These opening words, in the form of a letter from British Foreign Secretary Arthur Balfour to Lord Rothschild, a British Jew, were cleared in advance by Britain's new American ally, which in April had declared war against Germany. The following month, Balfour traveled to Washington and met twice with Brandeis. Between those two meetings, Brandeis spent forty-five minutes discussing the matter with President Wilson in the White House. By May 10, Brandeis could confidently inform Balfour of two things: First, the United States had no interest in being drawn into any kind of responsibility for a protectorate in Palestine or anywhere else in the Ottoman lands; but second, the United States would support the idea of a British protectorate in line with the project of European Zionists.[12]

There were political, religious, and ideological reasons for Wilson's support. Unions under Samuel Gompers' American Federation of Labor backed the idea in part because they wanted to keep Jewish immigrants, presumed competitors for American jobs, away from American shores. The Republicans, led by Wilson's bitter rival Theodore Roosevelt, were leaning toward support of a Jewish Palestine, "and no Democrat would willingly abandon the potential Jewish support in the big eastern cities to the opposition."[13] The deeply religious Presbyterian president was moved also by that biblical fascination shared by successor presidents: "To think that I, the son of the manse, would be able to help restore the Holy Land to its people," said Wilson, whose father had been a Presbyterian minister.[14] Finally, Zionism appeared to fit well with Wilson's liberal ideology of national self-determination: as indeed it did, but in bad ways as well as good. The Wilsonian vision for Europe was blurry on the problem of what to do about contending claims for national self-rule, and these contending claims would be part of the savagery of the second act in Europe's great civil war. Such contending claims would also prove a problem in Palestine, to put it mildly, with the added dimension that Europe's horrors, inflicted most comprehensively on Europe's Jews, thereby also helped drive a full century of claims and conflict in the Middle East.

Palestine's was among the many maps to be rolled out and—after a fashion—resolved at the post–World War I Versailles conference. The Balfour Declaration was also on the table. On the American side, Colonel House's "Inquiry"—a nascent think tank set up by the president to analyze postwar problems and which became the Council on Foreign Relations—was divided on the question. Opponents included Hines Page, the U.S. ambassador to Britain; the "Near Eastern Intelligence Unit," which consisted of one Jewish and strongly anti-Zionist American vice-consul based in Geneva named Samuel Edelman; Secretary of State Robert Lansing and many of his State Department colleagues who, among other worries, opposed the plan to preserve Anglo-French colonial control of the Ottoman lands; and important American Protestant missionaries allied to the Arab romanticism of Lawrence, and in any event knowledgeable and attuned to the worries of Christian and Muslim Arabs. The opponents lost this battle: Balfour was "enshrined," as Grose puts it, in the Versailles settlement and, hence, international law.[15] But it was enshrined in the form of a British mandate for Palestine, the terms of which were ambiguous, like the Balfour Declaration itself, on the actual form of a Jewish homeland. Certainly a succession of British governments over the next three decades were not unreservedly supportive of the Jewish cause, which they found difficult to balance with the interests of the Arabs under their rule.

Members of the U.S. Foreign Service were also trying to navigate and reconcile contending American interests and policies. They were, on balance, diffident about the Zionist project and wary of what they saw as White House political enthusiasm for it. For this the State Department and its WASP elites have long been accused of shaping policy from motives of anti-Semitism. Often cited as Exhibit A is the letter from Secretary Lansing to President Wilson suggesting that "many Christian sects and individuals would undoubtedly resent turning the Holy Land over to the absolute control of the race credited with the death of Christ."[16]

There was a serious strain of American anti-Semitism in the interwar years, epitomized by Henry Ford, that great and rancid American purveyor of the Protocols of the Elders of Zion, and other reactionary conservatives—including at least a few diplomats who, whatever they thought of American Jews, imagined Europe's Jewry as dark, dirty, and Bolshevik. But in general, American diplomacy framed the problem in neutral terms. It was not so much a matter of anti-Semitism as studied indifference to the problem of Jews in Europe. The American consciousness was, of course, not yet imprinted with the enormity of the Holocaust.[17]

When the darkest night imaginable descended on Europe's Jews, however, American policy regarding a homeland for those who could escape was characterized by the grimmest of ironies. Anti-Semitism did not significantly shape U.S. policy toward the Zionist project, but it did greatly affect U.S. immigration policy for refugee Jews. It left many who might have been saved to be exterminated by Hitler's executioners; it reached well into the State Department visa service, headed by the unmistakably anti-Semite Breckenridge Long; and it stains the historical legacy of a president, Franklin Roosevelt, whose many charms included a genuine philo-Semitism, but whose inattention to the abhorrent policy of sealing America's borders against desperate Jews cannot be erased from his record.[18] The grim irony was that—as postwar British politicians suspected—one consequence of wanting to keep a flood of Jews out of the United States was to make the case for a Jewish Palestine even stronger. (In private, Roosevelt had ruefully acknowledged that it was a bit rich for America to press Arabs to accept Jewish refugees that the U.S. was reluctant to admit to its own shores.)[19]

In a presidency filled with the crises of the Great Depression and a Second World War, the problems of Palestine were inevitably low on any list of presidential priorities. But FDR did latch onto it, starting a private file labeled "Palestine."[20] He was in favor of a Jewish homeland, though his ideas for it were vague and a bit wild. Like Wilson before him and Truman his successor, Roosevelt was fascinated by biblical geography. He was attentive to the Jewish vote and was competing for reelection in 1944 against New York governor Thomas Dewey, who was outspoken in his support for Zionism.[21] Roosevelt had notable Zionists in his so-called Brain Trust, Jewish protégés of Justice Brandeis, who were prominent enough to inspire the famous right-wing slur about Roosevelt's "Jew Deal." FDR did not find the slur at all funny; he abhorred this form of prejudice, and angrily rejected entreaties by prominent Jews *not* to nominate Felix Frankfurter, one of his Brain Trust members, as the second Jewish Supreme Court justice. (The lobbyists against the appointment feared that an overrepresentation of Jews would arouse American anti-Semitism.)[22]

Roosevelt's ideas for Palestine, when he did have time to think about it, were wild insofar as they sometimes included the germ of a plan to depopulate the land of its Arabs, moving them at his estimated cost of $300 million to Iraq or another Arab-majority area. Today this sounds both monstrous and naïve, and when mooted to the British they replied firmly that no sum of money would persuade Palestinian Arabs to leave voluntarily.[23] (In the event, of course, many Arabs were exiled, in just one episode of the larger tragedy of the vast population transfers that followed World War II.) Roosevelt's ideas were vague insofar as he was not always clear or consistent about the political construction of a Jewish homeland, or the political relations between these Jews and the Arabs who would live there if they could not be persuaded to leave. To be sure, as the Arab transfer scheme indicates, FDR seems to have envisioned complete Jewish sovereignty. But at the times when he realized that this might be at odds with reality, he was open to other ideas, including some sort of Jewish–Arab federation.

The intrusion of reality happened suddenly, on the USS *Quincy* in the Great Bitter Lake of the Suez Canal. Roosevelt was returning home from

Yalta, where, on the last night of the conference, he casually told Churchill and Stalin that he would be stopping to meet with the king of Saudi Arabia. Churchill was unhappy about the surprise and, though pro-Zionist, had already expressed skepticism about Roosevelt's ability to win over the Arabs. But Roosevelt, not for the first time, overestimated his charm and deal-making skills. He had already sent the king a letter assuring him "that it is the view of the Government of the United States that . . . no decision altering the basic situation of Palestine should be reached without full consultation with both Arabs and Jews."[24] Roosevelt didn't seem to register the polite yet clear replies of King Ibn Saud. But sitting with the king aboard the *Quincy*, there was no mistaking the answer. The president tried to pitch a grand deal coupling the Jewish homeland with massive economic development for the Arabs. Saud's reply, as recorded in State Department records: "The Arabs and the Jews could never cooperate, neither in Palestine, nor in any other country" and "the Arabs would choose to die rather than yield their lands to the Jews." This part of the meeting was a debacle. Roosevelt was perhaps only trying to salve an awkward encounter when he repeated the commitment in his 1943 letter to the king, and even elaborated: He "wished to assure his majesty that he would do nothing to assist the Jews against the Arabs and would make no move hostile to the Arab people."[25] Who knows what Roosevelt thought this was supposed to mean? Arabs, in any event, heralded the meeting as a great victory. When Roosevelt returned to the United States, he sent messages of reassurance to American Zionists. He several times suggested a "new formula" under which establishing and even protecting a Jewish state in Palestine would be the first task of the new United Nations Organization. Then he died.

HARRY TRUMAN has come down in popular memory as a great American friend—maybe the founding friend—of Jewish statehood. There are good reasons for this reputation. In many respects, however, Truman's initial ideas and commitments were as confused as Roosevelt's—and, in fact, the new president was quite uneasy about the implications of full "political Zionism." Like Roosevelt's, Truman's amiable philo-Semitism was rooted in his liberalism (and mixed, it should be acknowledged, with some common and casual anti-Semitic tropes that do not strike us as very important in assessing the man or his motives). Truman's liberalism was different in tone, perhaps, from Roosevelt's, because it was distinctively midwestern. It was also, by twenty-first-century standards, radical. Truman integrated the U.S. military; he ran for election in 1948 on a civil rights platform that started the process of steadily driving white southerners out of the Democratic Party; he pushed for a "Fair Deal" of economic controls, union power, expanded Social Security, subsidized housing, public works, and liberalized immigration; and he barnstormed for universal health care in both the 1948 and the 1950 midterm elections.[26]

Truman's liberalism drove his support for a Jewish homeland, but also his reluctance, or at least ambivalence, about endorsing a Jewish state. This was not, on the level of principle, contradictory. In the history of Zionism there was a tendency to ignore the fact of Palestine's Arab inhabitants—but they could not be ignored entirely, and their presence intruded awkwardly from time to time in the American consciousness. This was partly, but only partly, as a consequence of American interests, including oil interests, in the wider Arab region. Truman was also no doubt sincere when he worried that a state based on Jewish sovereignty would amount to a "theocracy" at the expense of Muslim and Christian Arabs.[27] There was a problem, however, with the somewhat fuzzy alternative of a "homeland" that would also be homeland to Arabs enjoying equal rights and equal sovereignty, whatever that might mean. It was simply unrealistic, as events would prove.

There were many other contradictory pressures pushing American policy in confusing directions. Access to Arab oil was seen not just as an economic imperative but as a strategic necessity as the wartime alliance with Stalin's Soviet Union dissolved into distrust and then a dangerous rivalry. The presumption that Stalin could exploit U.S. support for Zionism to curry favor with the Arabs seemed confounded when Moscow actually came out in favor of the Jewish state, but in fact over time the Soviets did earn some Arab credit as the United States was more closely identified with Israel.* There were in the halls of Washington recurring anxieties that any kind of

---

* It is important not to fall into the common error of assuming that the Soviet adversary's policies were more coherent or well-planned than Washington's. Though Stalin was about to embark on another vicious purge in which anti-Semitic paranoia would play an outsized role, the new Jewish state, as a "progressive" and socialist enterprise, fit the default template for a natural Soviet ally. It probably didn't hurt that the nascent state's fighters included organized terrorists who had engaged in such anti-British attacks as the bombing of the King David Hotel in Jerusalem. From Moscow's perspective, British imperial power in the Middle East was embedded in relations with "reactionary" Arab monarchs. Anything to weaken the British grip on the region could look like a

Jewish state or homeland in Palestine would require American troops to prevent another genocide of Jews, this time by the Arabs. Such a deployment was considered unthinkable, given the already competing pressures to bring American troops home after an exhausting world war, and to keep them in Europe as a guard against Soviet aggression.

On the other side of Truman's ledger, political pressures in favor of Zionism were becoming acute, after the single-minded Rabbi Abba Hillel Silver had taken prominent leadership of the American Zionist movement, helping to convert it into an organized Jewish lobby.[28] The biggest source of pressure, however, was the stunning reality of what had happened to the Jews in Europe, and the awful continuing plight of those who had survived. As Tony Judt starkly reminded us, the survivors throughout Europe had no viable home in the nations from whence they had been transported to eastern death camps: The attitudes of their gentile compatriots ranged from sullen indifference to outright hostility.[29] There were as many as 250,000 Jews in camps run by allies. Many wanted to go to Palestine, or were persuaded that they wanted to go to Palestine by Zionists in their midst; in any event, they were hardly welcome in large numbers anywhere else, including the United States. A decisive development for the Truman administration came in the form of an August 1945 report from Earl G. Harrison, dean of the University of Pennsylvania Law School, whom Roosevelt had appointed to investigate conditions in displaced persons camps. "Many Jewish displaced persons," Harrison wrote after his study mission to Europe,

> are living under guard behind barbed-wire fences . . . including some of the most notorious concentration camps [with] no clothing other than their concentration camp garb. . . . Most of them have been separated three, four or five years and they cannot understand why the liberators should not have undertaken immediately the organized effort to re-unite family groups. . . . Many of the buildings . . . are clearly unfit for winter. . . . We appear to be treating the Jews as the Nazis treated them except that we do not exterminate them. They are in concentration camps in large numbers under our military guard instead of S.S. troops. One is led to wonder

---

strategic gain for Moscow, and the Soviets may not have anticipated Britain's replacement, in the fullness of time, by the Americans.

whether the German people, seeing this, are not supposing that we are following or at least condoning Nazi policy.[30]

Harrison concluded in favor of "the quick evacuation of all non-repatriable Jews in Germany and Austria, who wish it, to Palestine."[31]

With this bleak report in hand, Truman persuaded British Prime Minister Clement Attlee to agree the formation of an Anglo-American Committee of Inquiry into the Palestine problem. On May 1, 1946, the committee recommended admitting 100,000 Jewish refugees to Palestine, in conjunction with a UN trusteeship leading to a binational Arab-Jewish state.[32] The idea of a binational state at least took account of Arab interests, and for quite a few months longer, Truman held on to the hope that such a federal arrangement might be possible. But the president mainly focused on the humanitarian case for letting the 100,000 go, while he prevaricated on the implications that renewed, large-scale Jewish immigration would have on future political arrangements.[33]

The British, with their grim experience of the Mandate, knew better, and their resentment at what they interpreted to be emotional and political (that is, Jewish-driven) American policy contributed to one of the several bouts of Anglo-American acrimony in the years after World War II. Britain had backtracked on the Balfour Declaration almost as soon as it was issued—in part because it had undertaken contradictory commitments to Jews and Arabs as it sought strategic advantage in World War I; in part because of the unrest, riots, and anti-Jewish attacks from Arabs who were acutely conscious of the implications of Jewish immigration for their own place in Palestine; and in part because Jewish terrorism, after a pragmatic pause during World War II, picked up in Palestine and hardened British attitudes against Zionism as well as aggravating some latent anti-Semitism in the UK. But Britain in its postwar exhaustion was also fed up with the Mandate, a feeling delicately expressed by one of the last commanders of British forces in Palestine, a notorious anti-Semite who bade farewell by urinating on the ground.[34]

With the UK unable to hold on, Jews and Arabs unwilling to live together, and the United States generally appalled by the prospect of deploying troops, the problem was handed over, as FDR had finally suggested, to the new and hopeful organization of the United Nations. The UN's first substantive act was the formation of the United Nations Special Committee on Palestine (UNSCOP), which, after studying the problem in Europe, the United States, and the Middle East, concluded there was not a viable alternative to partition. This was duly reported to the UN General Assembly when it convened in September 1947 outside of New York City.[35]

The United Nations was an American brainchild and another liberal enthusiasm, although it was supposed to be organized on more realistic principles than its ill-fated predecessor, the League of Nations. With Eleanor Roosevelt—presidential widow, liberal icon, and fervent Zionist—on the U.S. delegation, it carried a great deal of prestige. Not enough, however, to sway the U.S. State Department, whose forebodings were to be expressed in a series of memos by Policy Planning Staff Director George Kennan after the UN General Assembly voted for partition, and Palestine descended into war. "In the Mediterranean and the Middle East," Kennan wrote:

> we have a situation where a vigorous and collective national effort, utilizing both our political and military resources, could probably prevent the area from falling under Soviet influence and preserve it as a highly important factor in our world strategic position. But we are deeply involved, in that same area, in a situation which has no direct relation to our national security, and where the motives of our involvement lie solely in past commitment of dubious wisdom and in our attachment to the UN itself. If we do not effect a fairly radical reversal of our policy to date, we will end up either in the position of being ourselves militarily responsible for the protection of the Jewish population in Palestine against the declared hostility of the Arab world, or of sharing that responsibility with the Russians and thus assisting at their installation as one of the military powers of the area. In either case, the clarity and efficiency of a sound national policy for that area will be shattered.[36]

Kennan was often a maverick, but on this subject his views were fully in line with State Department orthodoxy.[37] That orthodoxy, in the formidable person of Secretary of State George C. Marshall, confronted the White House over the question of whether and when to recognize the self-declared Jewish state in May 1948, and lost. At a May 12 meeting in the Oval Office, Marshall was perturbed to find Truman's domestic policy adviser, Clark Clifford, not only present but invited to express his views. Partition was already happening on the ground, Clifford noted, and it would be good for America to have Israel as a democratic friend in the region, rather than forcing it to seek the patronage of Moscow. It is reported that Marshall, sitting through this, went red in the face. "Mr. President," he said, "I thought this meeting was called to consider an important and complicated problem in foreign policy. I don't even know why Clifford is here. He is a domestic adviser, and this is a foreign policy matter." A bit later in the meeting came Marshall's stunner: "If you follow Clifford's advice, and in the election I were to vote, I would vote against you." This, as Warren Bass has recounted, was a thinly veiled threat of resignation from Truman's most revered cabinet member six months before an election that Truman was widely expected to lose.[38]

Marshall did not resign, even though Truman did end up following Clifford's advice. Nor did Truman lose the election, though the Palestine question played little or no role in his surprise victory.[39] The whole recognition debate, though it looms large in the history of American attitudes toward Israel, was rather insignificant to what was happening on the ground in Palestine. There, Israel was giving birth to itself, in a violent process aided by confused Arab leadership. In November 1947 the UN General Assembly had called for partition and the establishment of two states, one Jewish and one Arab. The Arab League adamantly rejected this solution. In May 1948, as Marshall and Clifford faced off in the Oval Office, the armies of Egypt, Syria, Transjordan, Iraq, and Lebanon invaded for the putative purpose of destroying Israel at birth. But their armies were in fact fighting at cross purposes— Jordan's King Abdullah, for example, was really in it to secure a bigger share of Arab Palestine, rather than to prevent partition altogether[40]—and the Israelis actually enjoyed numerical superiority along with superior training and battle experience (although they were outgunned in heavy equipment).[41] Israel was also aided by the UN, which negotiated a one-month truce on June 11, during which the IDF was able to almost double its size and bring in armored vehicles and aircraft.[42]

The Arabs again played into Israel's hands by breaking the truce on July 8, one day before it was set to expire. The next phase of the war lasted only ten days, but they were decisive ones. Israel took control of Eastern and Western Galilee in the north, held Egyptian forces at bay in the south, and opened the road from Tel Aviv to Jerusalem.

It was at this point that Israelis' determination, both courageous and ruthless, to create and secure themselves as a state clashed decisively with Truman's humanitarian liberalism. In the first phase of fighting some 300,000 Palestinian Arabs had fled. Moshe Shertok, foreign minister of

Israel's provisional government, wrote in a June 15 letter of this "wholesale evacuation" as "the most spectacular event in the contemporary history of Palestine," and he added: "The reversion to the *status quo ante* is unthinkable." The next day the Israeli cabinet decided to keep the refugees out; the IDF was instructed to fire on Arabs who might seek to return. "That marked the beginning of the Palestinian refugee crisis," writes John Judis.[43] Though, for a time, Israel's defenders claimed that they fled spontaneously, subsequent scholarship, including from an important cadre of Israeli "New Historians," has made clear that the departure of many Arabs was intrinsic to the strategic logic of Israel's War of Independence.[44]

This is not to say that there were explicit orders to commit war crimes, and it is certainly not to discount the intentions and actual atrocities of the Arab forces. Arabs proclaimed their intentions proudly. "This will be a war of extermination and a momentous massacre, which will be spoken of like the Mongolian massacres and the Crusades." Thus spoke Arab League Secretary Azzam Pasha. As historian Simon Sebag Montefiore recounts, an ecstatic and fatefully overconfident fervor drove Arab fighters and commanders. "Secular nationalism merged with the fervour of holy war: it was unthinkable that Jews could defeat Islamic armies, and many of the Jihadist factions that fought beside the regular armies had long since embraced a fanatical anti-Semitism. Half the Egyptian forces were *mujahidin* of the Muslim Brotherhood, among them young Yasser Arafat."[45] Where they were able, Arabs did massacre Jews: in the Jewish quarter of Jerusalem's old city, for example; in the village of Kastel, where 50 Jewish prisoners were murdered and their bodies mutilated; and on the road to the Hadassah Hospital on Mount Scopus, where Arabs ambushed a convoy of ambulances and supply trucks, killing 77 Jews, mostly doctors and nurses.[46] Though Arab armies could not accomplish their promises on the avowed, blood-curdling scale, the fighting on both sides was desperate, and the notion that an Arab propaganda of extermination would not have influenced Israel's readiness to depopulate Arab municipalities is detached from reality.

There were some operations that seemed calculated to do that. On the other hand, many actions were ad hoc. It was a war for roads, and for villages that gave access to roads. Tactical needs led to fighting, and intelligent people do not wait to be killed; in that regard it was not a lie that many Arabs fled spontaneously. Benny Morris, a leading New Historian, has laid out in careful terms the contents of Operation Nachshon and Plan D, ordered by David Ben-Gurion to open the road to Jerusalem and secure the areas designated as Jewish in the UN partition plan.

> The plan gave the brigades carte blanche to conquer the Arab villages and, in effect, to decide on each village's fate—destruction and expulsion or occupation. The plan explicitly called for the destruction of resisting Arab villages and the expulsion of their inhabitants. In the main towns, the brigades were tasked with evicting the inhabitants of resisting neighborhoods to the core Arab neighborhoods (not expulsion from the country). The plan stated: "[The villages] in your area, which have to be taken, cleansed or destroyed—you decide [on their fate], in consultation with your Arab affairs advisers and HIS officers." Nowhere does the document speak of a policy or desire to expel "the Arab inhabitants" of Palestine or of any of its constituent regions; nowhere is any brigade instructed to clear out "the Arabs."[47]

Certainly the logic of Israeli state building was a logic of having fewer Arabs in the new Jewish state, as some local commanders understood very well. The Israeli journalist Avi Shavit has elucidated this dynamic in relation to the expulsion of Arabs from the small Arab city of Lydda, near the Tel Aviv airport on the road to Jerusalem. It was during the second phase, those ten days in July. After the city was taken, its military governor, Shmarya Gutman, imposed a curfew and confined thousands within the sweltering walls of the main mosque. In a state of tension, shots were fired, and the Israelis massacred 250 Arabs. It was not planned, but it happened. After the massacre, Gutman met with Arab dignitaries, who were grateful when he released those male prisoners still held in the mosque with the understanding that they would join the rest of the city in leaving.

> Gutman felt that he had achieved his goal. He had not planned it in advance, but occupation, massacre, and psychological pressure had had the desired effect. After forty-eight hours of hell, he did not quite order the people of Lydda to go. Under the indirect threat of slaughter, Lydda's leaders asked to go.[48]

Or, as Gutman himself told Shavit many years later, "War was inhuman, but it allowed one to do what one could not do in peace; it could solve problems that were unsolveable in peace." Just to be clear about the method and the meaning of that solution, Shavit depicts "a long, Biblical-looking column of thousands . . . marching into exile," and then, painfully, he records the memories of an Arab teenager who was part of that column.

> The road was narrow, the congestion unbearable. Children shouted, women screamed, men wept. There was no water. Every so often, a family withdrew from the column and stopped by the side of the road to bury a baby who had not withstood the heat; to say farewell to a grandmother who had collapsed from fatigue. After a while, it got even worse. A mother abandoned her howling baby under a tree. A cousin of Ottman's deserted her week-old boy. She could not bear to hear him wailing with hunger. Ottman's father told the cousin to go back and get her son, but the father, too, appeared to be losing his mind. Following the loaded wagon, he cursed the Jews and cursed the Arabs and cursed God.[49]

This was a familiar desolation in the postwar years; there were scenes like it throughout Europe, where evils and calamities on a biblical scale had been inflicted most directly on the Jews. Indeed, the evacuation of villages and towns such as Lydda was, in a very direct sense, the spillover of that European calamity. But Truman, in his liberalism, believed it should be possible to proceed on the basis of restored standards of civilization. The summer and fall of 1948, while Truman was battling for reelection, UN envoys Ralph Bunche and Count Folke Bernadotte tried to work out a settlement, but it was based more on Bernadotte's sense of justice than on a realistic sense of the facts on the ground and what the sides might be willing to negotiate. Bernadotte's proposal contained this language on refugees:

> The exodus of Palestinian Arabs resulted from panic created by fighting in their communities, by rumors concerning real or alleged acts of terrorism, or expulsion. It would be an offense against the principles of elemental justice if these innocent victims of the conflict were denied the right to return to their homes while Jewish immigrants flow into Palestine, and, indeed, at least offer the threat of permanent replacement of the Arab refugees who have been rooted in the land for centuries.[50]

The day after delivering this 130-page report and proposal to UN Secretary General Trygve Lie, Bernadotte and a French officer traveling with him were shot to death by members of the Stern Gang, a renegade Revisionist faction headed by Yitzhak Shamir, a future Israeli prime minister. This murder had the unintended effect of consolidating American support, albeit temporarily, behind Bernadotte's proposal. On September 21, Secretary Marshall, with the President's approval, issued a statement lauding Bernadotte and embracing his plan: "My government is of the opinion that the conclusions are sound and strongly urges the parties and the General Assembly to accept them in their entirety as the best possible basis for bringing peace to a distracted land."[51] But through the fall came continued cycles of fighting and truce, whereby Israel was steadily expanding its borders. On December 11, the UN established a three-member Palestine Conciliation Commission to negotiate an armistice that would encompass borders and refugees. Truman appointed the pro–civil rights editor of the Louisville *Courier-Journal*, Mark Ethridge, as the U.S. member of the commission. But Ethridge's mission to Palestine ran into an Israeli brick wall. It was enough for Truman to pronounce himself "disgusted with the manner in which the Jews are approaching the refugee problem."[52] And on May 28 Truman wrote to Israeli Prime Minister David Ben-Gurion that the U.S. government was "seriously disturbed by the attitude of Israel with respect to a territorial settlement in Palestine and to the question of Palestinian refugees." Without Israeli adherence to "the basic principles" of the Palestine Conciliation Commission, Truman threatened, Washington would "regretfully be forced to the conclusion that a revision of its attitude toward Israel has become unavoidable."[53]

But it was an empty threat based on a liberal illusion. Israel's struggle to be born was a demographic as well as territorial struggle, and it was not ready to compromise on either. It is not even clear that Israel could have compromised, and it is difficult to say that Israel was wrong on this. Shavit, who penned the harrowing scenes above on the exiled Arab population of Lydda, is a morally serious and liberally minded Israeli Jew, but of those who sent the Arabs into exile, he has concluded:

I will not damn the brigade commander and the military governor and the 3rd Battalion soldiers. On the contrary. If need be, I'll stand by the damned, because I know that if not for them the State of Israel would not have been born. . . . They did the filthy work that enables my people, my nation, my daughter, my sons, and me to live.[54]

Many years later, Ethridge would express bitterness that Truman had been unwilling to apply real pressure on Israel about refugees.[55] He believed that an Israeli willingness to repatriate 200,000 Arabs would have unlocked the refusal of Arab states to make peace with the new Jewish state in their midst. This seems unlikely: The gelling Arab nationalism of the postwar era of decolonization and postcolonialism needed an enemy, and Israel, a regional outpost of Europeans who had driven many Arabs from their homes, fit the bill perfectly. Indeed, the usefulness of this enemy to Arab monarchs and dictators struggling to assert their nationalist legitimacy in large measure explains why those Arab leaders have used the Palestinian refugees so persistently over the subsequent seven decades: The refugees' misery was a tangible and renewable resource for the anti-Israeli grievance that would remain a critical component of Arab nationalism.[56]

Ethridge, and many State Department officials, were also unrealistic about the amount of attention and political capital that Truman might have devoted to "pressuring" Israel. It is true that the president faced organized pressure from the nascent Israel lobby. But this was just one of many pressures. It was the beginning of the Cold War. The most urgent problem of summer 1948 was the Soviet blockade of Berlin—a crisis that continued until the following spring when Moscow relented because of the Western powers' successful airlift. As for the supposed need for American even-handedness to prevent Soviet gains in the Middle East, as we have already noted, the State Department position on this was, over the short term, simply wrong. (The long-term strategic consequences of U.S. support for Israel were more complicated, but not uniformly negative.)

The plight of Arab refugees from Palestine tugged at Truman's liberal conscience. But so too did the plight of Europe's surviving Jews. And once the actual fighting ended, through the diplomacy of Bernadotte's American deputy and successor, Ralph Bunche, the refugees could be—for a time at least—forgotten. Thus could the great liberal Eleanor Roosevelt, who genuinely worried about Palestine's Arabs as she was championing Israel's creation, conclude by April 1949 that "the many counties [in Israel] in which the Arabs remained are quite happy living side by side with the Jews and even taking part in the government of the community" cast great doubt on the allegation that "the Arabs were driven from their homes." Her conclusion was in line with what her husband had suggested a decade earlier: "The Arabs," Eleanor wrote, "will probably be better off if the funds already in hand are used to resettle them in some of the Arab countries where there are vacant lands that need people to work on them."[57]

Truman himself, as soon as he left the White House, appeared unburdened of the ambivalence he had felt about the nature of Israel's creation, or his own role in it. "I am Cyrus," he boasted to a New York Jewish audience in November 1953.[58] The ex-president intended, we can assume, some ironic hyperbole in comparing himself to the Persian ruler who restored the Jews to their homeland after the Babylonian exile. In the twentieth century it was mainly the Jews themselves who restored themselves to Israel. It was a great and epic achievement. Truman's ancient comparison had validity, however, insofar as it invites us to ponder the importance of a powerful and benign gentile empire to the fate of the Chosen People in their Promised Land.

Eisenhower and Suez

This chapter and the next consider the differences between liberal and conservative Americans' attitudes toward Israel. In examining the differences, however, we should not lose sight of the continuities. The next two American presidents did not have a high regard for one another, and in obvious ways they were very different men. Dwight D. Eisenhower was conservative and cautious—a military man of reserved rectitude. John F. Kennedy was brash, profane, charismatic, and liberal. Their approaches to Israel reflected these differing temperaments. Eisenhower, like George Marshall before him, viewed the infant Jewish state as a strategic nuisance, or worse, in the deadly serious context of a deepening Cold War. Kennedy, by contrast, embraced Israel in a fashion that arguably constituted the real beginning of a de facto U.S.–Israel alliance.[59]

Yet the two men and their respective administrations shared an important idea: that the United States had a Cold War leadership advantage because, alone among the Western powers, it could take a credible stand against the remnants of European colonialism. Both administrations attempted overtures to the avatar of that nationalism, Egypt's Gamal Abdel

Nasser. Neither overture was successful, but both caused great anxiety—and in Eisenhower's case, much worse—in Israel.

Eisenhower appeared at times genuinely vexed by Israel's actions. This vexation no doubt derived from a military man's cold appraisal of strategic interest, and it should not be confused with the appalling anti-Semitism of such of his World War II contemporaries as General George S. Patton.[60] There is zero evidence of such attitudes on the part of Eisenhower, who had been shocked when he toured the concentration camps in April 1945, and asked American journalists to visit and report on them.[61] But his administration decided early on that the Truman administration had "gone overboard in favor of Israel," as Secretary of State John Foster Dulles put it in 1953. In 1957, still angry about the Suez debacle, Dulles told Henry Luce of *Time* magazine, "I am aware how almost impossible it is in this country to carry out a foreign policy not approved by the Jews. Marshall and [Truman's Secretary of Defense] Forrestal learned that. I am going to try to have one." Eisenhower himself had told a friend, "I gave strict orders to the State Department that they should inform Israel that we would handle our affairs exactly as though we didn't have a Jew in America."[62]

This first Republican administration for a full generation spurned Jerusalem's appeals for American arms sales and a U.S.–Israel defense treaty. The State Department complained about civilian deaths from Israeli reprisal raids against *fedayeen* attacks that were usually launched from Jordanian or Egyptian territory. After one such reprisal, the U.S. assistant secretary of state for Near Eastern affairs, Henry Byroade, said Israel needed to shed "the attitude of a conqueror and the conviction that force and a policy of retaliatory killings is the only policy that your neighbors will understand."[63]

Eisenhower's coolness toward Israel set the conditions for appraising the proper response to turmoil in the Arab world. Nasser in 1952 helped topple an Egyptian monarchy weakened by its defeat at the hands of the new Jewish state. Nasserism would lead to regime change in several neighboring states, and appeared to threaten others, including the Hashemite Kingdom of Jordan.

Focused on the problem of Soviet encroachment, the new U.S. administration decided it had to balance support for the surviving monarchies with overtures to the leading Nasserite. In 1955, British Prime Minister Anthony Eden forged the anti-Soviet Baghdad Pact, which would eventually include Iraq, Iran, Pakistan, and Turkey, but, pointedly, not Egypt. As a gesture to

Nasser, the United States did not join either. But the gesture was too small: Angered by Washington's refusal to sell it arms, and unmollified by the fact that Israel was embargoed as well, the Egyptian president on September 27 announced an arms deal with Czechoslovakia—the beginning of a twenty-year strategic relationship with Moscow. But the Eisenhower administration did not give up trying to compete. A month before the Czech arms deal, Dulles proposed the "Alpha" peace plan, to include significant concessions of territory from Israel, a demilitarized Jerusalem with joint Israeli–Jordanian sovereignty, and return of 750,000 Arab refugees. In return, Israel was to enjoy access to the Suez Canal, economic relations with its Arab neighbors, and security guarantees from the major powers.[64]

The proposal went nowhere. Then Eisenhower made an appeal to Nasser's self-image as avatar of economic modernism. The United States would finance the massively ambitious Aswan Dam project to divert the upper Nile, expand Egypt's cotton production, and double the country's hydroelectric output. The overture was not handled with great skill. It was a hard sell in Congress, where American cotton interests, hardline cold warriors, and the Israel lobby united against it. Nasser himself was wary and diffident. But his ambassador to Washington persuaded the Egyptian president to accept the offer just as Eisenhower and Dulles decided they could not push it through— or at least, that it wasn't worth the trouble. This was a significant blow to Nasser's prestige, only partly offset when Moscow, sensing opportunity, offered a third of the financing. Nasser needed to react with something big, and so he did. He nationalized the Suez Canal.[65]

The nationalization of foreign assets with due compensation is well within the rights of nations. No matter: As Henry Kissinger would write decades later:

[O]nce Eden and Mollet had nailed their flag to the anti-appeasement mast, it should have become clear that they would not retreat. They belonged to the generation, after all, that viewed appeasement as a cardinal sin, and Munich as a permanent reproach. Comparing a leader to Hitler or even to Mussolini meant that they had moved beyond the possibility of compromise. They would have to prevail or lose all claim to governance— most of all in their own eyes.[66]

The three Suez conspirators—Israel, Britain, and France—can be ranked on a descending scale of legitimate panic. Israel was stronger than it thought, and faced weaker enemies than it imagined, but can be forgiven for observing that those enemies opposed its very existence and were vastly larger in population and area. France was in the midst of traumatic and violent decolonization: It had just suffered defeat in a brutal war to hold onto Indochina, and was determined not to lose the far more integral Algeria. France in general held Nasser and Nasserism responsible for the worsening Algerian civil war, and believed his removal would help solve the problem.

Britain was the most powerful conspirator and, arguably, the most confused. Prime Minister Eden himself had in fact pushed for compromise with Nasser when he was foreign secretary under the colonialist die-hard Winston Churchill, who was back in 10 Downing Street with a narrow government majority that included forty Conservative backbenchers dead set against any further British retreat from the Empire. Yet Churchill was ailing and fading in and out of real authority. By the time Eden had replaced him, Eden was also sick in a way that may have affected his faculties of perspective.

It was not as though Washington reacted to Nasser's move with equanimity. At the same time as it was putting together a plan to finance Aswan, the administration was implementing a secret plan, codenamed Omega, to constrain Egypt's economy while undermining its claim to Arab leadership.[67] But there was a fundamental disagreement between Washington and London. Washington wanted to tame Nasser and was convinced that any resort to military force would do the opposite. London was by now convinced that only regime change would solve its problems.

Transatlantic communications and intelligence sharing went quiet, and an agitated Eisenhower knew something was up. He could not quite have imagined, however, the outlandish details of the plot that Britain, France, and Israel cooked up. Israel was to invade the Sinai. When Egypt defended itself, France and Britain would issue an ultimatum for a cease fire. When both sides refused—Egypt having little choice since Israel's forces were not going to stop—the British and French would insert paratroopers to impose order and, incidentally, retake the Canal and dispatch Nasser. A key part of the plan was that Washington, though no doubt annoyed, would acquiesce.

Washington, however, refused to play its part. Eisenhower's fury at the elaborate plot was all the greater because the Suez War coincided with the Hungarian uprising and the Soviet move to suppress it. For good measure, Khrushchev threatened to defend Egypt by flattening London and Paris.

Eisenhower did his own flattening by organizing, in effect, a run on the pound. It was a humiliating demonstration of Britain's postwar immiseration and dependence on America. Britain surrendered. France and Israel followed suit, while Nasser survived, triumphant. (The Israelis, though required to pull back, did come out of the war with tangible gains, including the internationally guaranteed right of naval passage through the Strait of Tiran.)

Kennedy, Johnson, and the Six Day War

Michael Oren offers a somewhat simpler account of the Suez Crisis. "In 1956," he writes,

> Egyptian ruler Gamal Abdul Nasser, backed by the Soviet Union, nationalized the Suez Canal and threatened Israel's existence. Yet when Britain, France and Israel—America's friends—tried to stop Nasser, U.S. president Dwight D. Eisenhower turned against them. The invaders, Eisenhower concluded, represented imperialism while the Egyptian dictator somehow stood for liberation. Through America's intervention, Nasser was saved, yet he remained ungrateful. Two years later, he tried to overthrow virtually all the pro-American Arab governments. A chastened Eisenhower appealed to Britain, France, and Israel for help. The lesson: when dealing with the shifting loyalties of Middle Eastern autocrats, stick with your stable, democratic allies.[68]

This is a remarkable summary, with a "lesson" that hardly any American president attentive to the full range of national interests would be able to follow. Eisenhower's successor certainly did not conclude that one-dimensional support for like-minded Western allies was the antidote to the conservatism that he disdained. Indeed, John F. Kennedy continued to court Nasser, and had a more developed understanding of why it was a good idea. Kennedy propounded a distinctive vision of anticommunist progressivism, encompassing Green Beret special forces and the Peace Corps. His was actually a more ideologically coherent form of anticolonialism, which also brought him into some tension with European allies. As a young senator he made his foreign-policy debut in 1957 with a strongly worded attack on the folly of European "imperialism"—a word that he carefully equated with Soviet imperialism when he decried France's conduct of the war in Algeria, criticized U.S. arms supplies for that war, called for negotiations with the FLN, and worried that "the problem is no longer to save a myth of French empire. The problem is to save the French nation, as well as free Africa."[69]

In the White House, Kennedy's overtures to Nasser were extended, involved a thick and often friendly correspondence, and culminated in an outpouring of Egyptian public grief with the news of Kennedy's assassination in November 1963. The outreach was unsuccessful, foundering on the fact that Egypt employed poison gas in Yemen, among many other problems. But the outreach was serious and sustained. Meanwhile, Israeli anxieties were assuaged by a simultaneous American embrace. In part this was the natural resumption of Democratic Party affinity for Israel's pioneering socialism, an experiment still strongly supported by progressive elements in the United States. It was a time when America was roiled by civil rights struggles and dealing with Arab partners like Saudi Arabia that still practiced legalized slavery and demanded that any American military personnel on its soil be certified Jew-free. This was a comparison that made Israel look particularly good to such liberals as Harris Wofford, Kennedy's civil rights adviser, who pointed to the Israeli kibbutzim and labor unions as "models and teachers for the peoples seeking freedom in the developing world. . . . Pericles said that Athens was the school of Hellas. I have suggested that Israel and Gandhi's India are schools of the developing world."[70]

Kennedy presided over the first major American arms sales to Israel: HAWK surface-to-air missiles that the Eisenhower administration had refused. Warren Bass, a key historian of the period, considers this weapons deal the actual beginning of a U.S.–Israel alliance, which would quickly supplant Israel's strategic relationship with France. Despite misgivings, Kennedy also accepted Israeli claims about its nuclear energy program, even though JFK was the first American president who was preoccupied—almost obsessed—with the problem of nuclear proliferation.[71]

But Kennedy's presidency was tragically truncated. To assess it properly, as Robert Dallek has argued, we have to consider the Kennedy–Johnson administration as an eight-year whole. They were an odd couple—but there was a unity to their policies. Kennedy was a true liberal of progressive temperament, but also a pragmatic and sometimes ruthless politician navigating a ramshackle coalition of northern liberals and southern conservatives—in fact, pro-segregation racists. Johnson actually radicalized Kennedy's agenda, driven in part by the momentum of national grief over the assassination, and in part by his own hardscrabble experience in the Texas hill country. He drove landmark civil rights legislation through Congress and launched the Great Society expansion of the welfare state.

Johnson also launched America full tilt into the Vietnam War. He was relying on Kennedy advisers and believed he was continuing Kennedy's war, though recent scholarship offers evidence that JFK might not have deployed U.S. ground troops on a large scale.[72] We will never know. In any event, Johnson's war in Indochina had started to go as badly for America as it had for the French, and by 1967 it haunted every aspect of his presidency, including relations with Israel.[73]

Johnson called himself a "Jewish non-Jew" in whom Israel had found "an even better [friend]" than Kennedy.[74] But in his Vietnam torment, he was further discomfited by the leadership of American Jews in the antiwar movement. Israel did not occupy anything like the central place in American political discourse that it has today. Though the American Jewish community had played a large role in the Truman administration's embrace of the Jewish state, its relationship after two decades was ambivalent. Only 20,000 American Jews had emigrated.[75] Zionist activist Eliezer Livneh, dispatched to America by Israeli Prime Minister Levi Eshkol, concluded in a 1967 report that many American Jews resented Israel's dependence on the United States.[76] Esteemed Holocaust survivor Elie Wiesel told *Haaretz* that "The Jewishness of [American] Jewish youth can still be reached, but not through Israel."[77] It was an age of assimilation—what *Look* magazine in 1964 termed "the vanishing American Jew."[78]

Johnson was disappointed that U.S. Jews did not seem to take the problem of American "credibility" seriously. The then Israeli president, Zalman Shazar, would recall Johnson telling him that American "Jewish support for the Vietnam involvement was his due in light of his record of support for Israel."[79] In a White House meeting, as recorded in the official notes, LBJ warned the Israeli president that if,

> because of critics of our Vietnam policy, we did not fulfill our commitments to the 16 million people in Vietnam, how could we be expected to fulfill our commitments to 2 million Israelis? Yet some friends of Israel in the United States had publicly criticized US policy in Vietnam. . . . Our failure to carry through in Vietnam would be bound to affect our

ability to carry through in our commitment to other small states such as Israel.[80]

Israeli society was also not yet in a position to take the idea of an American special relationship for granted. Its first prime minister, David Ben-Gurion, had considered a close American alliance the prize to strive for, and after the chill of the Eisenhower years, as we have seen, he had made progress with Kennedy. Nonetheless, the Jewish state in its first two decades had strategic partnerships with the Soviet Union, Britain, and France, and the idea of American protection did not yet dominate Israeli strategic planning. Israelis in any event felt insecure. With the end of Holocaust reparations, the economy had slumped. Attacks by Palestinian guerrillas were increasing, particularly after a new radical Syrian regime came to power and started encouraging them more vociferously. Young Israelis were emigrating to Europe and the United States.[81]

With hindsight we know that in 1967 Egypt was not ready for war, and the increasingly belligerent language from Arab states was driven more by inter-Arab competition—what Malcolm Kerr called the "Arab Cold War"—than by intention to attack Israel.[82] But the rhetoric generated by that competition was bloody. The new Ba'athist regime in Syria, for example, was calling for a "total war with no limits" against Israel and promising "to drench this land with our blood, to oust you aggressor and throw you into the sea for good."[83]

For any historically minded Jew, this sounded like a plausible prelude to annihilation. And into this fearful mix was added Israel's own internal tensions and competitions, which damaged the ability to conceptualize and act strategically. The IDF policy of disproportionate retaliation to Palestinian attacks stoked the tensions between the IDF and its Chief of Staff Yitzhak Rabin, and more cautious government officials such as Foreign Minister Abba Eban, who worried about the impact on international opinion as well as the dynamics of crisis. Israeli historian Tom Segev explains the tensions clearly:

> For Rabin and the generals, most of whom were Israeli born, this [the reprisal policy] was not merely a professional military issue, but a question of their prestige, their dignity, and their image as Sabra warriors facing weak-spirited politicians. They viewed these Eastern Europeans, some of

whom were three decades older than they, as clinging to "Diaspora psychology." The belief that terrorism could be overcome by defensive means might bring about the construction of electric fences along the borders, said Rabin, and "they'll turn Israel into another ghetto." When speaking at General Staff meetings, Rabin used to refer to Eshkol and his ministers as "the Jews."[84]

Prime Minister Levi Eshkol was somewhere between these two camps, but he did worry about the consequences of disproportionate retaliation. After one such attack against Jordan escalated tragically, Eshkol, who thought in Yiddish, applied one of his homespun analogies: The IDF had meant "to give the mother-in-law a pinch, but instead . . . beat up the bride."[85] And indeed, the November 1966 IDF retaliatory raid on the Jordanian village of as-Samu' arguably set off the dynamics leading to the Six Day War. Jordan's King Hussein, whose relations with Israel were secretly friendly, was on that count insecure and vulnerable to the intra-Arab invective. He was accused of complicity in the Israeli attack on his own soil; the Syrians spoke of a plot between "the reactionary Jordanian regime and imperialist Zionism."[86] Nasser's state radio broadcast in similar terms. The King was impelled to yell back. The Jordanian delegation to an Arab League Defense Council meeting asked the Egyptians to explain: "Why didn't Egypt renew guerrilla attacks from its own territory? Why didn't they remove UNEF [the United Nations Emergency Force monitoring the Egypt–Israel armistice agreement] and transfer troops from Yemen to Sinai? And where was the touted Egyptian air force when the Israelis were attacking Samu'— where was Syria's commitment to Arab defense?"[87] In a separate statement King Hussein accused Nasser of "hiding behind the skirts" of the United Nations force.[88]

This was a potent charge because, like the Egyptian and Syrian accusations against Hussein, it was partly true. Nasser concluded that he had to stop hiding. He kicked out the UN troops, sent 80,000 of his own forces into the Sinai, and once more closed the Strait of Tiran to Israeli shipping, an act that Israel had always made clear would be regarded as casus belli. Yet Eshkol sent out repeated signals of reassurance both to Syria and to Egypt: Israel had no aggressive intentions. Israel's apparent desire to avoid war led Nasser to believe that he could threaten the Jewish state with impunity. Nasser was bluffing, because he knew he was not ready for war. Yet his rhetoric was a challenge to Israel's existence, as he made clear, for example, on May 29, stating: "Our basic objective will be the destruction of Israel."[89]

Meanwhile, Israeli Foreign Minister Abba Eban made a tour of Paris, London, and Washington—guarantee powers for the 1956 settlement—and got what must have seemed to Israel like a collective shrug. De Gaulle was especially dismissive. He warned Israel not to fire first.[90]

Israel ignored this advice. Early on June 5, its planes swept in low from the sea to destroy the better part of Egypt's air force. The war was effectively won, but Jordan and Syria, misled by Cairo's surreal propaganda, joined in Egypt's chimerical victory. King Hussein apparently believed that three-fourths of the *Israeli* air force had been destroyed.[91] Six days later, when a cease fire took hold, Israel had captured the Sinai up to the Suez Canal, the Gaza Strip, East Jerusalem, the West Bank of the Jordan River, and Syria's Golan Heights.

It was a stunning victory, and a triumph for the side that deserved to win. And it should have been prevented. There were American officials who had great foreboding about the consequences of a war in which Israel felt that it was on its own and had to act alone. And they had a simple solution: Don't leave Israel alone. The British were the first to raise the idea of an international flotilla, perhaps a NATO force, to reopen the Strait of Tiran and guarantee the safe passage of Israeli shipping. The idea had fervent advocates within the U.S. government, notably Under Secretary of State Eugene Rostow, and President Johnson did consider backing the plan.[92]

In the end, however, Johnson was precisely wrong about the consequences of America's commitment to Vietnam for the U.S. relationship with Israel. There is an opportunity cost to any military intervention, and especially one as painful, expensive, and divisive as Vietnam. The Vietnam commitment made America less, not more, willing to come to Israel's aid. Congress had a bad case of Tonkinitis. The American people were angry and succumbing to the Vietnam syndrome. The naval force to safeguard Israel's rights would not have been risk free—there was always a chance of confrontation with Egypt's Soviet patron—but there is good reason to believe it would have been prudent, inexpensive, and successful. However, "Rostow's flotilla"—as some in the U.S. government called it—never set sail.

At the time, of course, the Six Day War looked like it solved a lot of problems. Just on the American side, the Johnson administration, at a time when the hopelessness of Vietnam was sinking in, was quite willing to "bask"—as

Conor Cruise O'Brien once put it—in the "reflected glory" of an Israeli triumph involving American weapons against Soviet-armed Arabs.[93] This demonstration of Israeli prowess as a small modern state of moral courage and strategic genius made it a newly attractive ally to many millions of Americans, and it also made it a source of pride to American Jews. For Israel, victory brought the old city of Jerusalem and Judaism's most holy sites under its control. And it expanded its defense perimeter, if not its internationally recognized borders, to an area that coincided with Israeli strategists' concept of more easily defensible.

But the victory also brought many more Arabs under Israel's control. The occupation regime instituted by Defense Minister Moshe Dayan was humane and enlightened: It maintained Jordanian administrative control over many aspects of Palestinian daily life, including education, and it maintained an open border policy for Palestinians to move between the occupied territories and Jordan. Yet the very success of this regime bred some very dangerous illusions about the long-term consequences of Israeli military control over the Palestinians. The most dangerous of these was the idea that the new facts on the ground created by a relentless Israeli policy of establishing settlements in the occupied territories was either irrelevant to a negotiated peace, or might even constitute a useful bargaining chip. That Israel considered itself forced into the Six Day War did not relieve it, nor its new superpower patron, of the responsibility to think about the consequences of its new power over Palestinians whom it would not—and could not—offer citizenship or expel. The settlements policy was a historic mistake, greatly encouraged by Arab rejectionism. But even though most of the Arab states were refusing to negotiate in the 1970s and 1980s, enlightened self-interest should have led Israel to better prepare for the peace deal that would one day have to be negotiated. The settlements have made this negotiation far more difficult, and by now they may have made it impossible.

There is an irony here: In 1948 the Jews of Palestine made for themselves a state with a ruthlessness that explains and justifies the Arab memory of *Nabka*, "catastrophe." But the Jews of Palestine had no choice, and, as we argued previously, to judge them by contemporary standards is to ignore the danger and desperation of state building after the apocalypse of World War II. And while America tried to influence Israel's policy on the refugees, it was not wrong, on balance and given the many other problems facing the Truman administration, to support the birth of Israel. In 1967, Israel behaved more properly and Washington tried more seriously thereafter to pressure the Israelis for the purpose of saving it from its own mistakes. Washington immediately and consistently opposed Israel's settlement policy. But both America and Israel were fatefully remiss in not giving the issue the attention and priority it deserved. This was a significant failure of both Israeli and American liberalism.

June 1967 was the apotheosis of liberal Zionism's half century, coinciding with some of the worst fifty years in human history, years that included the European Holocaust, but also years of progressive advancement of which Zionism was a part. The year was also the high-water mark for about fifty years of American liberalism more generally. Vietnam helped to wash that liberalism away. On March 31, 1968, the president who had won the 1964 election by the largest landslide in American history went on television to say that, because of the torments of a divided country, he would not seek re-election. His Democratic party was suffering a crippling division between Cold War liberals and antiwar activists, as well as losing the southern segregationists who would migrate to the Republican Party, with a detour, in some cases, to George Wallace's third-party candidacy. The Vietnam divisions among Democrats also made it difficult to defend Johnson's Great Society accomplishments. Johnson later claimed that he knew this would happen:

> I knew from the start that I was bound to be crucified either way I moved. If I left the woman I really loved—the Great Society—in order to get involved in that bitch of a war on the other side of the world, then I would lose everything at home. All my programs. All my hopes to feed the hungry and shelter the homeless. All my dreams to provide education and medical care to the browns and the blacks and the lame and the poor. But if I left that war and let the Communists take over South Vietnam, then I would be seen as a coward and my nation would be seen as an appeaser and we would both find it impossible to accomplish anything for anybody anywhere on the entire globe.[94]

It was not a bad summary of the liberals' Cold War dilemma as it was starting to look by 1967. Regarding Israel, there is a coda for American liberalism that should not, perhaps, be mined for too much significance, but can be appreciated in literary terms. The following year, 1968, was America's *annus horribilis* of deepening war, protests, riots, and assassinations. On April 4 Martin Luther King Jr. was shot to death in Memphis, Tennessee, and American cities erupted into riot and flame. That night, presidential candidate Robert F. Kennedy landed in Indianapolis and delivered to his black supporters the news of Martin Luther King's murder, with tragic, poetic, calming words that probably saved the city from the violence that engulfed other American cities. Kennedy had always, and rather irrationally, despised his brother's vice president, and was never able to come to terms with LBJ's elevation to the White House. He had a well-deserved reputation for ruthlessness, and he had worked on the scurrilous committee of Senator Joseph McCarthy, who was godfather to his first child. But as a campaign adviser to his brother and then U.S. attorney general, he became genuinely devoted to the civil rights movement, and as senator from New York by 1968, the former hawk's decision to oppose the war also seemed to come from a sincere place. There was an inspiration and transcendence to RFK's run for president in 1968, and moments of grace, as when he spoke extemporaneously in Indianapolis. Kennedy may not have won the nomination, but he had a political plausibility that Eugene McCarthy, the other antiwar candidate, lacked. Kennedy brought together, for the last time in many years, a crucial Democratic coalition of blacks and Hispanics with Catholic, working-class whites. He also had strong Jewish support. This was helped by his strong support for Israel, which was perhaps de rigueur for a New York senator, but also grounded in his 1948 experience in Palestine as a correspondent for the *Boston Post*. Kennedy had been impressed by what he saw, and wrote of the "truly great modern example of the birth of a nation with the primary ingredients of dignity and self-respect."[95] When Kennedy visited Jerusalem, one month before Israel's declaration of independence, there was a four-year-old boy living there named Sirhan Sirhan. Twenty years later, Sirhan was living in Los Angeles, and saw that Kennedy, campaigning in the California primary, was promising if elected president to deliver fifty jet fighters to Israel. On June 5, Robert Kennedy won the primary. That night Sirhan Sirhan took a .22 caliber pistol to LA's Ambassador Hotel, waited until Kennedy finished his victory speech, and shot him in the head.[96]

2

The Rise of the Right

IN THE CLOSING SCENE of Steven Spielberg's 2005 film *Munich*, a tormented Israeli agent walks with his Mossad handler on the Brooklyn side of the East River. The agent, Avner Kaufman, has led a team of assassins through Europe and the Middle East against the planners of the terrorist kidnapping and murder of eleven Israeli athletes and a German policeman at the 1972 Munich Olympics. Avner in the preceding scenes has been depicted in the grip of posttraumatic stress disorder. On the waterfront he demands from Mossad an affirmation of certainty that the people he killed were in fact guilty of Munich. The handler dismisses the demand as naïve, and they part company. As the score rises and credits begin, the camera rests on the Twin Towers of the World Trade Center rising over lower Manhattan in the distance.

And it rests there for a long time. The towers were no longer standing, of course, when Spielberg shot the film, so he was making a point—though in art as opposed to propaganda, the point will not always be obvious.[1] The scene is not didactic, and neither is the film. But it is overtly ambivalent. *Munich* is a pro-Israel movie; its heroes are the men pursuing Israel's retribution for the 1972 murders; the depiction of those murders is horrific and haunting. But the film was controversial: Israel's partisans accused Spielberg of equating the retribution with the terrorism.[2] Though the accusation was false, it is certainly true that the film probes moral ambiguity, and it also asks in practical terms whether Israel has conducted an underground war of retaliation that it can never finish.

The film is thus in some measure a document in the growing ambivalence in the American liberal attachment to Israel. While we cannot read too much into one film director's choices, neither should we ignore that this was the same director who, twelve years earlier, had produced Hollywood's most significant film about the Holocaust, the brooding masterpiece *Schindler's List*. Nor can we ignore the contrast between *Munich's* torment and the liberal propaganda of Otto Preminger's *Exodus* four decades earlier. These were both serious Hollywood movies about Israel, but Hollywood's tone had changed.

American liberals' disillusionment with Israel was not immediate after 1967, was never complete, and is still ongoing. This liberal disillusionment crossed paths with a conservative ascendancy and right-wing hardening in both the United States and Israel. Neither trend has been straight and clear, but it is possible to trace, in the years after 1967, the jagged lines of both liberal decline and the rise of an alliance among right-wing Americans and Israelis. It started in the United States with Nixon, followed a decade later by the end of Labor rule in Israel and the coming to power of Menachem Begin's Likud. In Israel there would still be center-left governments under Shimon Peres, Yitzhak Rabin, Ehud Barak, and (depending on where you place him) Ehud Olmert. But these were exceptions. For roughly three out of the four decades since Likud first came to power in June 1977, Israel has been governed from the right.

Starting with Richard Nixon's election in 1968, the United States also experienced forty years of conservative ascendancy. On the matter of Israel, to be sure, U.S. Republican administrations have not strayed significantly from the liberal American foreign-policy consensus: They have opposed Israeli settlements in the occupied territories and favored UNSC Resolution 242. It is still the case, however, that the parameters of U.S. political debate moved to the right in the period 1968–2008, and this movement was in certain respects congenial for Israeli right-wing governments.

Nixonland

Richard Nixon was an anti-Semite. The record—a record we can play back, word for word, because Nixon famously (though at the time secretly) taped his White House conversations—is unmistakable.

"Most Jews are disloyal," the president can be heard telling his aide H. R. Haldeman in one of the many recordings.[3] In another, he blames revelations of American soldiers massacring civilians at My Lai in Vietnam on "those dirty rotten Jews from New York."[4] There were too many of them at too high levels of American society and government, and they were out to destroy him.[5] At one point, angered by insufficiently bullish analysis of a marginal drop in unemployment figures, Nixon ordered aides to make a count of Jews in the Bureau of Labor Statistics, and to weed them out of the agency. Nixon's order was implemented, in what one writer has called "the last recorded act of official anti-Semitism by the United States government."[6] Like many anti-Semites, the president made a personal exception for some friendly and trusted Jews, including Leonard Garment, William Safire, and Henry Kissinger. But he did not hesitate to goad and bully Kissinger, for example, on account of his Jewishness.[7] Kissinger would later write:

> Nixon shared many of the prejudices of the uprooted, California lower-middle class from which he had come. He believed that Jews formed a powerful cohesive group in American society; that they were predominantly liberal; that they put the interests of Israel above everything else; that on the whole they were more sympathetic to the Soviet Union than other ethnic groups; that their control of the media made them dangerous adversaries; above all, that Israel had to be forced into a peace settlement and could not be permitted to jeopardize our Arab relations.[8]

Nixon's anti-Semitism is important to this story for two reasons. First, it was motivated by the classic pathology of middle-class resentment. In Nixon's case the pathology drove him to political self-destruction through Watergate, but also fed a genius for demagogy that inspired his brilliantly successful "southern strategy." In reaction to a decade of civil rights advances, the Civil War Confederacy was drifting away from allegiance to the Democratic Party. The southern reaction against black equality was compounded by broader national anxieties about urban crime and social turmoil on campuses and in society at large. With appeals to states' rights and law and order, Nixon exploited these anxieties. "Cut the Democratic Party and country in half," wrote Nixon aide Pat Buchanan in a 1968 memo to the Republican candidate. "My view is that we would have the far larger half."[9] Nixon was able to bequeath to his Republican Party an emerging hegemony in the South, as he bequeathed to the country at large a potent mix of stoked resentments and cultural division. Historian Rick Perlstein devoted his magisterial book to the thesis that *Nixonland* was the same polarized country that made political life so bitter and raw in the Bill Clinton and George W. Bush administrations, and that even more venomously poisons the America of Barack Obama.[10]

Some elements have changed in the meantime. To begin with, the content of conservative politics has moved sharply to the right since the time of Nixon, whose actual policies would position him as a moderate-to-liberal Democrat by today's standards.[11] And although animosity toward Jews formed a salient part of Nixon's character, it is no longer an important ingredient of right-wing resentment. In the 1960s, conservative intellectual William F. Buckley took a forthright and important stand to purge the movement of anti-Semitism. (Buckley did not, it is worth noting, take the same principled stand against Jim Crow segregation.) In the intervening decades, moreover, right-wing politics has been shaped by vehemently pro-Israeli neoconservatism.

The second reason for paying attention to Nixon's prejudice against Jews is this: The Nixon record provides a kind of natural experiment into how real anti-Semitism affected U.S. policy toward Israel. Two things stand out. First, the general and overwhelming affections of the American body politic—represented strongly in Congress—dictated a certain minimum level of support. Second, however, the Nixon administration ranks in living memory as the administration most coldly focused on the unsentimental pursuit of American strategic interests. To appreciate just how unsentimental, it is worth remembering that their most important strategic achievement was to enlist China as a semi-open ally against the Soviet Union—at a time when Mao's murderous Cultural Revolution made Soviet autocracy look rather benign. On balance, with four more years of anguished and draining war in Vietnam, along with the ensuing trauma of Watergate weighing heavily on the negative side of the scale, Nixon and his key architect Henry Kissinger did serve and improve the U.S. strategic position. They did much to help America and its allies emerge, fifteen years later, as the non-collapsing protagonists of the Cold War.

In focusing on and pursing U.S. strategic interests, the Nixon administration supported Israel strongly. But this support was complicated, because the administration also appreciated and in significant ways accommodated the designs of Israel's most powerful enemy, Egypt.

Nixon in his first term was preoccupied with Vietnam, he had an aversion to Middle East issues because of his aversion to American Jews, and he did not trust his Jewish national security adviser to be objective about U.S. interests in the region.[12] So he was inclined to leave Middle East policy to the State Department, which for reasons of tradition and its own honest assessment of the situation tried to appear even-handed between Israelis and Arabs.[13] There was in any event a sea change after Israel's 1967 victory in the U.S. assessment of Israel's strategic value. The old view continued to dominate the State Department, but the White House, under both Johnson and Nixon, was more inclined to see the Israeli position as an American asset.[14] When Kissinger replaced William Rogers as secretary of state in Nixon's second term, he brought a more subtle cast to U.S. policy. Whereas his predecessors had fretted than an unbending Israel would drive Arab states into the Soviet camp, Kissinger decided that Israel's occupation of Arab land, and its intransigence about returning it, could be an exploitable asset. The Arabs had to be convinced that alliance with the Soviet Union offered them no hope of regaining any of their occupied territories. Only the United States could exert the subtle pressure to make Israel budge.[15]

Kissinger's strategy succeeded more quickly and completely than he probably could have imagined. It worked mainly because of the courageous iconoclasm of Anwar Sadat.

After their 1967 defeat, the Arab states at a summit meeting in Khartoum issued their infamous "three nos." They swore solemnly to one another that they would neither recognize, nor negotiate with, nor make any kind of peace with Israel. Nasser in early 1969 launched a war of attrition against the Israeli forces on the Suez Canal's east bank. The Israelis retaliated with bombing raids deep inside Egypt. In January 1970 Nasser appealed to Moscow for SAM-3 air defense missiles with Russian crews. When Brezhnev balked, Nasser threatened to resign and "hand over to a pro-American President."[16] His threat worked: The Soviets sent in missiles, missile crews, and military advisers. It was a major escalation of superpower involvement and a significant military shift against Israel. Within a year, however, Nasser had died. His successor Anwar Sadat quickly signaled a watershed reassessment of policy toward Israel, in direct contravention of the "three nos" of Khartoum. In February 1971, Sadat proposed to reopen the Suez Canal if Israel would withdraw its forces from the canal's east bank, adding that a timetable for further withdrawals could lead to peace. But the Israelis were wary, divided, and unresponsive.

Sadat needed for his own political survival to recover the Sinai and use of the Suez Canal. He decided that the situation required another war. Kissinger, in his memoirs, praises the Egyptian president's decision for war as an act of statesmanship. Sadat, in the American's account, fought not to win back territory, but to create a psychological shock that would bring both sides to the peace table. The Israelis needed to be jolted out of their complacent sense of military invincibility. The Egyptians needed to be liberated from their burning sense of national humiliation, which rendered them incapable of diplomatic flexibility. It was, according to Kissinger, an extremely rare case of a statesman who made the radical choice of war in order "to lay the basis for moderation in its aftermath."[17]

On Yom Kippur, October 6, 1973, Egyptian and Syrian troops attacked Israeli positions along the Suez Canal and Golan Heights. The attack achieved its intended surprise; by the third day of the war it became apparent that Israeli forces were in real trouble. The Syrian army, though suffering heavy casualties, remained intact; Egypt's army was proving fierce. Israel had lost forty-nine planes and 500 tanks and suddenly faced the prospect of a long war of attrition that a tiny country, surrounded by massed enemies, could not win.[18]

The United States started a low-key effort to resupply Israel and learned of a larger Soviet airlift to Syria. On October 12, after a week of war, the White House realized that Israel still had not broken the stalemate, and Nixon approved a full-scale airlift. Finally, after another perilous week, Israel was able to drive into Syria and to establish a bridgehead on the west bank of the Suez. The United States and the Soviet Union had now assumed the roles of diplomatic proxies for their Middle Eastern clients: Kissinger flew to Moscow, reached a cease-fire agreement with Soviet leader Leonid Brezhnev, then flew from Moscow to Tel Aviv and obtained the consent of a traumatized Israeli government.

But the cease-fire did not hold, and the prospect of Israel now turning the tables with another decisive victory over its enemies was one that the Nixon administration—mainly Kissinger, since Nixon himself was preoccupied by Watergate—considered potentially devastating to U.S. and, arguably, Israeli interests. By the time the cease-fire took effect, Israeli forces had nearly encircled the Egyptian Third Army on the east bank of the Suez. Having suffered 2,000 casualties and a new reminder of its national vulnerability, Israel found the temptation to destroy the trapped Egyptian forces hard to resist. As the cease-fire disintegrated, Israeli forces cut the Third Army's last supply route to Suez city. For Kissinger, who throughout the war had been in frequent contact with Sadat, this situation portended a disaster. Kissinger was convinced that Sadat could not survive the loss of his army, and if he fell, his replacement would be more pro-Soviet and more radically resistant to a long-term peace. The danger of Soviet gains seemed immediate. Moscow had suffered a setback in 1972 when Sadat, in preparation for his war, expelled his Soviet advisers. But now a desperate Sadat was appealing to the Soviet Union *and* the United States to send troops to enforce the cease-fire. The Soviets started to prepare an airlift to reintroduce its soldiers into Egypt. In response, the United States ostentatiously called its own military alert—including heightened readiness for its nuclear forces.

The crisis abated, the Third Army survived, and Kissinger embarked on five weeks of "shuttle diplomacy" between Cairo, Tel Aviv, and Damascus to negotiate the disengagement of Israeli, Egyptian, and Syrian forces. The United States had seen itself risk nuclear confrontation with the Soviet Union, in part for the sake of Israel, but this was also the beginning of close U.S. relations with Egypt.

Nixon and Kissinger were conservative realists, which meant, at least in their case, that they were historical pessimists. Nixon's pessimism was personal and paranoid. His volatile resentments against Kennedys, Jews, northeastern liberals—the composite Establishment that looked down on him—combined with his volcanic reaction to the antiwar agitation across the country and led him into the truly gratuitous self-harm of Watergate.

Watergate shook Washington like a series of earthquakes, and a big one hit during the October war. In the so-called Saturday Night Massacre, Nixon had demanded the firing of Watergate Special Prosecutor Archibald Cox, because Cox would not be deflected from his subpoena for seven of Nixon's recordings. The president had to accept the resignations of Attorney General Elliot Richardson and Deputy Attorney General William Ruckelshaus before, finally, Solicitor General Robert Bork, number three in the Department of Justice, agreed to fire Cox. Two days later, the House Judiciary Committee started discussing impeachment proceedings. Nixon was morose, withdrawn, and drinking heavily, and was judged to be out of commission on the night of October 24–25. The decision to raise alert levels, including for nuclear forces, and to more or less advertise this move to Moscow, was taken by a group of seven unelected officials headed by Kissinger, without the president's participation. For most of the October war, Kissinger directed not just American diplomacy, but U.S. foreign policy.[19]

Kissinger's pessimism was in some sense a realistic assessment of the collapse of presidential authority as well as the apparent decline of American power. The former was unmistakable; it was during this same month that the Congress overrode Nixon's veto to enact the War Powers Act, restricting a president's power to deploy military forces without congressional review (in practice the review has never turned out to be very stringent). The decline of American power was rather more complicated. On the one hand, events in the Middle East were moving the most powerful and important Arab country from Soviet to U.S. alignment, while the United States was also aligning more closely with an Israel that, after some weeks of peril, had once again decisively defeated Soviet-armed armies. The withdrawal from Vietnam, rather than tarnishing U.S. credibility, turned out in the long run to be the tonic for American self-confidence that war critics had long maintained it would be.[20] And the rapprochement with China helped to clarify a "correlation of forces" that would work increasingly to the United States' advantage and the Soviets' disadvantage.

This sanguine assessment, to be sure, relies on hindsight. There were at the time countervailing grounds for pessimism. OPEC delivered a most significant blow in the oil embargo and price hikes that constituted a revolution in the terms of trade between oil producers and the industrialized West. The prime architect of that OPEC revolution was Kissinger's hero, Sadat. The impact was a long-lasting aggravation of inflation and economic stagnation throughout the 1970s, adding to the sense of Western decline in the face of perceived (albeit fleeting) Soviet advances after the American defeat in Vietnam. And OPEC shrewdly used the embargo to drive a wedge between Washington and its European allies.[21]

On matters related to the Arab–Israeli conflict, the allies were easy to divide. European governments had from the outset of the war wanted to distance themselves from the U.S.–Israeli military partnership. Their view of the matter was perhaps less nuanced than Kissinger's complex embrace of both Israel and Egypt: The Europeans saw Arab armies fighting on what was internationally recognized to be Arab territory. "Is the attempt to put one's foot back into one's own house necessarily a surprising act of aggression?" is how French Foreign Minister Michel Jobert assessed the matter on October 8.[22]

From the first day of the war, Britain and France resisted American appeals for a common Security Council position for "return to the status quo ante." Jobert gave a speech to the French National Assembly blaming Israel for blocking peace and the United States and the Soviet Union for supplying the belligerents. This infuriated Kissinger, who would later write that Jobert had expressed "the moral equivalence of the two sides—the intellectual presupposition of European neutralism."[23] All NATO allies except for West Germany, the Netherlands, and Portugal banned overflight or use of their bases for America's airlift to Israel. And after the cease-fire disintegrated with Israeli moves to destroy the trapped Third Army, Bonn too informed Washington that German ports and bases were unavailable for the shipment of supplies.

At Sadat's behest, OPEC divided oil purchasers into categories based on their degree of support for Israel. The Americans and the Dutch were subject to a total embargo. The UK and France received uninterrupted supply. Everyone else was to be squeezed by 5 percent per month until Israel withdrew from the occupied territories.

The Europeans did not respond with conspicuous unity or heroism to the Arabs' use of their oil weapon, but the embargo's effects were, in truth, temporary and mainly psychological. The lasting impact came from the huge increase in the real price of energy. Through the Arab–Israeli conflict, OPEC discovered its unity and power as a cartel, but it would probably have found it anyway as the Western postwar economic miracle depended so much on cheap oil. The oil weapon, in any event, was two-edged: As the advanced economies drifted into prolonged periods of combined inflation and unemployment, OPEC producers had to start worrying about the health of their golden goose.[24]

The year 1973 was, in any event, a traumatic one for the West and for the United States in particular. Kissinger's Spenglerian gloom combined with evident self-satisfaction as the man of the hour who was in a position to manage American diplomacy as a partial corrective to American decline (or at least relative decline). The satisfaction was in large measure justified, but it also brought him to some odd positions. He wisely embraced Sadat for his courage and vision, yet he was disdainful of European governments whose empathy for the Arab position was not so very different in content from his own.

Neoconservatives and the Reagan Mythology

Whatever their own disagreements, Kissinger and European governments faced some American critics in common. In the 1970s there arose the important rightward intellectual and political movement of neoconservatism. This movement was born on the left, so its ascendance marks an important political defeat for American liberalism. Neoconservatism in its early and purest form comprised disillusioned leftists, including former Trotskyites, who became critical of what they saw as the failings of liberal Great Society domestic policies as well as efforts at conciliation with Soviet communism abroad.[25] Since both the Nixon White House and major European capitals— notably Bonn and Paris—were pursuing strategies of détente with Moscow, neoconservatives came to deeply distrust them all.

Many neoconservatives were Jewish, and the plight of Israel was a special concern. There was anxiety about the pro-Arab policies of European governments, and outrage at the global left's celebration of Palestinian terrorism. This was the era of terrorist spectaculars, including the hijacking and blowing up of Swiss, British, and American airliners in Jordan in 1970; the kidnapping and murder of the Israeli athletes at the Olympics; the kidnapping of ninety Israeli schoolchildren at Ma'alot in 1974 (twenty died in the rescue attempt); and the hijacking by German leftists, acting for jailed Palestinians, of an Air France flight to Entebbe, Uganda, in 1976. In this period the global anti-Zionist left was indelibly stained by active, murderous anti-Semitism. Honest leftists had to acknowledge this stain; it did not require a turn to neoconservatism, but it did impel a reckoning and a renunciation by such young leftists as Joschka Fischer, later Germany's foreign minister. For Fischer the shock of recognition was the news that at Entebbe, the German Revolutionary Cells hijackers, led by a popular Frankfurt leftist named Wilfried Boese, had organized a "'selection' of passengers, Jews on one side, non-Jews on the other, with the Jews slated for execution."[26] Arguably, the real selection criteria was "Israeli," but it was not the only time that airline hijackers went looking for "Jewish" passports among their hostages.[27] The Israeli commandos who interrupted the procedure included a young Ehud Barak and Benjamin Netanyahu's brother Jonathan, who was killed.

Part of the distinctly American appeal of neoconservatism was how it defined itself in large measure as a reaction against both fashionable leftism and the corruption of political language. The early neoconservatives were often brilliant polemicists—their Trotskyite training came in handy—and they were quick to link this Orwellian corruption of language to a culture of détente with communist totalitarians; romanticism, tinged with anti-Semitism, about the postcolonial rage of the Third World; and willful blindness to the evils of terrorism itself. A galvanizing event was the 1975 adoption by the UN General Assembly of a resolution equating Zionism with "racism."[28] With the Soviet Union joining a collection of blood-stained dictatorships in transparently anti-Semitic bluster, the vote was seen as an important symbolic defeat for humane values, and it was linked to what many regarded as America's ongoing strategic retreat, after defeat in Vietnam, Soviet advances in Africa and elsewhere in the Third World, and a whole culture of appeasement.

Such anxieties were serious, and one did not have to embrace neoconservative polemics to share at least some of them. The eloquent counterattack against the "Zionism Is Racism" resolution was led by then UN Ambassador Daniel Patrick Moynihan. For this and other reasons, Moynihan became a sort of patron saint for neoconservatism. Yet though he was, in certain respects, a neocon fellow traveler, Moynihan remained a Democrat, and when he later won a Senate seat from New York, he continued to champion liberal causes.

So the neoconservative insistence that acquiescence in moral double talk is morally corrupting was attractive and important. But their polemical certitudes did more harm than good, at least in more recent years. First, writing off the rhetoric of Third World leaders, especially Arab leaders, may have been satisfying and, in many respects, justified, but it also reinforced an unfortunate tendency of American discourse to render Arab populations more or less invisible. Second, and probably more damaging, the neoconservative assessment of a balance of power tilting toward the Soviets was simply wrong. But they never admitted as much, and helped to construct a potted history whereby the feckless Jimmy Carter was replaced by the resolute Ronald Reagan, who turned a losing game around and won the Cold War. This distorted history would have later consequences, inflating the confidence of neoconservatives regarding the utility of American military force.

RONALD REAGAN entered the White House in an era of American turmoil, exhaustion, and palpable malaise. The country had been humiliated by Iranian revolutionaries who held American diplomats hostage in their own embassy for 444 days. The economy had suffered a new demoralizing mix of high inflation and high unemployment, in part a legacy of the Vietnam War's deficit financing and consecutive oil-price shocks. After a period of détente, U.S.–Soviet confrontation had entered a very serious "second Cold War."

Reagan was lucky because, in the course of his administration, these problems corrected themselves for reasons only partly related to his policies. The hostage crisis was resolved through negotiations between the Carter administration and the Islamic Republic of Iran, facilitated by the government of Algeria (though, in a final insult to Carter, the Iranians delayed the hostages' release until the precise moment of Reagan's inauguration). Inflation was defeated because Paul Volker, a Carter appointee as chairman of the Fed, engineered a painful recession that lasted into the second year of Reagan's presidency. The subsequent recovery was boosted by the Keynesian effects of Reagan's increased defense spending (which also started under Carter) and tax cuts. The supply-side theory that the tax cuts would pay for themselves by encouraging investment proved as ridiculous as it sounds: When Reagan left office, he bequeathed the country large structural budget deficits. However, the underlying economy was strong enough that when Presidents George H. W. Bush and Bill Clinton reversed Reagan's fiscal policies, cutting defense and raising taxes, there were large budget surpluses by the end of Clinton's second term. Finally, the Cold War rapidly unwound when a new Soviet general secretary, Mikhail Gorbachev, launched radical reform at home and conciliatory diplomacy abroad. Reagan reacted with wisdom, courage, and skill when he embraced Gorbachev's radicalism, rather than distrusting it as many in his administration advised. The notion that Reagan's initial hardline policies actually produced the Gorbachev moment does not withstand historical scrutiny.[29] Some good things happened on Reagan's watch and soon thereafter, and he was able to take credit for them in ways that set the parameters of American political debate for the next generation.

In the Middle East, Reagan was handed a mixed legacy, and his administration turned in a mixed performance. The best part of the legacy was Egypt's treaty with Israel and alignment with the United States, a major shift managed skilfully by the Nixon, Ford, and Carter administrations. The worst part was revolutionary Iran, a problem the administration handled with murky morality, giving tacit support to Saddam Hussein's Iraq for its brutal, almost decade-long war against the Iranians. That support included, in effect, condoning Saddam's use of chemical weapons (discussed further in Chapter 6). Reagan's deployment of U.S. marines to Lebanon, arising in part from a humanitarian impulse to help manage the chaos from civil war and Israel's invasion, ended quickly after an Iranian-backed suicide terrorist killed 241 marines and other U.S. personnel, a Lebanese civilian, and himself with a truck bomb. Two minutes later a second truck bomb killed fifty-eight French paratroopers in their compound across the city. Reagan's decision to withdraw has been criticized as the *Ur* act of American appeasement in the face of Islamist terrorism, though one might also argue that he had the good sense to cut America's losses rather than persist in an unsustainable intervention. The Lebanon withdrawal was encouraged by the Pentagon and Defense Secretary Caspar Weinberger, who articulated the eponymous doctrine of strict limits on where and why the United States should go to war. Weinberger channeled the views of military officers who were haunted by Vietnam and averse to any comparable quagmire in the Middle East. As historian John Harper has observed, this created the historical irony that Reagan's was the "first (arguably the only) administration to adopt a clear and coherent position on avoiding future Vietnams."[30]

It wasn't the end of Reagan's woes in Lebanon, however, or of gestures that contained elements of appeasement. The taking of American hostages in Lebanon, and the torture (ultimately to death) of one of them, CIA station chief Christopher Buckley, convinced Reagan to approve a ransom plan in the form of weapons sales that Iran needed desperately for its war with Iraq. The humanitarian impulse was, again, laudable, but the damage to the administration's reputation was significant—even without the bizarre sideshow scheme to funnel profits from the weapons sales to *Contra* rebels in Nicaragua. Such was the real historical record, but the actual facts did not seem to affect the myth of Reaganite power, transcendent virtue, and idealist aggressiveness, which would be applied many years after Reagan left office, and to tragic effect, in Iraq.

While the Reagan administration was cautious about U.S. strategic commitments in the region, it was also forthright in seeing Israel as a valuable strategic asset in the framework of America's Cold War rivalry with the Soviet Union. This approach, in line with Nixon's, downplayed moral commitment in favor of a hard-edged analysis of the regional balance of power and the salience of Israel's location in the eastern Mediterranean. Even Israel's incursion into Lebanon in 1982, which the Reagan administration opposed when operation "Peace for Galilee" turned into the siege of Beirut, was seen as reinforcing deterrence vis-à-vis Syria and its Soviet patron. At this time, the United States established the Joint Political-Military Group with Israel, which brought the two militaries together for operational contingency planning and pre-positioning of U.S. equipment, fuel, and munitions at Israeli bases. Similar arrangements were attempted or completed with other regional states—including the cultivation of military access rights to facilities in the smaller states on the Arab side of the Persian Gulf—which the administration sought to knit into a cohesive and discrete network of defense cooperation.

The idea that Israel's strategic value as a partner against the Soviet Union would outweigh the damaging effect U.S.–Israeli military cooperation might have on Arab opinion was still resisted by the State Department and even by some within the Pentagon. At the same time, some in the U.S. Jewish community and in Israel itself worried that such explicitly strategic cooperation would be less enduring than the moral connection, and therefore a dangerous departure. Many Israelis, moreover, feared involvement in a U.S.–Soviet war. In any event, strategic cooperation deepened. A 1987 act of Congress designated Israel as a major "non-NATO ally," even though the two countries had not then and have not since concluded a formal treaty of alliance.[31]

With Reagan's departure, the instincts of the George H. W. Bush administration reverted to something more in tune with Eisenhower's ambivalence toward Israel. Israel again was viewed as a strategic problem as well as an asset. There were tectonic shifts in world order to be managed: the reunification of Germany, dissolution of the Warsaw Pact, and even, as it turned out, dissolution of the Soviet Union. Saddam Hussein's invasion of Kuwait, and the assembling of an international coalition to drive him out, drew Washington's focus back to the Arab side of the equation.

Washington's main request to Israel at this time was that it make itself scarce. The important thing was to keep the coalition with Arab states together. When Saddam fired Scud missiles at Tel Aviv and Jerusalem—in a largely successful effort to win support on the Arab street—Israel was given some not very effective American antimissile batteries, but was also expected to refrain from retaliating. When the IDF, thinking it might be called upon to mount retaliatory airstrikes anyway, asked Pentagon counterparts for "friend or foe" codes, they were refused. The brutal implication was that the Israeli planes could be shot down.[32]

The elder Bush administration did have reason to believe that its war against Iraq, with Arab states, including Syria, as part of the coalition, would serve Israel's immediate security and longer-term interest in being accepted by its neighbors. President Bush's October 1, 1990, speech at the UN asserted that confronting Iraq would create new opportunities for peace-making in the Middle East.[33] The administration followed through with the Madrid conference, which for the first time put Arab states other than Egypt at a table with Israel. The conference arguably set Israelis and Palestinians on track to the secret negotiations that would lead to the Oslo agreement two years later.

But the Bush administration became impatient with Israel's continued building of settlements, and blocked an automatic extension of housing loan guarantees unless the Yitzhak Shamir government could promise they wouldn't be used to house Jews in the West Bank. (This was a time when Israel was struggling to accommodate the influx of Russian Jews following the collapse of the Soviet Union.) Bush's secretary of state at the time, James Baker, banned then Deputy Foreign Minister Benjamin Netanyahu from the State Department building after Netanyahu said that U.S. policy was "based on lies and distortions." And Baker famously testified to Congress that the Shamir government did not appear ready for a "good faith, affirmative effort" to achieve peace. "I have to tell you that everybody over there should know that the [White House] telephone number is 1-202-456-1414; when you're serious about peace, call us."[34]

Baker has long denied the widely circulated story that he also said, privately, "Fuck the Jews, they didn't vote for us anyway." But if the statement was apocryphal, the math was genuine. Ronald Reagan in his first race against Carter won 39 percent of the Jewish vote—unprecedented for a Republican presidential candidate—against Carter's 45 percent. Eight years later, the elder Bush won 27 percent against the Democrat Michael Dukakis's 73 percent. In his failed bid for reelection, Bush received just 15 percent—the lowest Republican share of Jewish voters since Barry Goldwater in 1964. Bill Clinton in that election won 78 percent.[35]

The Clinton administration fit the familiar template of Democratic administrations' attitudes toward Israel. Emotion, not military logic, governed relations. Clinton spoke frequently to Israeli Prime Minister Yitzhak Rabin and freely expressed his admiration for both Israel and its prime minister. These feelings were reinforced by Rabin's personal style and the mood of optimism surrounding the initial post-Oslo period and the beginning of Israeli–Syrian bilateral negotiations. Israel was to be a partner in the transformation of the region by virtue of its participation in U.S.-brokered political and economic initiatives. Strategic military cooperation continued, but the president's focus turned to Oslo implementation and peace negotiations.

Rabin's 1995 assassination, a religious Jew's fanatical retribution for his willingness to divide the land with Palestinians, was a blow not just to the peace process and to Israel's political comity, but also to the bipartisan strength of U.S. support for Israel. After his close friendship with Rabin, Clinton's relations with Likud's Netanyahu during Netanyahu's first period as prime minister became extremely tense and bitter. After their first meeting in 1996, according to someone who was there, Clinton demanded of his staff, "Who the fuck does he think he is? Who's the fucking superpower here?"[36] Another Clinton aide of the time recounts an episode in which Netanyahu suddenly added new conditions to an agreement on Palestinian prisoners. Clinton erupted, yelling at the prime minister, "This is just chicken shit. I'm not going to put up with this kind of bullshit."[37] Two years later, as Clinton was facing the probe into his relations with Monica Lewinsky that would lead to his impeachment, Netanyahu came to Washington to meet and attend rallies with the president's most vociferous critics, including House Speaker Newt Gingrich, and right-wing Christian evangelists (and Christian Zionists) Pat Robertson and Jerry Falwell. (Falwell, founder of the Moral Majority, was at the time selling videotapes accusing the president of murder.)[38]

Clinton himself nonetheless maintained an enduring optimism about the prospects for a settlement. In the same year, 1998, he traveled to the West Bank and Gaza, where he was welcomed rapturously as a kind of Balfour for Palestine. At the same time there was among U.S. officials a rising sense of panic about the Palestinian explosion of rage that these officials correctly considered, in the absence of a settlement, to be just over the horizon. Together, this optimism and this panic led the administration to press for the deals that Netanyahu's successor, Ehud Barak, offered during the 2000 talks in Camp David and then Taba.

The failure of those talks led to hardened views about the supposed permanent incapacity of Palestinians and their leaders ever to accept Israel's existence and to make peace. According to these views, the Barak government was making a courageous gamble for a negotiated peace comparable in magnitude to Sadat's gamble in 1977. Arafat, in response, walked away from the offer and made a strategic choice for intifada and terrorism. To be sure, this conventional wisdom was soon challenged by a school of Camp David revisionism which noted the abundant reasons for Palestinian rage in the humiliations of an occupied status that had not been adequately ameliorated over nearly ten years of the Oslo process; in fact, the intrusion into Palestinian lives, especially limits on freedom of movement, had worsened in the Oslo years because of continued settlement growth and the security response to Palestinian terrorism. The revisionists also pointed to the failure of Israel (especially under Netanyahu) to fulfill commitments made under Oslo, and argued that the offer made at Camp David contained serious flaws.[39]

But American political discourse was generally preset to favor the Barak-courageous-gamble narrative over the revisionist one. And something then happened that pretty much solidified the narrative, at least for a number of years. Just as Palestinians' rage set off a new flood of violence and terrorism, the so-called "second intifada," the American psyche was wounded by al Qaeda's spectacular and horrific attacks on New York and Washington.

September 11

In respect to the American devotion to Israel, 9/11 had countervailing effects. At first, it sharpened those aspects of American politics and culture that have made Americans across the ideological spectrum ready to understand and embrace Israeli dilemmas and requirements. Over time, however, that very sharpening, and the second Bush administration's determination to turn it to the purpose of a radical departure in U.S. national security policy, led to an equally sharp polarization of the American body politic that is now affecting the debate about Israel as well. To put it simply: The Republican embrace of illiberal policies made it easier to accept illiberal aspects of Israel too. But that illiberal departure sat awkwardly with American traditions and, over time, it carried the support of only a minority—albeit a significant minority—of Americans.

President George W. Bush had an intense commitment to Israeli security. The strength of his attachment lay in the self-identification that has long characterized U.S. support for Israel; a belief that Israel is a valuable (and vulnerable) strategic partner; a religious empathy based on Bush's reading of biblical history and Protestant eschatology; and a perceived need to capture the Jewish vote in key states. This combination of motivations was unusual in U.S. politics, because it brought together traditional Republican and Democratic concerns in a mutually reinforcing way. It embodied both the Reaganite assessment of Israel as a strategic ally and Clintonite enthusiasm for the country and understanding of its dilemmas. These impulses received an important boost from the events of September 11. Instead of the Soviet Union, the United States was now battling the global scourge of terrorism. In this new war, Israel would again be a strategic partner against a common enemy, which had victimized both the United States and Israel. Israel, in Bush's view, was a country that had taken a premature risk for peace and been rewarded with terrorist violence.[40]

Bush's worldview was to become hugely divisive, but in the early months after September 11, most Americans shared it, just as they shared a special understanding of and devotion to Israel. In polls taken before the attacks on New York and Washington, 41 percent of those Americans surveyed expressed support for Israel and 13 percent for Palestinians. After the attacks, 55 percent backed Israel, while support for Palestinians fell by almost half, to 7 percent. CNN images of Palestinian women ululating in exultation after the World Trade Center's fiery destruction no doubt contributed to this disenchantment.[41]

What poll results do not readily convey is the degree to which American elites, and especially foreign policymakers and analysts, were distinctly more favorable to Israel than their European and other foreign counterparts. For example, it was difficult for Americans and Europeans to come to a common understanding of the moral significance of anti-Israeli terrorism. One of the present authors, in a conversation at the time with a British security expert, made what seemed to him the commonsense observation that Palestinian suicide bombers were engaged in the same moral and psychological ritual as the September 11 killers of 2,800 Americans. The British expert vehemently rejected the comparison. Yet the belief that a cult of suicide-murder is so heinous that it overshadows whatever grievances may lie beneath it was at the time central to the American reaction to the Palestinian struggle. *New York Times* columnist Thomas L. Friedman expressed this distinctly American view when he wrote:

Palestinians have adopted suicide bombing as a strategic choice, not out
of desperation. This threatens all civilization because if suicide bombing
is allowed to work in Israel, then, like hijacking and airplane bombing, it
will be copied and will eventually lead to a bomber strapped with a nuclear device threatening entire nations. . . . The Palestinians are so blinded
by their narcissistic rage that they have lost sight of the basic truth civilization is built on: the sacredness of every human life, starting with your
own. If America, the only reality check left, doesn't use every ounce of
energy to halt this madness and call it by its real name, then it will spread.
The devil is dancing in the Middle East, and he's dancing our way.[42]

Suicide terrorism in its evil and madness was indeed one of the most
striking and disturbing innovations of the previous two decades. Americans
after 9/11 felt that they intuited something about its historical significance
that informed the worldview that they shared with Israelis, and distanced
them from ostensible European allies who seemed, in this view, jaded and
complacent about the terrorist threat. Intuition is not an adequate guide to
policy, however, especially when it combines with panic and fear to put liberal values and principles of common sense at risk.

Illiberal Temptations

The 2003 U.S. invasion of Iraq was centerpiece of a grand strategic plan to
reconstruct the Middle East on liberal principles. The neoconservatism of
its ideological proponents has been categorized, correctly, as a kind of liberal imperialism. Yet wars of invasion are highly problematic vehicles for
liberal transformations. As this one went awry, the illiberal side of American right-wing politics became a driving force of the Republican Party.
This was evidently against President George W. Bush's best intentions. To
be sure, Bush himself bears major responsibility for the most egregious
abandonment of American liberal values in the decision to ignore long-
established laws of war to humiliate and torture terrorist suspects (along
with common prisoners of war and victims of mistaken identity) at Abu
Ghraib, Bagram, Guantánamo, and various black sites. And he bears responsibility for taking America to war on pretenses that, knowingly or not, were
false. But Bush also took admirable pains to set an example of ecumenical
respect for the world's two billion Muslims, and he appeared to understand,

at least by the end of his presidency, that some effort at justice for the Palestinians was a necessary token of that respect.[43]

Unfortunately, the party he led was at the same time undergoing a process of ugly transformation. Rallying to a civilizational "war on terrorism," it became the face of a retrograde nationalism. The 2012 presidential candidates of this transformed party were to outbid one another in support of torture.[44] Rhetoric about Muslims was borderline racist.[45] Unsurprisingly, this American illiberalism meshed neatly with illiberal elements of the Israeli right to put forward new and increasingly unattractive rationales for the U.S.–Israeli alliance.

Several months before the invasion of Iraq, one of the present authors attended a small conference in Berlin. Among the participants was Ahmad Chalabi, whose fairy tale that a quick and easy victory against Saddam Hussein would usher in a peaceful, democratic and pro-American Iraq was taken at face value by the mostly conservative Americans in the room. Another session was devoted to the Israel–Palestine problem. In response to Dana Allin's suggestion that Palestinian aspirations and dignity must somehow be accommodated, Arizona's Republican Senator John Kyle replied with a blast of indignation. Kyle's bluster was typical of an emerging conservative argument that the only way to deal with Palestinians in general was to defeat them. Once they were defeated, and understood that they were defeated, they would be forced to make peace on Israel's terms.

There emerged at the time an American right-wing version of an old but never widely credited Israeli idea about dealing with the problem of Gaza and West Bank Palestinians by "transferring" them off the land. This was something new among U.S. conservatives. House Majority Leader Richard Armey in May 2002 was probably the first high-level Republican official to publicly endorse the idea of expelling from the occupied territories their Palestinian inhabitants. "There are many Arab nations that may have thousands of acres of land and soil and property and opportunity to create a Palestinian state. I happen to believe the Palestinians should leave."[46] Other Republicans such as Mike Huckabee and Newt Gingrich were to make similar statements, which coincided with a resurgence in Israel of the idea that the real solution to the Palestine problem was for most Palestinians to move to Jordan.[47] This was a particularly ugly manifestation of convergence between the American and Israeli right, and it underscored the shaky moral ground on which U.S. foreign policy in general, and its support for Israel in particular, could find itself if it departs from the secular-humanist foundations that have guided it for half a century. But, of course, part of the problem was that a growing source of U.S. support for Israel was anything but secular.

Christian Zionism

On a warm September evening in 1978, twenty-year-old Dana Allin sat in the packed common room of Yale's Timothy Dwight College. With fellow students he watched television as President Jimmy Carter spoke to a joint session of Congress; Israeli prime minister Menachem Begin and Egyptian president Anwar Sadat sat in the balcony. The three leaders had just finished thirteen difficult days at the presidential retreat of Camp David, Maryland, concluding an agreement on a framework for peace. Toward the end of his remarks Carter read from the 85th Psalm: "I will hear what God the Lord will speak: for he will speak peace unto his people, and unto his saints: but let them not return again unto folly." Then Carter concluded. "And I would like to say, as a Christian, to these two friends of mine, the words of Jesus, 'Blessed are the peacemakers, for they shall be the children of God.'"[48]

Allin remembers watery eyes and a surge of emotion that felt like a form of religious exaltation. It is important to state here that Allin was (and remains) religiously agnostic. Yet his religious response to the promise of peace in the Holy Land was a profoundly American response. If he grew up and was socialized into a secular milieu—the East Coast professional middle class of the 1960s and 1970s—it was a milieu that was significantly shaped by mainstream churches and multidenominational religious organizations like the National Christian Leadership Conference for Israel. And he was connected to more extended historical memory as well. Imbued with a biblical sensibility, early Americans experienced the country as a promised land and saw themselves entering a new Canaan. A drive across America today reveals town after town named for Old and New Testament sites such as Hebron, Bethlehem, Bethesda, and Salem (short for Jerusalem). For that matter, the residential college where Allin watched Carter's speech was named after the theologian who had helped launch America's Second Great Awakening of religious fervor in the early nineteenth century.

So Christian influence on U.S. policy toward Israel was not always or necessarily in the form of a right-wing Christian Zionism, as Carter himself demonstrates. The Georgia governor was deeply, even awkwardly, a man of faith. His improbable political rise and capture of the White House occurred in the unusual circumstances of the immediate post-Watergate election. The secular political and media establishment did not quite know what to make of a southern politician who, in an interview with *Playboy* magazine, confessed that he had "looked on a lot of women with lust" and had "committed adultery in my heart many times . . ." Many Americans first encountered the concept of being "born again" in reference to the somewhat strange man who would, in a few months, be elected as their president.

In 1973, the year before he announced his candidacy for president, Carter traveled with his wife Rosalyn to Israel. Prime Minister Golda Meir lent them a car and driver, and they drove into the West Bank and washed in the Jordan River. It was, for Carter, a deeply moving pilgrimage, though he also saw things that disturbed him. Lawrence Wright, in an account of the Camp David talks, recounts that Carter returned to see Meir and warned her with some nervousness—because he knew she was a secular Jew—that Israel's empty synagogues portended the bad things that happen to Jews when they turn away from God.[49]

So here, in the White House, was another president, like Wilson, Roosevelt, and Truman, who was fascinated by Israel of the Bible and knew its geography better than that of his own country. Beyond fascination and devotion was a religious fervor unmatched by any of his predecessors except, perhaps, Woodrow Wilson. Of the Camp David agreement, Wright concludes:

> There would be no peace treaty without Carter's unswerving commitment to bring this conflict to an end. He was fueled by his religious belief that God had put him in office in part to bring peace to the Holy Land . . . in truth, there was no candidate as sufficiently powerful and impartial as the United States to fill that role. And yet, until Carter, no American president had been willing to risk his prestige and perhaps his office to pursue such a distant goal.[50]

Devotion to God moved the president of the United States to invest himself and his office into a cause that massively enhanced Israel's security: After the treaty with Egypt, there would be no other Arab army that could truly threaten the Jewish state. Yet Carter took seriously what he regarded as an Israeli pledge as part of the agreement to halt the building of settlements on occupied territory; he was angry that Prime Minister Begin broke that pledge, and despite his irrefutable service to Israel's security, Carter came to be accused of hostility to Israel.

Ronald Reagan was a far more casual Christian than Carter, but his politics were more attractive to the newly energized and politicized Christian right. Where Carter won a thin majority of self-styled Evangelicals, Reagan won 78 percent in his 1984 reelection.[51] Their contribution to American polarization was profound, and was evident in everyday life. Dana Allin spent his high school years in an area of rural Maryland that belonged culturally to the Bible Belt. Though its conservatism was palpable—especially to someone too stupid to cut his shoulder-length hair after frequent hallway beatings—it was also mainly apolitical.[52] But in 1996, twenty years after his high school graduation, Allin returned for a class reunion. He was astonished to receive a lecture from his old friend, a dairy farmer, on the evils of "secular humanism." His friend's tone was affable; still, this was not a conversation they would have conducted at cross-country training on any autumn afternoon in 1975.

Politicized, right-wing Christianity gave a major impulse to the emerging intimacy between American and Israeli conservatives. Neither the American nor the Israeli right consisted exclusively of the religious faithful, but there was a critical mass of true believers in both countries whose biblical literalism was fixed upon the books they shared in the Hebrew Bible and the Old Testament. From the Book of Genesis, one verse in particular commanded attention:

> The LORD said to Abram . . . "Lift up your eyes and look from the place where you are, northward and southward and eastward and westward, for all the land that you see I will give to you and your offspring forever. I will make your offspring as the dust of the earth, so that if one can count the dust of the earth, your offspring also can be counted. Arise, walk through the length and the breadth of the land, for I will give it to you." [Genesis 13:14–17, English Standard]

In the nineteenth century, Protestant "dispensationalists" such as the Irish preacher John Nelson Darby promoted the idea that God's distinct dispensations of grace included the land promised to Abraham and his descendants, and that—*pace* Augustine among others—nothing had superseded that promise to the Jews. In the twentieth century, this dispensationalism became popular in America through the influence of such writers as Cyrus Scofield, whose Scofield Reference Bible appeared in 1909, and Hal Lindsey, a political conservative and Christian writer whose 1970 book *The Late Great Planet Earth* interpreted the tumultuous events of the mid-twentieth century through the lens of dispensationalism and apocalyptic eschatology. Lindsey's book was a publishing phenomenon, selling something like thirty-five million copies in fifty-four languages. (His achievement was surpassed, a generation later, by the *Left Behind* series of sixteen novels coauthored by Tim LaHaye and Jerry B. Jenkins, which depicted the End Time in a similarly wild—and contemporary—theological framework.)[53] Of course, as Paul Miller has noted, the publishing successes of Scofield and Lindsey bracketed a rather significant real-world event:

> The unlikely return of a political entity called "Israel" to the eastern shore of the Mediterranean nearly 2,000 years after the abolition of the Roman province of Judea seemed nothing short of miraculous, and was taken as a clear confirmation that those who had predicted Israel's return long before it was remotely possible had been right. "The one event which many Bible students in the past overlooked was this paramount prophetic sign: Israel had to be a nation again in the land of its forefathers," Lindsey wrote.[54]

What comes next, however, is harrowing. The contemporary gathering of the Jews in Israel is necessary for their participation in the final battle that will be fought there at the end of history. The state of Israel is therefore an essential validation of scriptural history and a vital prerequisite for Christian redemption. Some have argued that the supposed affection of Christian Zionists for Israelis is suspect, given that the last cataclysmic confrontation requires the remaining Jews' conversion to Christianity—or their slaughter and condemnation to everlasting hell. Frankly, however, this apocalypse will be rough on most people, so the Christian believers who anticipate it are not being particularly hard on the Jews.

The more serious problem is that revealed, monotheistic faith—where the revelations are interpreted in literal terms—creates harsh ground for political compromise. In 2002, the neoconservative pundit William Kristol was pointing to and celebrating the growing religiosity of Israel and (as it then seemed) America as an important link that distinguished both countries from more secular European societies.[55] He meant it as a compliment, a mark of U.S.–Israeli exceptionalism. Yet it was also a link that tied them to the religious revivalism of the Islamic world, and the companion of religious revivalism in all three cases has been religious fanaticism.

The carnage inflicted by Islamic fanaticism has, in contemporary times, been the greatest by orders of magnitude. Yet it is also true that the fanatics from all three Abrahamic religions share some common tropes. Thus Anwar Sadat, one of Carter's blessed peacemakers, was gunned down on a Cairo reviewing stand in 1981. His crime was apostasy, his execution duly sanctioned by the religious authority of the "Blind Sheik," Omar Ahmad Abdel Rahman. (Years later Rahman, somehow ensconced in Newark, New Jersey, gave spiritual guidance to the first plotters who attempted to destroy the World Trade Center.) Among Sadat's sins: making peace and thereby accepting a Jewish state in Palestine. Fourteen years later, the Jewish divinity student Yigal Amir approached Israeli Prime Minister Yitzhak Rabin in the parking lot next to the Tel Aviv square where Rabin had just addressed a peace rally, and shot him to death. Amir believed that the murder was rabbinically sanctioned in what amounted to a Jewish fatwa. In being prepared to hand over sacred Jewish land, Rabin was judged to be endangering the redemption of the Jewish people as a whole. Amir later explained: "Without believing in God, I would never have had the power to do this. . . . If not for the Halakhic ruling . . . made against Rabin by a few rabbis I knew about, it would have been very difficult for me to murder." He did not name the rabbis, but it was certainly the case that luminaries of the Orthodox rabbinical establishment, including Rabbi Shlomo Goren, a former head chaplain of the Israeli Defense Forces, had instructed Jews to "disobey any order to evacuate Jewish settlers from Jewish land." Goren also wrote that Jews should be ready to "give our lives in the struggle against the vicious plan of the government of Israel [to evacuate settlements] and be ready to die rather than allow the destruction of Hebron."[56]

The textual link between American right-wing Christianity and these murderous fanatics does not justify imputing any guilt by association. Our point, however, is that American support for Israel should not be based on literal readings of sacred texts. At best, that would mean affirming Menachem Begin's claim of four decades ago that the United States would back maximalist Israeli claims because it is written in the Bible.[57] This indeed is the logic of the affable Mike Huckabee—preacher, presidential candidate, diet guru, and Fox News commentator—when he says that the Palestinians can have a state so long as it isn't in Palestine. At worst, it implicates America in a potential Israeli civil war, not just between Arabs and Jews, but among Israel's Jewish citizens. Yitzhak Rabin's murder was an opening shot in that latent civil war. The injection of apocalyptic eschatology into modern politics is an invitation to murderous violence. As Steven Simon and Daniel Benjamin wrote after 9/11:

> The scriptural emphasis on warfare has armed successive generations with powerful mental images of an embattled world. The community of the faithful is perpetually in crisis or at its edge. When a religious group believes that its identity is fundamentally threatened, it may turn to stories of apocalypse that describe the end of earthly history. . . . In Christian and Jewish apocalyptic literature—exactly as in the Muslim literature, which is based largely on the earlier-born faiths—the reversal of fortune is a stock theme. The righteous advance from suffering under the murderous rule of a terrible beast to a restored community of believers who enjoy eternal life in the presence of God. . . . This is a violence-prone cast of mind.[58]

The most horrific End Time ideology is propagated by the butchers of ISIS in Syria and Iraq.[59] But religious militancy influenced the Christian Identity movement in the United States, which inspired Timothy McVeigh to detonate a truck bomb in front of the Alfred P. Murrah Federal Building in Oklahoma City, killing 168 people and injuring another 600. In Israel, a Jewish messianism grew out of the more religiously oriented Zionism that started to compete with classical secular Zionism after the June 1967 war brought the most holy places of Judaism under the control of the Jewish state. The Gush Emunim ("Bloc of the Faithful") movement arose after the traumatic events of 1973. Menachem Begin's coming to power in 1977 seemed promising, but his signing of the Camp David Accords was deemed a massive betrayal. In 1978, Yeshua Ben-Shoshar, Yehuda Etzion, Menachem Livni, Gilead Peli, and several others started stockpiling explosives for their intended plot to blow up the Dome of the Rock in Jerusalem, the third holiest site for Islam. This act, they believed, would usher in the millennium. As Etzion put it, "We exist in the world in order to actualize destiny."[60] The plot was never carried out because the plotters could not find a rabbi to bless it.

But the lack of rabbinical dispensation did not stop another Jewish fanatic, Dr. Baruch Goldstein, from killing twenty-nine Muslim worshipers, and wounding another 150, at the Tomb of the Patriarchs in Hebron. Goldstein, American-born, followed the American Rabbi Meir Kahane, who advocated expelling Israel's Arabs and would himself later be killed by a Muslim fanatic. For Kahane and Goldstein, the Jews' struggles of millennia continued. The battle was existential, and the Jews could afford no compromise.[61]

American Exceptionalism

Most Jews and most Christians, it should go without saying, are not biblical literalists or fanatics. The presidency of George W. Bush was, in our view, damaging on many levels to American interests. Yet, whatever signals to American Evangelicals were embedded in code by Michael Gerson, his talented speechwriter, Bush was no religious fanatic, and nothing in his personal relationship with Jesus Christ precluded the establishment of a Palestinian state.

Bush's moral and strategic overreach did demonstrate, however, how American religiosity has injected another kind of Messianic impulse into the American creed: the idea of American exceptionalism. This messianic impulse is far gentler, obviously, than those discussed above, but it can carry problems, not least in its relevance to the American relationship with Israel. There is a well-considered, secular vision of exceptionalism, embraced along today's ideological spectrum from Robert Kagan to Barack Obama. Kagan has been a thoughtful and influential reinterpreter of neoconservatism for the twenty-first century. In his important essay "Power and Weakness," a key argument is that the "exceptional" role of America in the world had mainly structural rather than moral or cultural causes.[62] America's immense military capabilities shaped the national psychology about when it is useful to employ military force, while its historical traditions made it a natural champion of universal liberty.[63] Barack Obama, asked at a Strasbourg press conference early in his presidency whether he believed in American exceptionalism, delivered a lengthy response that conveyed some of the same ideas argued by Kagan.[64] Obama took care, however, to add the commonsense observation that other nationalities could feel that their countries were pretty exceptional too.

There are more extreme versions of exceptionalism shaped by religious conviction. These carry theological implications beyond our comfort zone—though we feel reasonably confident in asserting that even a personal deity would not be in the business of picking individual countries on planet earth over others. In any event, like many religious ideas, this one can be taken to virulent extremes, invoking not the transcendent inclusiveness of God's grace, but the sectarian otherness of the outsider. In the years since 2008, it has been lashed to the most virulent attacks on the allegedly un-American strangeness of Obama and his schemes.

"From the moment Barack Obama appeared on the national stage," Peter Beinart has noted, "conservatives have been searching for the best way to describe the danger he poses to America's traditional way of life."[65] Eventually they settled on a unifying conclusion: Obama denies and refutes the truth of American exceptionalism. According to the Factiva database, as cited by Beinart, the term appeared 3,000 times in English-language publications during the entire George W. Bush presidency, but more than 10,000 times in just the first five years of Obama's.

In the run-up to Obama's 2012 reelection, the denials of his devotion to both his own country and that country's Israeli ally turned into a full and steady stream. One became inured to the language, but it was really quite remarkable. Obama, it was alleged, intended with full malice aforethought to turn America into the kind of barren, socialist dystopia that was somehow the "Europe" of the right-wing imagination. "I want you to remember," said Mitt Romney in a campaign speech after winning the New Hampshire primary, "when our White House reflected the best of who we are, not the worst of what Europe has become."[66] Obama sought a "European-style entitlement society. . . . This president takes his inspiration from the capitals of Europe; we look to the cities and small towns of America." Such rhetoric went on and on.[67]

The American tradition of Europe-bashing, albeit often less crude than this, is an old one: It goes back to founders' disputations about whom to align with in the wars between Britain and France. There is a certain logic insofar as passionate exceptionalism requires a defining contrast, for which Europe has served since at least the time of Jefferson. In the campaign against Obama, moreover, there was a natural fit between the conservative claim that he did not properly love America, did not love Israel, and in fact preferred

Europe—the place that American neoconservatives, in particular, have long distrusted as pro-Arab.[68]

The attacks on Obama as not authentically American did not end with his reelection. In February 2015, Rudy Guiliani, the political hero of 9/11, was speaking at a New York dinner of wealthy conservatives, and said the following:

> I do not believe, and I know this is a horrible thing to say, but I do not believe that the president loves America. He doesn't love you. And he doesn't love me. He wasn't brought up the way you were brought up and I was brought up through love of this country.[69]

This was an extraordinary statement. But, attempting to take it more seriously than it perhaps deserves to be taken, can we stipulate that Guiliani was perhaps caricaturing a genuine difference in worldview? The answer is that Obama's impulses and themes derived from quintessentially American traditions and themes, but they were to an extent reimagined by an acutely intelligent and imaginative politician with a distinctive experience and formation.

Obama's embrace of American exceptionalism was at once more complicated and more serious than that of his critics. In his March 18, 2008, speech on race, he said that "for as long as I live, I will never forget that in no other country on Earth is my story even possible."[70] This was debatable. Yet, it does seem palpably true that there is something distinctive in the American energy to reinvent itself, that the election of a black man as president was an expression of this moral genius, and that, equally, the achievement could only be appreciated against the context of America's faults and sins and ongoing struggle to create "a more perfect union"—as Obama titled that speech, and repeated many times in many subsequent speeches.

Just as American exceptionalism can only be understood as an ongoing struggle against real American demons, the purposes of American power abroad can be considered benign only if understood to be imperfect and not always friendly to the objects of American attention. Inside a bubble of our own propaganda, Americans might convince themselves that their actions are always accepted as virtuous by the rest of the world, but that does not make it so. Hence, Obama's Cairo speech was indeed an important one. He delivered it early in his presidency, on June 4, 2009.

I've come to Cairo to seek a new beginning between the United States and Muslims around the world. . . . I do so recognizing that change cannot happen overnight. I know there's been a lot of publicity about this speech, but no single speech can eradicate years of mistrust, nor can I answer in the time that I have this afternoon all the complex questions that brought us to this point. But I am convinced that in order to move forward, we must say openly to each other the things we hold in our hearts and that too often are said only behind closed doors. There must be a sustained effort to listen to each other; to learn from each other; to respect one another; and to seek common ground.[71]

As a bid for a "new beginning," the speech was certainly ambitious, and now, near the end of Obama's presidency, we can conclude that the ambition has, in many though not all respects, failed. But that doesn't mean it wasn't worth a try. And we can attest from long observation and, in the case of one of us, from working directly with the president, something else. The allegation that Cairo somehow embodied a naïveté about the world in general, and Muslim societies in particular, a naïveté that has been carried through in the policies of his presidency, is false.

So while there was a genuine newness in Obama's approach at home and abroad, we should never exaggerate the differences. Obama's liberalism is very much in the mold of his liberal predecessors, including FDR, Harry Truman, John F. Kennedy, and Bill Clinton. His understanding of American exceptionalism as a struggle between American ideals and America's original sins is a perfect echo of Lyndon Johnson's understanding, when Johnson stood before the U.S. Congress, a week after the brutal beatings of unarmed protestors in Selma, Alabama, to call for a new voting rights act and to intone, "We shall overcome."

Moreover, Obama's realism has been very much in the mold of Richard Nixon's and even Ronald Reagan's. It was conveyed in a seminal moment during his first long presidential campaign, when he was asked, during a YouTube debate, "Would you be willing to meet separately, without preconditions, during the first year of your administration, in Washington or anywhere else, with the leaders of Iran, Syria, Venezuela, Cuba, and North Korea, in order to bridge the gap that divides our countries?" Obama's answer: "I would." The answer was considered a faux pas, not least by his campaign aides who immediately conferred on how to undo the damage. But Obama, according to *The New Yorker*'s Ryan Lizza, overheard them and said "something to the effect of 'This is ridiculous. We met with Stalin. We met with Mao. The idea that we can't meet with Ahmadinejad is ridiculous.'"[72]

Thus Obama has been a carrier of recognizable American traditions. There are, nonetheless, two ways in which his presidency marks a new era. First, if he is a conventional liberal in the mold of Truman or Johnson, it is also arguable, as we will indeed argue in subsequent pages, that after a forty-year eclipse by the conservative ascendancy, American liberalism is moving back toward a dominant position. Second, Obama is black man of multiracial formation and experience, and it would be silly to argue that this formation has nothing to do with how he sees the world. Obama represents a departure, not in the main lines of U.S. foreign policy, but more in the nature of American society—in what America is becoming. Obama was not an aberration, he is the future.

As Obama's Israeli critics may have intuited, this future has implications for the future of U.S.–Israeli relations. It does not mean American hostility toward Israel, but it could impose greater American expectations. These are expectations that Israel could be unwilling, or even unable, to meet.

PART II
The Crisis

3

Obama, Netanyahu, and the Palestinians

BARACK OBAMA cultivated Jewish leaders—and voters—in Chicago during his Senate run and through his presidential campaign. For the most part, these were progressive Jews who embodied the values of a generation that marched through Selma, Alabama, linked arm in arm with Martin Luther King, Jr. The avatar of this generation, Rabbi Abraham Joshua Heschel, was no longer alive when Obama began his association with the circle of a liberal Chicago Jewish community, but Heschel's values animated the group.[1] The connection between the American rabbinate and the civil rights movement in the 1960s was close, even intimate. Most of these clergy were from the Reform movement, but there were Orthodox and Conservative rabbis as well. Heschel, who is immortalized in the famous Selma photo of King, Ralph Abernathy, and Ralph Bunche, was an institutional conservative, that is, centrist in his doctrinal preferences but largely orthodox in personal practice. Rabbis had organized freedom rides as early as 1961, and Jewish lawyers had worked side-by-side with black legal experts at the NAACP, the board of which included a rabbi. For the most part, rabbinic participants in the civil rights movement were, like Heschel, staunch opponents of the war in Vietnam. Their public policy concerns were rooted in the Hebrew Bible. The Jews, like the blacks, had been enslaved for centuries. They were expected by God to identify with the suffering of slaves everywhere. This, of course, is one of the motifs of the Passover seder ceremony, and in the 1960s Jews celebrated "freedom seders." The peasants of Vietnam slotted neatly into this narrative.

With the ghetto riots of the late sixties, the stigmatization of Jewish landlords, and radicalization of young urban blacks, the relationship between liberally inclined Jews and the black community soured. The Jews felt that their collaborative efforts earlier in the decade were disregarded, while the radicalized street leadership in the black community condemned these efforts as patronizing and the narrative of collaboration as mere self-congratulation by a comfortable part of the white establishment that had actually risked rather little for their principles. Black radicals' support for the 1975 United Nations General Assembly resolution equating Zionism with racism helped complete the break. It has never really healed, as the air-brushing of Jews from Ava DuVernay's *Selma*, the 2015 biopic about King, seems to suggest.[2]

Nevertheless, the impulse that thrust Heschel and other prominent rabbis into the civil rights protests of the 1960s did not fade completely. Glowing embers were fanned to life by the rabbis and Zionist leaders who connected with Obama in Chicago. It was their reading of Jewish tradition and of Zionism that Obama absorbed. He was influenced especially by Newton Minow, a discreet lawyer who had long felt that Israel's occupation of Palestinian territories was unjust and unwise. Minow, briefly famous as chair of the Federal Communications Commission in the 1960s for declaring that television of the day offered a "vast wasteland," was a Zionist who believed Israel's policies toward the Palestinians had betrayed the ideals of the Jewish faith, which he equated with his own liberal temperament. Judge Abner Mikva, who served as a congressman, circuit court judge, and White House counsel for two years in the Clinton administration, was another such influence. Bettylu Salzman, whose father, Philip Klutznick, had been a philanthropist and Jewish community leader, was an important member of this circle. (Klutznick was ultimately repudiated by the mainstream Jewish organizations he helped found as they moved to the right in recent decades.) David Axelrod, Obama's political advisor, was introduced to the future candidate in Chicago by these liberal Jews and shared their overall sense that Israel had gone off the rails.[3]

Obama was exposed to harsher rhetoric about both Israeli and American foreign policy from Trinity United Church of Christ pastor Jeremiah Wright. Wright was close to the Obamas, officiating at their wedding and baptizing their daughters. The preacher tended to express himself in a kind of rococo prophetic rhetoric. But this was between Wright and his parishioners until he attracted a degree of notoriety for the circulation of videos of his sermons, including one in which he declared that the United States has brought the 9/11 attacks upon itself by inflicting horrific violence on the rest of the world for decades. He honed these themes in the ensuing years in a way that jeopardized Obama's political standing. Eventually, campaign politics necessitated a break. Wright attributed his exclusion from the White House to "them Jews" around Obama.[4] Yet whatever impact Wright's preaching might have had on Obama's worldview more generally, it seemed to have no impact on Obama's views on the Jewish state. By all accounts, he considered the creation of the Jewish state a marvelous thing and admired its accomplishments. Steven Simon in his time with the Obama administration certainly never heard anything different.

Obama came into office seeing Israel in much the same way as his liberal Zionist backers saw it: as a flawed miracle. The Chicagoans believed that Israel's governments had pursued policies that damaged the long-term interests of the Jewish state while punishing the Palestinian people, whose troubles they took seriously.

Israel's center-right American friends don't completely disregard Palestinian suffering. The difference between center-right and center-left is the latter's view that there is a parallel of sorts between the horrors that punctuated Jewish history and the dispossession of the Palestinians. For the center-right, this parallel is an offensive and false equivalence that trivializes the Holocaust. But the policy implication for those who take the parallel seriously is that Israel has an obligation to make the concessions necessary for a resolution to the conflict. And for the center-left, there is yet another consideration that the center-right rejects: Because Israel is the stronger party, it is obligated to accept disproportionate risks in pursuit of a just agreement with the Palestinians. Obama seemed to subscribe to both of these beliefs, to the intense discomfort of an Israeli political establishment that rejects both.

In the period leading up to the election in 2008, the Obama campaign tacked somewhat to the right. Swirling suspicions about Obama's views on Israel led his team to tone things down and distance the candidate from two lightning rod advisors, Robert Malley and Daniel Kurtzer. Both are Jewish. Malley is a brilliant lawyer and academic who had served as the chief aide to Bill Clinton's national security advisor, Sandy Berger, and had also functioned as a peace process expert on the NSC staff. Cosmopolitan, shrewd, and low key, Malley grew up in France and was educated at Harvard and Oxford. He achieved a kind of notoriety by breaking with the consensus regarding culpability for the failure of the Camp David and Taba talks in 2000 and 2001. Then president Clinton had put the blame for the breakdown of talks squarely on Palestinian leader Yasir Arafat, to whom he has recalled saying, "I'm a colossal failure, and you have made me one."[5] Malley's reconstruction in the Rashomon-like parade of postmortems following the talks was cooler and more nuanced; his was a leading voice in the school of "Camp David revisionism." Like the biblical Jacob, Malley's name soon "reeked among the people of the land." Branded an apologist for Arafat by the right and left and cast as disloyal to the Clinton peace team, he was judged a liability by Obama's team and ejected from the campaign. (These problems tend to fade with time, and by 2015 Malley was once again on the National Security Council staff, responsible for coordinating policy toward the Middle East region, including negotiations with Iran over its nuclear program.)

Kurtzer's background is equally uncommon. An ordained Orthodox rabbi with a Columbia doctorate in Middle Eastern studies, he scaled the heights of the Foreign Service, in which he served as ambassador to Egypt, then Israel. As the U.S. envoy in Tel Aviv during the George W. Bush administration, he was viewed as a problem by the White House because of his assertive stance toward Israeli activities, particularly settlement construction, that were seen to impede U.S. diplomatic objectives. Elliott Abrams, who refers to himself as the "White House Middle East guy" in his memoir, describes Kurtzer as "a political enemy of Ariel Sharon."[6] This was not meant to be a compliment. The implication was that Kurtzer was pursuing his own anti-Zionist agenda in carrying out his instructions from the State Department, which, in Abram's view, was a renegade faction of the U.S. government seeking to undermine the president's authority. Strained relationships between Foggy Bottom and the White House are nothing new, of course, but the bitterness evident in Abrams' account, especially toward career diplomats, was unusual.

In any event, this story line about Kurtzer's performance as ambassador turned out to have legs. Despite early involvement in Obama's campaign, Kurtzer's dovish reputation risked reinforcing suspicions about which side of the conflict Obama was really on, and he was sidelined. Although he was an informal counselor to Obama's first national security advisor, Jim Jones, and his focus on settlements clearly influenced Obama's first-year game plan, Kurtzer never really got back in the game. He was crowded out by Dennis Ross.

Ross is another exceptional character. He combines all the qualities essential to success in the official policy community. A powerful patron is, of course, a prerequisite. Superb briefing skills are also indispensable; without these, there can be no powerful patron. And a powerful patron affords access and credibility in elite circles—a platform for briefing skills in increasingly decisive settings. Ross's patrons during his decades in Washington included James Baker, both Clintons, and, in the Obama administration, Tom Donilon. Ross's seductiveness owes a great deal to his easygoing West Coast demeanor, languid air, and breathy voice. He has the reassuring qualities of the doctor you really hope you will have if you are ever diagnosed with a fatal illness. In an arena where most of the news is bad news, senior staff who possess this attribute are the messengers least likely to be shot. In the Obama administration, they were known as "whisperers." The other essential quality is to be able to boil complex issues down to a couple of basic propositions, sanded and planed to a perfectly smooth, impermeable, and nicely shaped argument. Deployed as mantras, these could seem incredibly perceptive, yet somehow obvious at the same time, with the result that the briefing recipient is impressed without being threatened. Ross was just magnificent. In 2008, he was also someone who could direct these powers toward a skeptical Jewish electorate, with all the credibility of a person who is widely understood to be a true friend of Israel.

It's impossible to say how important this rightward maneuver was in electoral terms. Obama did well in states with large Jewish populations in 2012, at a time when his opponent was accusing him of betraying Israel, so it seems unlikely Obama's prospects would have suffered in 2008 if he had not taken the fireproofing steps he took during the campaign. Nevertheless, Malley and Kurtzer were out and Daniel Shapiro, a young, liberally inclined Orthodox Jew who had worked for Congressman Bill Nelson, was in. Ross was given a job at the State Department, where he was an advisor to Hillary Clinton on matters relating to Iran, about which he was in a position to reassure the Israeli government regarding U.S. intentions.

Tactical shifts in the heat of a campaign to shore up the base, especially among critical constituencies, are business as usual. The rhetoric wrapped around these repositioned policies can sometimes constrain an incoming administration's options. One might have expected this phenomenon to play out this way regarding the administration's peace process agenda. But that is not how it turned out. The White House made it clear from the very beginning of the first term that despite tacit signals to the contrary in the latter part of the campaign, the peace process would be a priority and that the focus of intervention would be on Israeli settlement activity.

Unsettlement

Israeli settlements in the West Bank were established shortly after the IDF ejected Jordan from west of the Jordan River during the Six Day War of 1967. A combination of messianic zeal and practical military thinking led to a fairly rapid expansion of the settlement enterprise. When Obama took office in January 2009, the settler population was over 478,000, about 40 percent of whom were living in East Jerusalem, the sector of the city that had been in Jordanian territory until the 1967 war, or in suburban enclaves clustered along the old cease-fire line. The rest live in settlements scattered throughout the West Bank.[7]

The settler population has changed in important ways since the early days of settlement construction and habitation nearly a half-century ago. Until the early 1990s, population growth resulted from Israelis moving into the West Bank. The implication was that if there were a policy decision to remove incentives for immigration or simply to prohibit it, the growth of settlements could be slowed or halted. By the late 1990s, however, settler population growth due to births within the settlements had exceeded growth owing to immigration. In 2011, for example, 3,600 Jews moved to the West Bank, but nearly 11,000 were born there.[8]

Demographers expect this trend to accelerate because of the growing number of ultra-Orthodox that have been relocating to the West Bank (excluding Jerusalem). In 1991, only about 5 percent of the settlers were ultra-Orthodox. By 2011 they constituted over 30 percent of the population. By the end of this decade, their share of the overall settler population will be closer to 40 percent. The total fertility rate among ultra-Orthodox women—that is, the number of children on average that a woman will have in her fertile years—is an astonishing 7.7. For comparison, West Bank Palestinians have a total fertility rate of 3.1, just a hair more than the Jewish women within the

Green Line. Settlers of all religious stripes have high total fertility rates, on average a bit over 5.0. At this stage, nearly 20 percent of the entire West Bank population is made up of Israeli settlers, and a large plurality of these are ultra-Orthodox. It is not hard to see how the Israeli settlement project has created difficulties for any Israeli government in pursuing a peace settlement, while making a deal less plausible or even desirable to Palestinians.[9]

Settlements have complicated the task of negotiating an agreement by populating parts of the West Bank so densely with Israelis, especially ultra-Orthodox Israelis, over such a long period of time that the return of these conurbations to Arab sovereignty has become hard to imagine. Hence the need for the parties to agree on territorial swaps. This, in turn, makes an already freighted negotiation even more challenging, since the only land available to swap for territory around Jerusalem is fundamentally undesirable. It's very hard to find areas that are as habitable and productive as the territories that Israel will likely retain in an eventual deal. This was what Israeli proponents of settlements meant nearly a half century ago when they spoke of "creating facts on the ground."

Settlements are also problematic because they interrupt the contiguity of Palestinian land. The various bits of Palestinian territory are separated from each other by areas that are settled by Israeli Jews. All the development models of a successful Palestinian state show that contiguity is vital to the economic growth needed to sustain an increasing Palestinian population. The need to go through multiple checkpoints introduces transaction costs that hobble economic activity while necessitating the duplication of assets and infrastructure in areas that are cut off from each other. If Palestinian refugees were to return to a new Palestinian state, the demographic pressures would naturally be greater, along with the need for territorial contiguity.

Every American administration has opposed settlement activity, usually relying on a rhetorical formula combining the concepts of illegitimacy and unfairness. In the years immediately after 1967, the U.S. position was that settlements were illegal under the provisions of the fourth Geneva Convention, which forbids occupying powers to transfer their own population to conquered territories. Like legal arguments everywhere, this one was contested in the combative world of diplomacy and international law; it was fiercely challenged by Israel's lawyers, and Washington soon gave up pressing the point. The fallback was to point out that settlement activity was in effect prejudging the results of negotiations by removing from the chessboard land that the other side laid claim to and which the two sides were supposed to be bargaining over. This was the fairness argument. Invoking legitimacy was meant to convey the sense that settlements were illegal without getting mired in endless legal argument.

So Obama's was certainly not the first U.S. administration to oppose or make an issue of the settlements. Ronald Reagan, for example, had tried to take a firm stand in the wake of the Lebanon War of 1982. Reagan declared that:

> The United States will not support the use of any additional land for the purpose of settlements. . . . Indeed, the immediate adoption of a settlement freeze by Israel, more than any other action, could create the confidence needed for wider participation in these talks. Further settlement activity is in no way necessary for the security of Israel and only diminishes the confidence of the Arabs that a final outcome can be freely and fairly negotiated.[10]

When the U.S. ambassador previewed Reagan's speech for Israeli Prime Minister Menachem Begin, Begin lamented that it was "the saddest day of his life."[11] Reagan's initiative died swiftly, but the problem of settlements was subsequently raised in other contexts. As we have seen, the administration of the elder President Bush got into a bruising fight with Israel's Shamir government over settlements. And, in a forlorn effort to stem the spiraling violence of the al Aqsa intifada in the fall of 2000, the George W. Bush administration convened a summit at the Egyptian resort town of Sharm al-Sheikh, which established a fact-finding commission of prominent men—the EU's Javier Solana, Turkey's Suleiman Demirel, Thorbjoern Jagland from Norway, and from the United States, two distinguished former senators, Warren B. Rudman and George J. Mitchell—to get to the root of the problem and recommend a way forward for the warring parties. Among its many recommendations, the commission stated that "The [Government of Israel] should freeze all settlement activity, including their 'natural growth.'"[12] (Natural growth is an Israeli term referring to additional construction to house the growing populations of existing settlements.)

The settlement question then found its way into the "Roadmap for Peace" that the Quartet of the UN, EU, Russia, and the United States devised during the first term of the Bush administration. The Roadmap charted a phased arrangement whereby the Israelis and Palestinians would each meet specific obligations, which would unlock additional positive actions in a sequence ultimately leading to a final status accord. According to the Roadmap, in the first phase of the process, "Consistent with the Mitchell Report, the [Government of Israel] freezes all settlement activity (including natural growth of settlements)."[13] In any event, the Palestinian Authority was never able to stanch the terrorist attacks that hammered Israel during this period. With Israeli civilians being massacred within the Green Line, there was no possibility that the Israelis would make concessions on settlement growth. The Bush administration was sympathetic to Israel's position and chose not to push then Prime Minister Sharon on the issue, especially given their perception of Sharon's political vulnerabilities. It was an intractable chicken-and-egg scenario. Israel would not take symbolic steps desired by the Palestinians because Abbas could not get a grip on Palestinian attacks against Israel and Abbas could not get traction because he was seen as unable to wring concessions from Israel. To make matters worse, neither side believed the other would deliver even if reciprocal concessions were agreed upon. Despite the failure of the Roadmap to foster progress toward a settlement, it did make clear that settlements were seen to be a problem that had to be tackled if the process were ever to advance—a thesis clearly endorsed by the Bush administration.[14]

Although Israeli public opinion was increasingly divided about the settler movement, many Israelis saw it as the embodiment of a pioneering spirit that was central to Israel's national myth. In reality this spirit had long since leached out of Israel's urbanized culture. But this only made the myth more essential to Israel's identity. Israelis are not the first to have gone through this disorienting process of profound social change. As the United States changed from a rural agrarian society to an urban industrial one after the First World War, and the frontier gave way to a unified continental society, cowboy movies—those proverbial "horse operas"—dominated the country's cinematic production. The more the Great Plains were fenced and farmed and cowboys disappeared, the more these laconic, rugged individualists on horseback appeared on screen and in the American imagination. For a changing Israel coming to grips with the end of its own pioneer days, settlers filled an analogous emotional gap. So, even before the settler movement burgeoned into a politically potent force in its own right, it had become a difficult thing for the United States, let alone Israeli governments of whatever political stripe, to challenge.

And the complex politics of the issue within Israel enabled successive prime ministers to argue that the issue was beyond their ability to manage. Hence if progress in the peace process were to happen, it would have to happen despite settlements. Eventually, this argument gave way to the claim that settlements were actually a good thing, because they would incentivize the Palestinians to negotiate in earnest. By this reasoning, the more settlements the better. The reality, of course, was that the effect on Palestinian motivations was precisely the opposite. If the Israelis were serious about returning land, why were they building on it?

The George W. Bush administration did depart in one respect from the way previous administrations had handled the settlements issue by agreeing in a 2004 letter to the Sharon government that, as far as the United States was concerned, the major settlement blocs would remain in Israeli hands in the context of a final status accord with the Palestinians.[15] On one hand, this was a concession to what many already assumed—that the large suburbs clustered on the Green Line and around Jerusalem were so solidly established and so densely populated that the return of the land they encumbered was inconceivable. On the other hand, it appeared to signal the Palestinians that the United States was officially rejecting the idea that the 1967 cease-fire line was relevant to negotiations. For the Bush administration this concession seemed to make sense because Sharon was preparing to remove all Israelis from the Gaza strip and dismantle the settlements there. Sharon had also said that he would remove four small settler outposts in the northern West Bank, suggesting that what he had done in Gaza he might be prepared to do in the much more sensitive West Bank. Although unilateral withdrawal, as opposed to negotiated withdrawal, was viewed skeptically in Washington, it was still thought to be better than nothing. Sharon, who was being battered by his own party over the withdrawal from Gaza, deserved something in Bush's estimation, so the concession on settlement blocs seemed a sensible and even small price to pay.

The Bush approach evolved over time, however, especially once Condoleezza Rice moved from the White House to the State Department. Control of peace process policy and diplomacy moved with her, isolating the neoconservative Elliott Abrams and injecting a new flexibility into the administration's thinking. (When Steven Simon briefed Abrams in 2005 about the RAND Corporation's study *Helping a Palestinian State Succeed*, Abrams thanked him for taking the trouble but observed, perhaps just a bit mischievously, that "there isn't going to be a Palestinian State.") The White House would have also been conscious in 2007 of the commitment made earlier to Tony Blair that the United States would revive the Middle East peace process, implicitly intended to help Blair counter the unpopularity of Britain's involvement in the invasion of Iraq.[16]

In a sense, Rice's view of the problem resembled the views of the Chicagoans surrounding Obama, who at about this time was already planning to compete for the Democratic nomination. In pushing back against criticism of the 2007 Annapolis peace summit, she pointed to restrictions on the movement of Palestinians within the West Bank, comparing them to acts of racial discrimination that had angered her as a black youngster in Alabama. Abrams derides her characterization of the issue, describing Rice's outrage in the sarcastic terms of his own countervailing outrage. "Never before had I heard Condi cast the Israelis as Bull Connor and the Palestinians as the civil rights movement."[17]

The Annapolis conference failed to produce an agreement. Controversy continues to surround it. It was in fact a dramatic event. Virtually all the Arab countries were represented by heads of government or foreign ministers, although the Saudis and others churlishly refused to shake Olmert's hand or allow themselves to be photographed with Israelis. The conference initiated a detailed planning process led by Tzipi Livni and Abu Ala'a that produced studies and draft agreements on a range issues in which Israel and the Palestinians had a common interest. These talks were carried out bilaterally, without U.S. participation. And Palestinian president Mahmoud Abbas met one-on-one perhaps dozens of times with Prime Minister Ehud Olmert on the core issues. On these, they came up with a plan that broadly resembled the Clinton proposals of Camp David II and Taba talks: a Palestinian capital in Jerusalem, internationalization of the Holy Basin, the return of nearly all the West Bank to Palestinian control (up to 93.7 percent of the territory with negotiated land swaps for another 5.8 percent), a Gaza–West Bank corridor, and a "humanitarian gesture" that would allow for a certain number of Palestinians returnees without conceding a right to return.

Abbas eventually rejected the offer, in part because it did not entail a right of return; in part because the Israelis appear not to have conveyed an authoritative, detailed map of the territorial aspects of the proposal; and in part because Olmert's legal troubles overwhelmed him (he was to be indicted and convicted of bribery) before the Palestinian side could formulate a coherent response to what he had put on the table. To Israelis, Abbas's rejection of the offer was incomprehensible—a repeat of Arafat's behavior at Camp David. The offer, in the Israeli view, was self-evidently better than anything the Palestinians would ever again be offered. When he spurned it, Abbas signaled to many centrist Israelis, who were already spooked by Palestinian violence during the al Aqsa intifada, that they really did not have a partner for peace.

The truth is probably more complicated. For Palestinians, doubts about Olmert's ability to deliver were superimposed on fears about their own ability to deliver. These combined with suspicions raised by Israel's refusal to present a detailed map, and led, ineluctably and perhaps tragically, to rejection of a deal. But Abbas apparently believed that negotiations could continue. This was a mistake, not least because the U.S. government at the time lacked the focus to keep the negotiations going. Having established the process, the administration in effect abstained from managing it. There seemed to be little confidence that the parties would really agree and therefore little incentive to invest time or effort, either by providing bridging proposals where the negotiators were stuck or, in the grim endgame, a U.S. framework for an agreement. The objectives themselves were in dispute, with Abrams working against the State Department to substitute American backing for the development of Palestinian institutions—what he called a bottom-up approach—for the top-down diplomatic effort aimed at a final agreement and Palestinian statehood that Rice had set in motion.[18] Internecine squabbling over the purposes of U.S. involvement compounded the disorientation of a White House distracted by an unfolding disaster in Iraq and the implementation of a new war strategy—the surge. There then erupted another bout in the recurring battle between Israel and the Hamas forces in Gaza, with 1,400 deaths and wrenching suffering inflicted on the Palestinians there, while Israelis huddled in bunkers under an avalanche of rockets. This Gaza War, "Operation Cast Lead," which began in late December of 2008 and ended right before Barack Obama's inauguration, killed whatever negotiating momentum might still have existed.

Obama's Difficult Start

Bush's legacy to Obama was therefore both complicated and difficult. The problem seemed to call for a new approach. Obama appointed former Senate Majority Leader George J. Mitchell, who had chaired the Sharm al-Sheikh Commission, to lead the effort. Before that he had been the U.S. special envoy to Northern Ireland. In that capacity, under President Clinton, he chaired the all-party peace talks that produced the Good Friday peace agreement of 1998, ending a hundred years of political and religious war. A record of resolving apparently intractable conflicts seemed like a good qualification and, as former negotiator Aaron David Miller pointed out at the time, Mitchell's appointment indicated the new administration's serious commitment to the peace process.[19]

Obama was determined to put a tougher U.S. stand against Israeli settlements at the center of this process. He may have been freer to do so in part because there were no peace process professionals in the West Wing to tell him it would probably not work. This was not necessarily a bad thing; the triumph of hope over experience can lead to bad outcomes, but so can the triumph of experience over hope. In this instance, the White House chief of staff, Rahm Emanuel—judged by the *New York Times* in 2009 as "perhaps the most influential chief of staff in a generation"—believed that it could and would work. Emanuel's father had been a member of the Irgun, the right-wing Jewish militia that flourished in mandatory Palestine. His uncle had been killed by Arabs in 1933. Rahm himself had spent two weeks on an Israeli military base in 1991 as a kind of volunteer cum tourist. He and others seemed to feel that this pedigree would fireproof him against charges of anti-Zionism or pro-Palestinian bias. In one meeting shortly after Obama took office, Emanuel—well known for his over-the-top and bellicose delivery of messages—told officials responsible for Middle East policy that the United States would compel Israel to concede to the administration's demands regarding the settlements question. As he told *New York* magazine, "We were enunciating twenty-plus years of U.S. policy. The difference was we weren't just lip-synching it."[20]

Attention now turned to Benjamin Netanyahu's first trip to the United States in his second stint as prime minister. Following a close Israeli election, Netanyahu had formed a coalition government just two months after Obama's inauguration. The countercyclical pattern of a liberal U.S. president entering the White House just when a conservative prime minister takes the helm in Jerusalem has rarely produced a happy relationship (though the juxtaposition of Democrat Carter and Likud's Begin in producing the 1979 Camp David Accords was an arguable exception). Netanyahu met with Obama on May 18. Obama proposed that Netanyahu order a halt to all settlement activity to pave the way for renewed negotiations with the Palestinians. Astonishingly, Obama's request took Netanyahu completely by surprise. After leaving the Oval Office, the prime minister walked down the hall to Vice President Biden's office, where, by the time he had arrived, he was completely white. He paced around as though caged in Biden's smallish office, lamenting that he was being asked to do the impossible, something required from none of his predecessors. The avuncular Biden did his best to calm the agitated Netanyahu, but there was little the vice president could say. A settlement halt was what the president expected.[21]

Netanyahu's next station on the Via Dolorosa was Congress, where he must have expected a degree of relief. Netanyahu traveled down Constitution Avenue to Capitol Hill that day expecting milk and cookies, but on settlements he just got more of what he had heard in the Oval Office. With the Senate in Democratic hands, the White House had been able to coordinate in advance with the informal Israel caucus on the settlements issue. U.S. Jewish community leaders, mostly on the Democratic side, were also consulted in a process that continued at least through the summer, culminating in a mid-July meeting convened by Obama with the leaders of fourteen Jewish groups, including Alan P. Solow, chairman of the Conference of Presidents of Major Jewish Organizations, and AIPAC president-elect Lee Rosenberg. There was little if any pushback. Settlements were just hard to defend.[22]

The joint press conference on May 18 reflected the difficult nature of the visit. The two leaders sparred. Netanyahu, playing to his Israeli constituency, devoted most of his opening statement to the Iranian threat. On the peace process, he insisted that there could be no progress unless the Palestinians recognized Israel as a Jewish state. Obama, who had not raised settlements in his opening statement, must have found Netanyahu's insertion of this requirement somewhat jarring. Thus, in the question-and-answer segment of the press conference, after explaining Palestinian obligations, he said:

> Now, Israel is going to have to take some difficult steps as well, and I shared with the Prime Minister the fact that under the roadmap and

under Annapolis that there's a clear understanding that we have to make progress on settlements. Settlements have to be stopped in order for us to move forward. That's a difficult issue. I recognize that, but it's an important one and it has to be addressed.[23]

Jerusalem and Washington immediately began battling over what Obama meant, with the Israeli government spokesman trying to create the impression that this was no big deal and framing the issue as a question of family values:

We want to move on the issue of illegal outposts because, first and foremost, it is an issue of law and order and it has to end. . . . Our position on settlement expansion is that within existing communities there has to be normal life. . . . Will we be able to continue building within the existing boundaries of an established settlement? We hope so.[24]

Secretary Clinton, in rebuttal, speaking at a May 28 press conference with the Egyptian foreign minister, brushed aside the Israeli reaction:

With respect to settlements, the president was very clear when Prime Minister Netanyahu was here. . . . He wants to see a stop to settlements— not some settlements, not outposts, not natural growth exceptions. We think it is the best interests of the effort we are engaged in that settlement expansion cease.[25]

Obama himself took the opportunity of his Cairo speech on June 4, 2009, to reinforce this point. "Israelis," he said,

must acknowledge that just as Israel's right to exist cannot be denied, neither can Palestine's. The United States does not accept the legitimacy of continued Israeli settlements. This construction violates previous agreements and undermines efforts to achieve peace. It is time for these settlements to stop.[26]

How to stop them was an unanswered question. Trying one approach, the president sent letters to about seven Arab states asking for public gestures toward recognizing Israel, to give Netanyahu cover to take steps on settlements. Typically, in the delicate U.S.–Israel diplomacy regarding the peace process, such initiatives would result from an Israeli proposal. Although such a move to internationalize the peace process was hardly unprecedented, White House staff feared it could become a delaying tactic. In their assessment it was an opportunity for Israel to put the onus on Obama and wriggle out of a straightforward diplomatic challenge. Next Israelis would ask Obama to fetch Bilbo Baggins's ring from Sauron's evil mountain. Obama, however, felt that Netanyahu's position was not unreasonable and told his aides that he would go directly from Cairo to Riyadh to convey the request in person to King Abdullah of Saudi Arabia. No one, it seemed, thought this was a particularly good idea, least of all the Saudis. But Tom Donilon, Obama's deputy national security advisor, wanted to support the president's impulse to test Netanyahu's bona fides, so preparations began.[27]

The trip was a disaster. The Saudi monarch harbored a deep distrust of Netanyahu and, it seems, was not predisposed toward Obama himself. The fact that the U.S. president, from King Abdullah's perspective, was representing Netanyahu's interest did little to override whatever preexisting skepticism the king might have had toward Obama personally. The Saudi foreign ministry tried to wave off the trip because they foresaw precisely where it would lead. Obama's requests on one level were trivial—perhaps a Saudi trade office in Israel, or overflight rights for commercial aviation headed toward Israeli airports from Asia—but in the context of the king's perception of Israeli treatment of Palestinians, these minor concessions looked like a cosmic betrayal. The king, according to a published source, launched into a "tirade" against Israel.[28]

This episode had several ramifications. It got relations between the new administration and the Saudi leadership off to a bad start. Obama had taken a risk in choosing this issue as the substance of his first encounter with the Saudi king; Abdullah, for his part, should not have abandoned diplomacy and might have at least indicated the possibility of concession if Netanyahu were to demonstrate an intention to follow through on settlements. One could have conceived of several plausible formulas. In the event, the effort collapsed and sourness never really seemed to dissipate. For the peace process, it meant that Obama would have to go back to Netanyahu having failed to deliver, thereby conferring on Netanyahu something of the moral high ground, if such a place could be said to exist. For the organization of the White House staff there were consequences as well. Donilon, who would naturally have been on the receiving end of Obama's annoyance at the outcome of the Riyadh meeting, concluded that he had been ill served by his Middle East office and decided that they needed adult supervision, as staff members subsequently described it. Supervision would be provided by Dennis Ross.[29]

The position created for him was a new one, senior director for the Central Region, which was intended to correspond to the military's Central Command, with an area of responsibility (AOR) stretching from Marrakech to Bangladesh, as their public affairs officers like to say. Unlike the commander of Central Command, the NSC senior director had no troops, but he did have proximity to the West Wing. The other difference is that one country not included in military's Central Command AOR—Israel—is one that is very much a part of the NSC's directorate for the Central Region domain. Ross had long cultivated a close relationship with Israel, and Israelis were very much a part of his professional and social life. For the bulk of his career, this would have been inevitable, given his responsibility under successive administrations for the peace process. For Ross, empathy for Israel's sense of vulnerability and isolation has always been the key to Israel's readiness to take risks for peace.

There is a logic to Ross's approach. It does stand to reason that Israel is the party that must be satisfied if there is to be a peace agreement. American ideas, let alone peace proposals, according to this logic, must find acceptance first by Israel; only then does it make sense to bring them to the Palestinians. Not for nothing did former negotiator Aaron David Miller dub the American peace negotiators, among whom he specifically included himself, "Israel's lawyers."[30]

The weakness of this logic, however, is that it entails a disregard for Palestinian requirements, which, over time, has left them as distrustful of Washington as they are of Jerusalem. Complaints about Ross from the Palestinian side were common. These were unfair to his motivations, but not necessarily to the policy approach associated with his diplomatic role. And the policy approach was coextant with Ross's overriding role in peace process diplomacy for decades. It was, in effect, the Bush administration's approach as well until the end game in 2007–2008, when there was an important but ineffectual shift in emphasis.

The Israel-first strategy had limited appeal to the new Obama administration, not necessarily because it violated anyone's sense of justice, but because it did not seem to be working. Obama's settlement gambit had been an attempt to change the strategy. It too failed, for several reasons. It took too long for the administration to negotiate it with the Israelis, during which time the Netanyahu government unleashed a blizzard of building permits, tenders, and contracts to get as much settlement construction underway as possible before the moratorium clock started to tick. This was not unlike the normal intensification of fighting before a cease-fire takes effect as both sides try to maximize their positions before they have to stop shooting. In this case, though, only one side was in a position to shoot. From a Palestinian perspective, therefore, the proposed settlement freeze produced more settlement activity, or laid the ground for it, than would have occurred had there been no freeze. Their mood was consequently dour.

The publication on September 15, 2009, of the UN-mandated report on the previous year's Gaza conflict was another factor. The report, known by the name of the South African jurist, Richard Goldstone, who headed the fact-finding mission, was severely critical of Israel's conduct of the war. The initial response of the Palestinian Authority was to raise the Goldstone Report's finding to the Security Council in order to generate a condemnation of Israel and showcase the Palestinians' cause. The report was also critical of Hamas's conduct, but the Palestinians were justified in thinking that Hamas's culpability would be overlooked. The Israeli reaction was vehement. In the usual pattern of Israeli–Palestinian interaction, it was clear that no settlement freeze would be thinkable if the Palestinians followed through on their plan to take the Goldstone report to the Security Council. To salvage its initiative, the administration had no choice but to lean hard on Abbas to abandon his UN ploy. Abbas complied, only to face an atrocious backlash not just from the Palestinian street, but also from within the ranks of the Palestinian Authority and Fatah, his own party. The personal and political abuse hurled at him left him badly wounded. The result was that the administration's peace team felt that they could not immediately begin twisting Abbas's arm to get his approval on a settlement freeze that from a Palestinian perspective was woefully incomplete.[31]

This was the third factor. Netanyahu bargained hard to limit the scope of the moratorium. His aim was to satisfy the administration's minimal standard for what would constitute a moratorium, while maximizing the construction that could continue under its terms. This made sense in the narrow definition of keeping both Washington and his more right-wing cabinet members off his back. There was a missing element, however, in the form of the Palestinians, who were expecting, partially on the basis of the administration's own rhetoric, a really complete freeze. To them, this meant a halt to construction in Jerusalem as well as within the settlement blocs and other settler communities within the West Bank. Combined with American unwillingness to press Abbas because of the gauntlet Obama had already forced him to run over the Goldstone Report, Washington's acquiescence in Netanyahu's terms for a settlement freeze was a useful, perhaps inevitable, pretext for Abbas to avoid a resumption of talks with his more powerful neighbor. This had the anticipated effect of validating Israeli claims that they had no partner for negotiations, even when they were willing to make difficult sacrifices regarding settlements.

There was not much the administration could do at that point. The settlements freeze that Netanyahu was willing to offer, however limited, was the only achievement Washington could claim in its marquee attempt to restart talks between Israel and the Palestinian Authority. It could not just be abandoned. Yet the clock was ticking toward the end of the ten-month partial freeze. If the Palestinians failed to engage before the clock ran out, the administration's hard-won concession from the Israelis would amount to a Pyrrhic victory.

In May 2010, the administration sent the vice president along with George Mitchell to reassure Israel of the U.S. commitment to its security and to start a round of proximity talks, in which Mitchell would shuttle between Jerusalem and Ramallah, the capital of the Palestinian Authority on the West Bank, in the hope of prodding the two sides to meet directly before the freeze expired. While Biden was pledging the administration's "absolute, total, unvarnished commitment to Israel's security," the Israeli interior ministry announced that 1,600 new housing units would be constructed in Ramat Shlomo, an ultra-Orthodox community that butts up against the Palestinian towns of Shuafat and Beit Hanina north of East Jerusalem. The Israelis have annexed the land on which Ramat Shlomo was built and therefore define it as part of the municipality of Jerusalem; the international community regards it as occupied and Ramat Shlomo as a settlement.[32] The announcement lit the fuse on a vice-presidential stick of dynamite. Given Biden's status, his expressions of solidarity with Israel, and the diplomatic process he was in Israel to foster, the insult was nearly incomprehensible. Netanyahu's office said that the prime minister had no idea the announcement was in the works and it is quite possible that the interior minister, a Shas politician who shifted the party to the right after his predecessor was jailed for corruption, acted independently. In any case it was left to Netanyahu to repair the damage, first by explaining that construction, if it were to happen, would not happen immediately. Biden had little alternative but to accept this, but as one prominent Israeli columnist wrote, "To wipe the spit off his face, Biden had to say it was only rain. Therefore, he lauded Netanyahu's assertion that actual construction in Ramat Shlomo would begin only in another several years."[33] The president and high-level aides like Rahm Emanuel were unmollified, and Secretary Clinton was instructed to express the American displeasure to Netanyahu in a long and "tough phone call," as the State Department characterized it publicly.[34] In a classic case of mixed messages, the vice president then reached out to Netanyahu with a conciliatory call, undercutting Clinton and reinforcing Israel's generally dismissive approach to the administration's periodically tough messaging.

Netanyahu nevertheless moved to lower the temperature by extending the freeze to include Jerusalem for a three-month period. Unfortunately, the Palestinians were not yet ready to return to direct talks. Assiduous diplomacy by Mitchell over the course of that summer ultimately got Abbas back to the table, but by then, the freeze period was nearly over, and Abbas had declared that he would not negotiate unless the freeze remained in effect. He had climbed very far up that tree and it did not appear as though he had plausible way back down. Another crisis was therefore in the offing. The administration attempted to head it off by persuading Netanyahu to agree to a two-month extension of the freeze, to give the direct talks that had begun a month before a chance to develop some momentum. There was always the remote chance that this might perpetuate both the freeze and progress toward an agreement.

This sparked something of a frantic search for a package of political and military inducements the administration might be able to offer the Israelis. At this juncture, the Israelis held all the cards. It was the Palestinians who had spurned direct talks, despite the extension of the partial freeze to include Jerusalem. And, given the high importance the White House had attached to the peace process as a signature initiative, Obama clearly needed the freeze extension more than Netanyahu did.

The difficulties were compounded by the undeniable fact that Netanyahu did not have the cabinet backing he needed to agree to a freeze extension.

The governing coalition in 2010 commanded seventy-four seats. Likud controlled the largest segment; Labor, under Ehud Barak, held another sizable chunk; the right wing, consisting of Lieberman's Yisrael Beiteinu, Eli Yishai's Shas, and the Orthodox Habayit haYehudi and United Torah Judaism, made up the rest. This presented Netanyahu with a political challenge, given that many of his own party's ministers along with the right-wing and religious parties were opposed to an extension of the freeze. Netanyahu did have the option of ejecting these smaller parties from the government and replacing them with Tzipi Livni's Kadimah party, but their mutual antipathy would have precluded it, even if Livni did not have the forlorn hope that the government would break up over this issue and pave the way for elections that her party might win. The White House was tracking these cabinet dynamics carefully, but hoped against hope that the right package of incentives would enable Netanyahu to agree to the freeze without risking the collapse of his government.

In the crazed environment of the United Nations General Assembly meeting in New York, where leaders of scores of nations and their aides were jammed into the Waldorf Astoria trying to choreograph as many meetings as possible during the week-long international jamboree, Ross worked on a package he thought might do the trick. The political part of the deal would be the release of Jonathan Pollard from prison. Pollard, who is Jewish, was sentenced in 1987 to life for espionage on behalf of Israel. Requests for his release on humanitarian grounds were a hardy perennial in U.S.–Israeli diplomacy for years even though Pollard did not become eligible for parole until November 2015 (when he was, in fact, released through the normal parole process). Early release was a big decision, in part because the U.S. defense and intelligence communities were vehemently opposed, and in part because a decision to play him was a card that could be used only once. There were questions, naturally, as to whether trading Pollard for a two-month extension of a negotiating process that looked likely to fail made much sense. Ross thought it did, however, and he appears to have gotten Obama's go-ahead to put Pollard on the table.

The security-related offer consisted of a squadron of F-35 aircraft, the most advanced in the U.S. inventory. The U.S. Navy version costs a bit more than $330 million per aircraft. Early delivery of these aircraft was to be made on a concessionary basis, although it is not clear what the terms were because the deal was being devised under so much pressure by distracted officials that no one was quite sure at the time. Normally, these deals result from months of painstaking negotiation between large teams of experts. Hillary Clinton's game attempt to explain the terms to Netanyahu over the phone was burdened by uncertainty about the financial specifics, which neither side had had time to puzzle out. This part of the deal was controversial as well since it linked—for the first time since Camp David in 1978—an infusion of military aid to secure a specific Israeli gesture in the context of a negotiation. It differed from Camp David, however, because of the mismatch between the large scale and undefined price of the weapons system offered by the administration and the relatively minor concession requested from the Israelis in return. At Camp David, the aid offered was quite significant, but the quid pro quo, peace with Egypt, reshaped Israel's strategic environment by ending the prospect of war between Israel and Egypt and dealt a major blow to Soviet pretensions in the region. This looked like a huge bribe for a trivial gain; observers wondered whether it would set a precedent that de-linked military assistance to Israel from its real-world security requirements and transformed it into just a form of currency used to buy Israeli cooperation in diplomatic talks. In the event, Netanyahu never responded to the offer.[35]

Thus ended the first phase of Obama's attempt to advance the peace process. It had obviously not gone well. The relationship between the two countries, and their leaders, had been damaged. Abbas's position had been weakened by the stresses on him during this period, and he had grown even more suspicious of Israeli intentions and U.S. capacity to influence Israel. The administration's desire to protect the talks that had finally begun in the late summer of 2010 exuded an air of desperation symbolized by the sudden offer to release Pollard and supply advanced aircraft in return for a brief extension of the freeze. It was time to take a break and review the options.

The London Process

Ross, in the meantime, was pursuing a separate effort he believed would produce a breakthrough where Mitchell's effort had failed. He began to meet in London with his Israeli counterpart, Isaac Molho, and with Hussein Agha, a Palestinian academic based in Britain, to draft a set of principles that would serve as the basis of an Israeli–Palestinian final status accord.[36] The idea was to generate the document outside of the three governments, but with the knowledge of the leaders of all three parties. If the negotiators came up with an agreed text that was quietly blessed by the leaders, it could be introduced as a *deus ex machina* into whatever lumbering, official peace process maneuvers were taking place at the time and lead to a relatively rapid resolution of the conflict. There was nothing intrinsically wrong with this approach. The Oslo Accords had started out in much the same way, and although the assassination of Rabin, followed by the al Aqsa intifada, had erased Oslo's gains, it had been an impressive achievement. The London process, as it came to be known, also suited Ross's style. He had long felt that diplomacy works best when diplomats have the freedom to react to events or to seize opportunities quickly, working directly with decision makers to lock in gains before events altered the mood or the operational context in which an initiative was being pursued. As a diplomat, however, you could not be fleet of foot if you were enmeshed in a bureaucratic process that subjected your game plan to analysis, a variety of other viewpoints, and what amounted to a vote on its validity. The process simply takes too long, highlights risk and induces caution, increases the possibility of leaks, and robs your plan of its timeliness and audacity.

The London process from this perspective was perfect. It entailed a very small group, was secret, but most crucially was outside of government and therefore of the web of constraints and encumbrances that would drain the energy from an official effort. The problems with it were that the Israeli and Palestinian negotiators were mismatched and neither of them had any reasonable expectation of their work ever being recognized by their leaders.

Molho (pronounced Molkho) was Netanyahu's personal lawyer. Ariel Sharon had also used a personal lawyer as his envoy and negotiator; it is accepted practice in the Israel system. Perhaps Woodrow Wilson's Colonel House is the American analogue, although House was not a lawyer (or a colonel). The scion of a family that had settled in Israel over a century ago, Molho is wealthy, self-assured, and well connected. He has philanthropic interests and was central to the stunning renovation of the Israel Museum in Jerusalem. His status as Netanyahu's lawyer put him very nearly in the position that Ross aspired to at the White House, namely, outside the interagency process and answerable only to the country's leader. The Ross–Molho partnership probably contributed to Mitchell's eventual departure from the administration. With Ross and Molho communicating via secure phone directly from their respective desks in the United States and Israel and each of them within arm's reach of their president and prime minister, respectively, Mitchell and his team could never really be sure what was going on. In fact, this was never really clear to Ross's colleagues at the NSC. Ross's close relationship with Donilon, who by this time had replaced General Jones as national security advisor, reinforced his independence. The Israelis were in the uniquely advantageous position of being able to choose their American interlocutor. They could communicate seriously and substantively with Ross, who they felt had a more sympathetic grasp of their concerns as well as access to the president, while according Mitchell merely formal recognition.

The mismatch between Molho and his Palestinian counterparts was like having a careful, unrelenting divorce lawyer negotiate with an opera diva. The diva in the London process was brilliant and a gifted debater, but not the forensic and unforgiving lawyer he needed to be to cope with the combination of Ross's irrepressible inventiveness and Molho's detailed focus on textual nuance and subtle advantage. It was clear from the later versions of the London document that the Palestinians had been outmaneuvered on at least one issue, the location of the Palestinian capital, and possibly others. The document also incorporated interesting ideas that had been floating around regarding refugees, whereby the forced migration of both Jews and Arabs as a consequence of 1948 would be recognized and compensated; and a path toward Palestinian recognition of Israel as a Jewish state via revival of an old UN Security Council resolution. On the formal side of the peace process, Molho was paired with Saeb Erekat, another diva, whose capacity for self-expression in a range of emotional states was ill suited to Molho's implacable precision and composure.

While Molho, like most Israelis, particularly of his generation and background, probably wanted an Israeli–Palestinian agreement that would end the conflict, he had the wrong instincts to play a constructive role. This assumes, of course, that he had any flexibility, which seems doubtful. One of Molho's more memorable tropes was the need he perceived to "punish" the Palestinians in general and Abbas in particular for their attempts to end run the negotiating table, where they were clearly overmatched, with spastic and essentially ineffective appeals to the UN or Arab multilateral bodies, or by initiating yet another futile stab at reconciliation with Hamas. Molho's idea was probably to deter Palestinian reliance on these stratagems by raising the cost of deploying them. They had to be taught a lesson. With each lesson, most of which involved withholding tax revenues that would inevitably be released because of the risk that unmet payrolls could trigger unrest on the West Bank, trust eroded further and the possibility of productive negotiation receded even more. This feedback loop of punishment and provocation resembled the pattern in American high-security prisons, where the result is endemic mental illness and prolonged incarceration.

Arab Aspirations

During early 2011 the administration had to grapple with the spiraling revolutions of the Arab Spring, which began in December 2010 in Tunisia. The challenge of understanding precisely what was happening across the region and what the implications were for U.S. interests absorbed much of the administration's energy and focus. The rest was consumed by the planning for a military drawdown from Iraq and another down the road for Afghanistan. The peace process was crowded out by other crises.

This was the period when Steven Simon was asked whether he would be interested in returning to National Security Council staff to replace Daniel Shapiro, whom Obama had appointed as the new ambassador to Israel. Simon took over as senior director for the Middle East and North Africa in late April, as the administration was deciding that the president should deliver an Arab Spring speech. The impulse was to declare U.S. support for the revolutions and celebrate the recasting of Middle Eastern history by a new generation of activist youth. Obama would make it clear to a domestic and foreign audience that his administration stood on the right side of history and with demonstrators throughout the region who were putting their lives on the line for democracy. In retrospect, this is all rather melancholy, but at that moment the administration, like many others at home and in the region, sensed a new beginning and was eager to seize the opportunities it would present.

There was no way that such a speech could omit the Israel–Palestine peace process. The question was what it should say. Should it contain the president's view on how the parties should resolve all four major issues at stake—Jerusalem, refugees, territory, and security—or be limited to the so-called secular issues of territory and security that did not invoke core concerns relating to identity? Simon and his staff referred to these options as the "full Rabinowitz" and the "half Rabinowitz." In large government decisions like this, differences are nearly always split, so the likelier outcome would be a section of the speech that laid out Obama's view on the half Rabinowitz, leaving the identity issues to be dealt with later, once a resolution of the secular issues had injected a certain mutual confidence and trust into the Israeli–Palestinian relationship.

The timing of the speech proved difficult to pin down. Obama's travel schedule, including a planned swing through Asia, was one factor. Another, which was unknown to most of the staff at that stage, was the operation to kill Osama bin Laden. The impact of the speech was obviously going to be greater with a successful raid in the background, but given the nature of the operation it couldn't be planned months ahead for a specific day. The result was that the speech drafters were never quite sure how much time they had to work with. The text was still being tweaked as Obama mounted the podium. And even if the outcome were predetermined by policymakers' hard-wired preference for a middle solution—the half Rabinowitz—the issue still had to be debated and, at the end, put to the president for decision. The key cabinet member on the National Security Council in this deliberation would naturally be Secretary Clinton. Not until the meeting with the president actually unfolded in the Situation Room would her advice be known. As the participants gathered, one of her aides distributed a paper that seemed to advocate a speech text that covered all four of the core issues. This, thought Simon, was going to be an interesting encounter. But in the ensuing discussion, it became clear that she was in favor of a speech confined to the two secular issues and reserving the more wrenching identity issues for later. This, of course, was Ross's preference, as well as Simon's, and Ross had been in periodic touch with Clinton. With this decision out of the way, the next question was when to tell the Israelis that the president would be making a speech that would lay out the administration's ideas about territory and security. Because of the tight time frame available for the speech and the very short interval between the setting of the date and the delivery of the speech, the Israelis would necessarily not have very much warning.

There was really only a single passage that needed to be previewed, and it was this one: "We believe the borders of Israel and Palestine should be based on the 1967 lines with mutually agreed swaps, so that secure and recognized borders are established for both states."

The initial call from the NSC to Netanyahu's close aide Ron Dermer, a wealthy, Orthodox Floridian, drew a reaction that was stunned and angry.

You could hear the shouting down the hall. Dermer was furious over reference to 1967 lines as well as the short notice. Attempts to explain were rejected. Israelis immediately began mobilizing their first line of defense, members of Congress.

Obama thus gave the speech as two sides girded for battle. The State Department was chosen as the venue to suggest that diplomacy would be Obama's first recourse, unlike that of his predecessor, and that the State Department's role in managing the U.S. response to the upheavals of the Arab Spring would be prominent. He situated the language about borders and swaps in a frank discussion of the larger strategic problem that Israel would confront in the absence of a deal with the Palestinians. To evaluate the Israeli response, it is worth reproducing Obama's discussion at some length:

> For over two years, my administration has worked with the parties and the international community to end this conflict, building on decades of work by previous administrations. Yet expectations have gone unmet. Israeli settlement activity continues. Palestinians have walked away from talks. The world looks at a conflict that has grinded on and on and on, and sees nothing but stalemate. Indeed, there are those who argue that with all the change and uncertainty in the region, it is simply not possible to move forward now.
>
> I disagree. At a time when the people of the Middle East and North Africa are casting off the burdens of the past, the drive for a lasting peace that ends the conflict and resolves all claims is more urgent than ever. That's certainly true for the two parties involved.
>
> For the Palestinians, efforts to delegitimize Israel will end in failure. Symbolic actions to isolate Israel at the United Nations in September won't create an independent state. Palestinian leaders will not achieve peace or prosperity if Hamas insists on a path of terror and rejection. And Palestinians will never realize their independence by denying the right of Israel to exist.
>
> As for Israel, our friendship is rooted deeply in a shared history and shared values. Our commitment to Israel's security is unshakeable. And we will stand against attempts to single it out for criticism in international forums. But precisely because of our friendship, it's important that we tell the truth: The status quo is unsustainable, and Israel too must act boldly to advance a lasting peace.

The fact is, a growing number of Palestinians live west of the Jordan River. Technology will make it harder for Israel to defend itself. A region undergoing profound change will lead to populism in which millions of people—not just one or two leaders—must believe peace is possible. The international community is tired of an endless process that never produces an outcome. The dream of a Jewish and democratic state cannot be fulfilled with permanent occupation.

Now, ultimately, it is up to the Israelis and Palestinians to take action. No peace can be imposed upon them—not by the United States; not by anybody else. But endless delay won't make the problem go away. What America and the international community can do is to state frankly what everyone knows—a lasting peace will involve two states for two peoples: Israel as a Jewish state and the homeland for the Jewish people, and the state of Palestine as the homeland for the Palestinian people, each state enjoying self-determination, mutual recognition, and peace.

So while the core issues of the conflict must be negotiated, the basis of those negotiations is clear: a viable Palestine, a secure Israel. The United States believes that negotiations should result in two states, with permanent Palestinian borders with Israel, Jordan, and Egypt, and permanent Israeli borders with Palestine. We believe the borders of Israel and Palestine should be based on the 1967 lines with mutually agreed swaps, so that secure and recognized borders are established for both states. The Palestinian people must have the right to govern themselves, and reach their full potential, in a sovereign and contiguous state.

As for security, every state has the right to self-defense, and Israel must be able to defend itself—by itself—against any threat. Provisions must also be robust enough to prevent a resurgence of terrorism, to stop the infiltration of weapons, and to provide effective border security. The full and phased withdrawal of Israeli military forces should be coordinated with the assumption of Palestinian security responsibility in a sovereign, non-militarized state. And the duration of this transition period must be agreed, and the effectiveness of security arrangements must be demonstrated.

These principles provide a foundation for negotiations. Palestinians should know the territorial outlines of their state; Israelis should know that their basic security concerns will be met. I'm aware that these steps alone will not resolve the conflict, because two wrenching and emotional issues will remain: the future of Jerusalem, and the fate of Palestinian refugees. But moving forward now on the basis of territory and security provides a foundation to resolve those two issues in a way that is just and fair, and that respects the rights and aspirations of both Israelis and Palestinians.

Now, let me say this: Recognizing that negotiations need to begin with the issues of territory and security does not mean that it will be easy to come back to the table. In particular, the recent announcement of an agreement between Fatah and Hamas raises profound and legitimate questions for Israel: How can one negotiate with a party that has shown itself unwilling to recognize your right to exist? And in the weeks and months to come, Palestinian leaders will have to provide a credible answer to that question. . . .

That is the choice that must be made—not simply in the Israeli–Palestinian conflict, but across the entire region—a choice between hate and hope; between the shackles of the past and the promise of the future. It's a choice that must be made by leaders and by the people, and it's a choice that will define the future of a region that served as the cradle of civilization and a crucible of strife.[37]

The fury that erupted really did raise questions about the fundamental willingness of Netanyahu and his American supporters to grapple seriously with the question of borders at all. It is true that U.S. policy statements over the years had generally avoided referring specifically to "1967 borders"— what the storied Israeli foreign minister Abba Eban had called "Auschwitz borders"—and opted instead for a variety of circumlocutions. Lyndon Johnson in 1968 said: "It is clear . . . that a return to the situation of 4 June 1967 will not bring peace."[38] Reagan in 1982 stated, "in the pre-1967 borders [the] bulk of Israel's population lived within artillery range of hostile armies. I am not about to ask Israel to live that way again."[39] Bill Clinton in 2001 referred implicitly to the 1967 borders when he said:

I think there can be no genuine resolution to the conflict without a sovereign, viable, Palestinian state that accommodates Israelis' security requirements and the demographic realities. That suggests Palestinian sovereignty over Gaza, the vast majority of the West Bank, the incorporation into Israel of settlement blocks. . . . To make the agreement durable, I think there will have to be some territorial swaps and other arrangements.[40]

Then there was George W. Bush's 2004 letter to Ariel Sharon, in which he wrote,

In light of new realities on the ground, including already existing major Israeli population centers, it is unrealistic to expect that the outcome of final status negotiations will be a full and complete return to the armistice lines of 1949, and all previous efforts to negotiate a two-state solution have reached the same conclusion. It is realistic to expect that any final status agreement will only be achieved on the basis of mutually agreed changes that reflect these realities.*[41]

And yet this was precisely the actual content of Obama's supposedly radical speech. The statement seemed both unobjectionable, given that changes to a border could only be made with reference to a baseline, and unthreatening since the reference to mutually agreed swaps could only mean that the resulting border would be different from 1967. In any event, the aftermath of the speech was more about political damage control than geopolitical analysis. Israel's friends in Congress and the media had to be placated but without going back on a policy statement that Obama earnestly believed would serve Israel's vital strategic interest. He had to explain two things: that the U.S. position was not that Israel must return to the 1967 borders, but

---

* A couple of years before, however, Bush did refer explicitly to 1967 in the context of references to UN Security Council Resolution 242, which referred to the return by Israel of territories conquered during the Six Day War. "Ultimately, Israelis and Palestinians must address the core issues that divide them if there is to be a real peace, resolving all claims and ending the conflict between them. This means that the Israeli occupation that began in 1967 will be ended through a negotiated settlement between the parties, based on UN resolutions 242 and 338, with Israeli withdrawal to secure and recognized borders." His mention of "mutually agreed changes," by following Clinton's reference to "territorial swaps" in his establishment of the "Clinton Parameters" for a peace agreement, showed the direction U.S. policy had already begun to take. During Obama's first year in office, Secretary Clinton offered this formula: "We believe that through good-faith negotiations the parties can mutually agree on an outcome which ends the conflict and reconciles the Palestinian goal of an independent and viable state based on the 1967 lines, with agreed swaps, and the Israeli goal of a Jewish state with secure and recognized borders that reflect subsequent developments and meet Israeli security requirements." By describing 1967 borders as a Palestinian goal, with which the United States clearly sympathized, and juxtaposing it with an Israeli goal also backed by the United States, she got the ideas out there but without igniting a firestorm.

rather to think of these borders as the cartographic and diplomatic reference point required for any detailed negotiation of territorial arrangements, and that mutually agreed swaps necessarily implied adjustments to the 1967 border that would reflect demographic and security imperatives.

The annual AIPAC policy conference was less than a week away, so the right venue was available at the right moment for this clarification. A new speech, tailored to address the concerns of this important constituency, was drafted and the president's speaking slot scheduled. Within the vast hall enveloping nearly 20,000 attendees, the president received a polite reception. After reassuring the audience of his commitment to Israel's security against Iran and a range of other threats, he turned to the controversy unleashed by his previous speech.

> And since my position has been misrepresented several times, let me reaffirm what "1967 lines with mutually agreed swaps" means. By definition, it means that the parties themselves—Israelis and Palestinians—will negotiate a border that is different than the one that existed on June 4, 1967. (Applause.) That's what mutually agreed-upon swaps means. It is a well-known formula to all who have worked on this issue for a generation. It allows the parties themselves to account for the changes that have taken place over the last 44 years. (Applause.) It allows the parties themselves to take account of those changes, including the new demographic realities on the ground, and the needs of both sides. The ultimate goal is two states for two people: Israel as a Jewish state and the homeland for the Jewish people—(applause)—and the State of Palestine as the homeland for the Palestinian people—each state in joined self-determination, mutual recognition, and peace. (Applause.)
>
> If there is a controversy, then, it's not based in substance. What I did on Thursday was to say publicly what has long been acknowledged privately. I've done so because we can't afford to wait another decade, or another two decades, or another three decades to achieve peace. (Applause.) The world is moving too fast. The world is moving too fast. The extraordinary challenges facing Israel will only grow. Delay will undermine Israel's security and the peace that the Israeli people deserve.[42]

It did not really work, and it enabled critics to gloat that they had been able to get Obama to change his tune in the course of the week, insisting against all evidence and common sense that the terms laid out in the second speech differed somehow from the first. Netanyahu, who was in Washington to speak at the conference as well, was also invited to speak to a joint session of Congress. There he decisively rejected the president's case to the howling admiration of members, who interrupted Netanyahu eighteen times with standing ovations. The speech took on Obama's points one-by-one. "I stood before my people and said that I will accept a Palestinian state; it's time for President Abbas to stand up before his people and say, 'I will accept a Jewish state,'" reiterating the equivalence of these propositions and ignoring the longstanding Palestinian recognition of the State of Israel. He then stated that Jerusalem would never be divided and, by extension, there could be no Palestinian capital within the city; that the refugee problem would be resolved "outside the borders of Israel"; and that there must be a long-term Israeli presence along the Jordan River, where Netanyahu recalled having fought terrorists as a younger man. In a conversation with Abbas, Netanyahu defined a long-term presence as forty years.[43] Netanyahu then described how the Palestinian economy had flourished under occupation and speculated how much better it would do if there were peace. Yet peace would prove elusive if Palestinians continued to reject the legitimacy of Israel as a Jewish state and incited hatred against it in Palestinian schools.[44] The prime minister elaborated on these themes in his Oval Office meeting with Obama, where he lectured the president and the press corps on the basics of Jewish history and Israel's physical vulnerability to its enemies (the lecture described in the first page of this book). Netanyahu's condescending posture was widely noted by the media and commentators, as it was meant to be. In part this was aimed at a domestic audience that relished the spectacle of an Israeli leader humiliating an American president, but it was also a reflection of Netanyahu's apparently deep contempt for Obama.

The entire episode had been nothing less than a fiasco. But an alternative scenario is difficult to conjure. If, for example, the White House had had more time to preview the Arab Spring speech with the prime minister's office, Israeli officials would have leaked it to Congress and the media to whip up the political opposition and Israel's friends in the same terms they used after the speech to mischaracterize Obama's reference to 1967 borders, while ignoring the qualifier of mutually agreed swaps. In fact, Israeli officials did just that the night before the speech. In this alternative history, the environment would have been poisoned well before Obama's voice on the issue could even be heard. The only course that might have obviated this rancorous situation would have been to drop discussion of the Israel–Palestinian impasse entirely. Successive U.S. administrations have been unable to do this, however, and Obama's was no exception.

Nonetheless, the remainder of the first term dealt mostly with a range of U.S.–Israeli issues that were unrelated, or only tangentially linked to the peace process. There was an ongoing, closely held but not secret bilateral process intended to keep Israel and the United States on the same path toward Iran, an effort to cajole the Turks and Israel to patch up their squabble over the Israeli raid on a Turkish ship that had killed several Turkish citizens in 2010, and an endless game of whack-a-mole, whereby the United States staved off—or tried unsuccessfully to block—Palestinian plays at the UN, usually in the form of requests for membership in UN organizations.

There were issues related to the peace process as well, but these were not decisive. Work was required to manage the legal implications of Palestinian reconciliation attempts throughout this period. Under U.S. law, the administration could not provide funding for the Palestinian Authority if Hamas was part of the Palestinian government, unless Hamas recognized Israel, denounced violence, and embraced existing Israeli–Palestinian agreements. Since Hamas was not going to agree to any of these things, the situation required delicate negotiations with Congress, the Palestinian Authority, and Israel to avoid a cutoff of assistance that might push a cash-poor Palestinian Authority into bankruptcy.

The Jordanians, in the meantime, offered to try to get Abbas and Netanyahu back to the table. Although it seemed like a risky maneuver for a king who was coping with serious political and economic challenges, the administration thought that the effects of failure on the king's standing in Jordan were best judged by him, so they gave the go-ahead. The effort foundered on, among other things, the inability of the two sides to agree on terms of a prisoner release that Abbas had set as a requirement for continuing talks and on the Palestinians' continued efforts to lodge themselves as a kind of recognized entity at the UN. This was but a taste of what was to come.

The administration's posture for the remainder of the first term was set by late 2011 and reflected in Ross's evolving views and his departure from the White House. In the wake of the confrontations with Israel over Obama's speech and the lack of give on either the Israeli or Palestinian side, Ross embraced a new, sensible formula to the effect that the conflict had to be managed; there was too little trust between the protagonists to make meaningful progress. This captured the overall mood while presaging Ross's loss of interest in a process that was clearly going nowhere. And since being outside of government would make it easier for him to play in the London process, it was not as though he were saying goodbye to Israeli–Palestinian negotiations. To the contrary; he could now focus on the real thing. But Simon's impression was that his time was running out in any case.

Denis McDonough, now Obama's chief of staff, was then the deputy national security advisor and therefore in charge of the day-to-day coordination of U.S. foreign and defense policy. Unlike most occupants of this spatially infinitesimal but bureaucratically powerful office, McDonough was a close confidant of the president and especially determined to protect his back. Given this orientation, he was unsurprisingly disturbed by the sheer volume, let alone the intensity of the flak directed at the president over initiatives in which Ross had played an outsized role. McDonough's impulse was to clip Ross's wings a bit and ensure that Ross's diplomatic maneuvers were subject to supervision and review—that is, to put them in the same category as the administration's other diplomatic policies and plans.

At the same time, faith in Netanyahu's intentions was diminishing. One of Ross's carefully cut and polished rhetorical gemstones was dubbed by Simon's staff "the Two Bibi's." The gist of the argument was that Netanyahu as a person and political leader was divided. There was the Bibi who clearly understood that a two-state solution was essential to a prosperous, secure, and democratic future for Israel, but there was also the Bibi who was not only still in thrall to dreams of a territorially "greater Israel," but more importantly was not the sort of politician inclined to take bold risks for peace. In Ross's analysis, the United States had to strengthen the first Bibi while working over time to help overcome his more cautious instincts. By the early fall of 2011, Obama seems to have concluded that there was in fact only one Bibi and that it was the second—the Bibi that someone within the increasingly exasperated White House eventually dubbed "chickenshit."[45] There was one particular moment that autumn when Ross attempted to explain to Obama about the two Bibi's—as though Obama were Lenny in *Of Mice and Men* asking George to tell him about the rabbits again—and the president made it clear that he had had enough.

4

Peace Impasse

OUTSIDERS MIGHT be surprised at the relative isolation of working-level White House staff from partisan politics. However, in 2012 the White House at every level did notice when Benjamin Netanyahu intervened on Governor Mitt Romney's side of the general election campaign. Israel's government denied, of course, that he was doing anything of the sort, and the intervention did enjoy some plausible deniability. Netanyahu, his spokesmen said, was simply representing Israel's national interest when he excoriated the sitting U.S. President Barack Obama for failing to stop Iran's nuclear program, and it was not his fault if his words were featured in Romney's campaign commercials. These denials did not pass the laugh test. An Israeli prime minister who wanted to influence the American president, rather than unseat him, would have pressed his case through established private channels rather than appearing on every U.S. Sunday talk show, on multiple Sundays, to accuse the incumbent, in effect, of appeasement.[1]

Angry Democrats and likeminded commentators called Netanyahu's behavior "unprecedented," forgetting perhaps that it was certainly not unprecedented for an *American* administration to take sides in *Israeli* politics. Veterans of the elder Bush administration have expressed satisfaction over their role in helping dispatch Likud Prime Minister Yitzhak Shamir, who was replaced by Labor's more congenial Yitzhak Rabin.

Netanyahu's behavior was nonetheless foolish, for two reasons. First, it was rather more dicey for the junior partner to engage in such machinations against the political leadership of his country's strategic protector.* More seriously, Netanyahu's gambit reflected a fundamental misreading—indeed, a surprising ignorance—of American politics. This constitutes a serious liability arising from the deepening Likud–Republican alliance. Netanyahu was educated and worked in the United States; he speaks English like a native. But his American-born adviser, Ron Dermer, came from the neoconservative right; his major campaign donor is the billionaire Sheldon Adelson, who has lavished hundreds of millions of dollars on right-wing American candidates and causes. By the fall of 2012 it was looking increasingly likely that Barack Obama would win reelection. He was consistently ahead in well-polled swing states. But Republicans were trapped in an epistemic bubble of their own creation. *Wall Street Journal* columnist Peggy Noonan had seen Romney "quietly rising" because "the Republicans have the passion now, the enthusiasm. The Democrats do not. Independents are breaking for Romney." *Washington Post* columnist George Will predicted a Republican landslide. It was impossible, conservatives argued, that blacks, Hispanics, and the young—all of them disillusioned by this failure—would turn out in numbers comparable to 2008. Yet turn out they did. Obama took every swing state except North Carolina. Mitt Romney was reportedly "shellshocked." So, we can surmise, was Netanyahu.[2]

The United Nations

In mid-November, days after the president's reelection, more fighting broke out between Israel and Hamas. It was a brief confrontation that ended without an IDF incursion. During the same month, the administration had to cope with another battle between Israel and the Palestinians at the United Nations. This diplomatic arena had become, and will continue to become, increasingly attractive to the Palestinian leadership. Israel hates it because the Israelis believe that the UN—and international opinion more broadly—is biased against it, and that the agenda of Palestinian sympathizers is to "delegitimize" Israel's right to exist as a sovereign state. The Palestinians can respond, also not without reason, that if they have abjured violence, if the decades-old peace process has gone nowhere, and if the United States in its

---

* Although, as we saw in Chapter 2, that had not stopped Netanyahu himself from similar antics against Bill Clinton in the late 1990s.

mediation will always build its proposals around Israeli bottom lines, then their only recourse is a moral appeal to the court of world opinion. All of this invariably puts the United States in an awkward situation. Its longstanding position is that the dispute can only be settled through direct negotiations between the parties. And it has almost always supported Israel at the UN. But this support has not only isolated it internationally; it has also required the contortion of voting against resolutions the substance of which it supports.

This had happened already in early 2011, when the Palestinian Authority sought a Security Council resolution condemning Israeli settlement expansion. The Palestinians deepened the quandary by cleverly inserting language very similar to the words that President Obama and Secretary Clinton had used in condemning settlements. Moreover, the Palestinian bid came in the context of the unfolding Arab Awakening. In a White House meeting, Jeffrey Feltman, assistant secretary of state for Near Eastern affairs, argued that a U.S. veto of the resolution would make America a target of the Arab demonstrators—something that, so far at least, had not happened. Feltman's argument received strong support from UN Ambassador Susan Rice and Defense Secretary Robert Gates, a respected Republican who has made no secret of his decades-long view that the U.S.–Israeli relationship is unbalanced in Israel's favor. Dennis Ross, on the other hand, recalls that, listening to these arguments, "I could barely contain myself." He responded, according to his own account:

> No one in [Cairo's] Tahrir Square or elsewhere in the region is thinking about settlements or Palestinians. No one is paying attention to this. They are thinking about self-determination for themselves, justice for themselves. They are preoccupied with defining the relationship between ruler and ruled. I am not saying they are indifferent to the Palestinians, but they are completely absorbed by what they see as an internal revolution— it is a moment of release and loss of fear. We should veto this resolution because we told the Palestinians not to do it. And we can veto this resolution because the people in the region are consumed by upheaval that has nothing to do with the Palestinians or Israelis.[3]

In narrow terms, Ross was probably correct about the regional ramifications. In this case, the administration tried to get the Palestinians to back off by promising, as Ross recalls, to "formally accept 1967 with mutually agreed swaps as the basis for final borders"—words that would set off a firestorm when Obama used them in a speech a few months later. But the resolution went ahead and Obama issued his first UN veto—against an otherwise unanimous Security Council that included America's closest European allies, and over a resolution with which he essentially agreed.

Now, on the eve of Obama's second term, it was happening again. On November 29, the UN General Assembly voted overwhelmingly to accord the Palestinian Authority nonmember observer state status in the United Nations. The only countries to vote against this symbolic measure were the United States, Canada, Israel, Micronesia, Palau, Panama, and the Marshall Islands. In the months preceding the vote, the White House tried to manage both Israelis and Palestinians carefully in the hope that the Palestinians could be persuaded not to proceed and the Israelis would take steps that might induce Palestinian restraint or, in the event that the Palestinian initiative came to a vote, that the United States and Israel would not look absurdly isolated.

During this period, a succession of high-level Israeli visitors made the trip to Washington to plot a course to deter the Palestinians, as well as member states inclined to vote for them, from going ahead. The national security advisor, Tom Donilon, personally handled these encounters, which unfolded along set lines. The Israeli official would insist that Washington act to prevent a vote, or to fortify the "against" column should a vote prove unavoidable. Donilon would say, in effect, fine, what would you like us to do? The Israeli visitor would suggest, for example, a mix of U.S. diplomatic demarches in capitals urging the host government to vote the right way alongside threats that the United States could use with Palestinian president Abbas to ensure that he understood the risks he was running of Israeli retaliation. Donilon would record these requests and indicate that he would personally ensure that they were carried out. He would then say that none of these actions would affect the prospects for or outcome of a vote in the slightest. But, he continued, we would follow through. What, he would then ask, was Israel going to do? Surely there were steps that Israel could take that could be used to show key UN member states—"quality" Western European countries, or Japan—that there were good reasons to give Israel the benefit of the doubt and at least abstain when Palestine's status came up for a vote. The answer was, no, there was not anything to offer because a concession at that stage would simply reward the Palestinians for taking a provocative step. The appropriate response was threat of punishment, not appeasement. Donilon would say, well, okay then, we will proceed with your requests and take stock in a week or two. With the arrival of the next Israeli delegation, Donilon would take out the list and run through each item, explaining the specific actions the U.S. government had taken to implement the last round of Israeli requests. The cycle would then repeat with the Israeli visitors putting forward additional requests, Donilon turning them into a to-do list, and asking what the Israelis were going to do. In the days before the vote Steven Simon's phone was ringing off the hook with calls from counterparts in European governments asking if the United States could get Israel to pledge even some relatively minor concession to enable their leaders to abstain or even vote against. But the United States had nothing to offer. In the end, the vote had something of a bitterly comic edge, not because the Palestinians won—that was a foregone conclusion—but because no "quality" votes apart from the United States and Canada could be mustered.

The Peace Process, Again

With the Palestinians' symbolic UN victory and the inevitable recriminations about whether the United States had done all it could to prevent the humiliating rebuke of Israel, thoughts turned again to the question of what the second-term administration would do about the peace process. In early December, there was small, informal meeting in the Situation Room, in which White House and senior State Department officials discussed whether it was time for another effort. Some proposed exploring the prospects of some sort of "coordinated unilateral withdrawal" from the West Bank. The term is obviously a kind of self-contradiction, but the idea was basically that a negotiated final status agreement was probably unattainable for the foreseeable future so alternative arrangements had to be considered. The last time Israel had unilaterally withdrawn from occupied territory was in 2005, from Gaza. Because that move was not coordinated with the Palestinians and only barely with the United States, there had been no time to arrange an orderly transfer of authority within Gaza. The result was a Palestinian mini–civil war and the ascendance of an entrenched and violent Hamas dictatorship in Gaza. Perhaps discrete discussion with the Israelis on how the benefits of unilateral withdrawal might be realized for both sides while minimizing the inevitable risks would be useful. This idea was shot down immediately.

Another view was that reconstituting a peace process would be pointless unless and until there was a "train wreck" that persuaded both sides to negotiate seriously. The problem with this, in the view of others, was that a train wreck in the form of a third intifada would likely strengthen hardliners and make both sides more resistant to compromise. There was also the question of the president's role. For a negotiation to produce results, the power of the presidency had to be fully applied. Given the uncertainties involved and the president's other priorities, was another round of peace talks a sensible investment of the president's scarce time and perishable credibility? Despite the skepticism voiced by participants in the meeting, however, Simon's own sense was that the West Wing commitment to a two-state solution would impel another effort. And that is what happened.[4]

The first step was the presidential trip to Israel that had not happened during Obama's first term. There were a number of reasons to do it now. The trip was certainly attractive to Netanyahu, who could use the visit to show Israeli critics that his treatment of Obama during the first term had not really damaged the relationship between the two countries. Netanyahu involved himself personally in the selection of a logo for the visit, a kitschy depiction of the U.S. and Israeli flags blending into a single red, white, and blue image adorned with the standard American meme of an "unbreakable alliance" and, in Hebrew, "covenant of nations."

For Obama, the political utility of the visit was somewhat less obvious. He had just been reelected by a comfortable margin. But his administration thought in terms of "reset buttons." The White House remained skeptical of Netanyahu's intentions.[5] But the new secretary of state, John Kerry, was more inclined to trust the Israeli prime minister, who continued to make private assertions that he was ready to drop his right-wing coalition partners if he saw the real possibility of an agreement with the Palestinians. The U.S. administration was also making a frank effort to reach out to a young Israeli public over the heads of its government. In the trip's keynote speech, delivered to an enthusiastic audience of Israeli university students, including Israeli Arab students, Obama stated explicitly, "as a politician—I can promise you this, political leaders will never take risks if the people do not push them to take some risks."

The speech began on a conciliatory note, with Obama downplaying in an amiable way the apparent animosity between him and Netanyahu. All the bad blood had just been a joint effort to provide juicy material for *Eretz Nehederet*, the Israeli version of *Saturday Night Live*. He then revisited the themes of his AIPAC speech nearly a year before. The Arab Spring meant that peace would have to be between peoples rather than between governments; that technology in the form of long-range missiles would make the idea of defensible borders obsolete; that demographics west of the Jordan River meant that Israel could be a democracy or a Jewish state controlling the West Bank, but not both; and that Iran would not get a nuclear weapon on his watch but that principled diplomacy was the best path to this objective. In all this there was nothing new. What was new was the appeal to an open-minded and adventurous cohort of young Israelis who constitute Bernard Avishai's "global Israel," referenced in the Introduction. Part of the appeal was a warning about "the undertow of isolation" that Israeli policies toward the Palestinians had generated, especially in Europe. This undeniable trend was contrasted with the evident desire of the audience to partake in a global culture of ideas, commerce, and technological innovation. But global integration, he implied, would have to begin with empathy for the Palestinians.

> Put yourself in their shoes. Look at the world through their eyes. It is not fair that a Palestinian child cannot grow up in a state of their own. (Applause.) Living their entire lives with the presence of a foreign army that controls the movements not just of those young people but their parents, their grandparents, every single day. It's not just when settler violence against Palestinians goes unpunished. (Applause.) It's not right to prevent Palestinians from farming their lands; or restricting a student's ability to move around the West Bank; or displace Palestinian families from their homes. (Applause.) Neither occupation nor expulsion is the answer. (Applause.) Just as Israelis built a state in their homeland, Palestinians have a right to be a free people in their own land. (Applause.)[6]

Obama clearly struck a chord, but with a university student audience predisposed to his message. The one large Jewish college in the West Bank, Ariel University, was excluded from the lottery process that distributed tickets to the event. One assumes that this was not an oversight; it was probably an embassy staff decision. The Ariel student association put up banners featuring Shepard Fairey's acrylic image of Obama from the iconic "Hope" poster, but with the slogan "No We Can't."[7] Obama's view was that it was his responsibility to lay out a vision for Israel's future even if no outsider could compel Israel to share it.

John Kerry, however, was going to try. Among the first calls he made as secretary of state in February 2013 were to Netanyahu, Shimon Peres, and Mahmoud Abbas.[8] He was probably encouraged by the new government coalition that Netanyahu was pulling together. The cabinet would include Yair Lapid, a television host with an inexplicable reputation as a maverick, whose total avoidance of meaningful discourse on Arab–Israeli issues was interpreted by hopeful observers as bold and unconventional thinking about a peace process, and Tzipi Livni, who actually did think in these terms but lacked the constituency and security credentials to press them effectively.

Kerry quickly assembled a team to carry out the negotiations. The Middle East envoy, David Hale, was slated to take the embassy in Beirut, a decidedly better prospect than embarking on yet another round of negotiations that he expected would be futile. He resisted Kerry's pressure on him to forgo Beirut and stay on the Palestinian–Israeli beat. Waiting in the wings was Martin Indyk, a director at the Brookings Institution and a fixture in Democratic Party Middle East policymaking since 1992. Stylish and even debonair, he had started out as a White House staffer, which, like his later successor Dan Shapiro, he parlayed into the job of ambassador to Israel. From there, he was made head of the State Department's Near Eastern Affairs Bureau.

Indyk paid a call on Tom Donilon in 2012 to share his assessment of the Israel–Palestine situation. He indicated, on the basis of conversations he was having with Israelis, that there might be some room for maneuver. Donilon was courteous but did not really engage. He had a more accurate sense of the real room for maneuver, which he judged infinitesimal. But Simon had the feeling in that meeting that Indyk was rehearsing for a renewed attempt.

In the year between the beginning of Kerry's initiative in April 2013 and its demise in late April of 2014, the secretary of state made eleven trips to Israel. This is an extraordinary level of commitment, on par with Henry Kissinger's travels in pursuit of an Israeli–Syrian disengagement agreement following the Yom Kippur War of 1973. Both the Israelis and Palestinians recognized that their interests would be best served by going along because neither wanted to be blamed for opposing peace. Netanyahu declared that he was "determined not only to resume the peace process with the Palestinians, but to make a serious effort to end this conflict once and for all."[9] Abbas signaled his willingness to cooperate but only on the basis of conditions that Israel regarded as inconsistent with the spirit of the enterprise. He told Kerry that release of prisoners was a "top priority." He also wanted a map showing the proposed borders of Israel and Palestine and a settlement freeze. As a sign of his own good intentions, he offered to suspend Palestinian efforts to join UN organizations, a constant source of aggravation in Jerusalem, for two months. Jordan was to have a role in helping the United States get the Israelis and Palestinians to work out a solution regarding Jerusalem, for which King Abdullah II has a proprietary role.[10]

In May, the administration enlisted General John Allen to revive the security talks that had begun in the first term under General "Hoss" Cartwright. These U.S.–Israel "mil-mil" talks aimed to define ways that Israeli security—the integrity of the "envelope"—could be maintained in the absence of Israeli forces, particularly along the Jordan River. The underlying idea was that military officers working shoulder to shoulder on technical issues could produce interesting ideas that might help close the gap between the parties. The first attempt under General Cartwright failed, not because the teams couldn't come up with good ideas, but because the IDF could not get the political cover they needed from the prime minister's office to proceed. Their instinct for self-preservation prevented them from advancing ideas that politicians might disown as weakening Israeli security. There was a debate within the peace process team about whether to go down this route again. Some thought that recreating the security process would enable Israel to put off discussion of other core issues until their security concerns were met, which meant never. Others pointed out that if Israel's security concerns were not assuaged, there would not be an agreement in any case, so the best course would be to take the bull by the horns. This faction won the argument.

For Israel, the issue came down to response capability rather than warning. All could agree that there were multilayered technical surveillance and reconnaissance solutions that if properly deployed would give Israel plenty of warning that bad actors were on the way. This was all well and good from an Israeli perspective, but who would actually stop these bad actors once they were detected? On this point, there was no satisfactory reply since the

Israelis themselves had ruled out a third-party force along the river to interdict intruders.

The fact that for years the first line of defense was the four Jordanian brigades on the eastern side of the river, a formidable capability given the relatively small area they needed to patrol, was not sufficiently reassuring. The Israeli view was that a West Bank unencumbered by an IDF presence would quickly devolve to a warren of missile factories and launch sites that would threaten Ben Gurion International Airport, which lies quite close to the Green Line, and bring Israel's economy to a halt. Indeed, heavy mortars could do the job. In Simon's conversations with Israeli military officers they asked, not unreasonably, whether the Palestinian Authority, let alone a third party, could react quickly and decisively on intelligence about a bomb factory in the *casbah* of Nablus. Their reasoning was difficult to counter. Even if the Palestinian Authority would be inclined to act in such a situation, the politics of action would be complicated. To underscore this point, one Israeli general officer asked Simon if he was familiar with the problem of settler violence. Of course, Simon said. The general then asked rhetorically what the Israeli government's response was. His answer was "catch-and-release." He explained that the politics were just too complicated for any government to grapple effectively with the problem. He concluded by saying that there was no reason to expect Palestinians to be more effective in controlling terrorists than it was for Israel to control settler violence. The clear implication was that the IDF could not afford to vacate the West Bank.

The problem was made worse by what the IDF planners called the *ma'atefet*—the envelope. This term represented the perimeter of the West Bank. If the envelope were not sealed, extremists incubated in the cauldron of the Arab uprisings would exploit the weaknesses of the Palestinian Authority to set up infrastructure in the West Bank, which they would transform into a launching pad for attacks against Israel. A senior military intelligence officer put the problem to Simon in social science terms. The one indisputable characteristic of the Arab Spring was the weakening of the state and the fracturing of societies. Although this might not be true of Egypt, or even Jordan (just yet), it was a defining feature of Libyan, Syrian, Iraqi, Yemeni, and Bahraini politics. If powerful praetorian states like Syria have come apart under these pressures, why, he asked, would anyone expect a government as pathetic as the Palestinian Authority to be immune? Thus, the Obama administration's plan for "the IDF to stand down in the West Bank as the Palestinian Authority's security forces stood up" flew in the face of observable and ineluctable realities. This was Israel's analysis of the situation well before the Gaza eruption of 2014 and was a serious impediment to a peace process.

In late June and then mid-July, Kerry travelled to Tel Aviv, Jerusalem, Ramallah, and Amman and succeeded in getting the two sides to resume negotiations on the basis of 1967 lines, mutually agreed swaps, and the principle of two states for two peoples. Abbas and Netanyahu both got pushback from their respective cabinets. Saeb Erekat, the chief Palestinian negotiator, with support from the Palestinian intelligence chief Majid Faraj, privately told Abbas that Netanyahu would "take you, Kerry and everyone else for a ride."[11] Abbas had to produce a document signed by Kerry stating that "this letter is to confirm that the position set forth by President Obama in his May 2011 speeches, that Palestine's borders with Israel should be based on the 1967 lines with mutually agreed swaps, still represents our position. As negotiations begin I reiterate our commitment to this position."[12] He also pressed Kerry to deliver 104 Palestinian prisoners as evidence of both Washington's clout and Netanyahu's seriousness. Kerry delivered, more or less. Netanyahu agreed to a release, but in tranches, for fear that Abbas would receive the prisoners and then bail out of the talks. He also limited the release to eighty rather than 104 prisoners because some of the requested prisoners held Israeli identity cards and were not eligible for expatriation. Kerry did not catch this detail, probably because he got the commitment in a one-on-one meeting with Netanyahu, so there was no note taker or other aide to grasp the difference in positions. This meeting style drove his staff crazy for just this reason. It was a difference that turned out to be significant. The mistake was compounded by a misapprehension of the settlement freeze, or restraint in the government's parlance, offered by Netanyahu. Kerry thought that the proposed cap of 2,000 units was comprehensive. Netanyahu believed that he was capping only the number of housing units that were already open for bidding, but that new building plans as well as building in East Jerusalem would not be limited.[13]

With the delivery of the Kerry letter, the first round of prisoner releases in mid-August, and the murky pledge on settlement restraint accomplished, talks resumed. Progress was limited. Israel released another tranche of prisoners on October 29, but the gaps were still too wide. Kerry expressed disappointment with the pace, but said that the talks "were on the right track."

By early December the lack of agreement had soured the mood. Kerry met with Netanyahu three times between December 4 and 6 and once with Abbas. Participants were beginning to characterize the process as "futile"; Palestinians derided the U.S. security proposals as "very bad ideas that [they] could not accept," while an unusually circumspect Erekat described the talks as "still very difficult and matters are complicated."[14] Israel's continued settlement activity and insistence on a long-term presence along the Jordan generated friction. The Palestinians were not the only ones who were vexed by the U.S. approach. Kerry presented General Allen's security plan during this visit. It was dismissed by Israel's Defense Minister Moshe Ya'alon as "not worth the paper it's written on."[15]

Kerry returned to Israel on December 12. He met with both Netanyahu and Abbas. The Palestinians were getting increasingly restless with what they saw as the United States giving in to Israeli demands. The Israelis were neuralgic about what they saw as a lot of Palestinian energy directed at the conditions for talks, but precious little actual talking. Abbas was especially annoyed by U.S. backing for a continuing presence of IDF troops along the Jordan during the implementation phase of an agreement. When Kerry visited Ramallah he brought General Allen with him, but to no avail. At this juncture, Kerry started to talk about a near-term framework agreement that would allow Israelis and Palestinians to state their "reservations" about specific provisions, but they would still be expected to sign it. As a practical matter, this meant saying yes while meaning no, but it could be presented to skeptical publics as progress. Kerry envisaged six to twelve months of negotiations to turn the framework and the parties' "reservations" into a final status accord that would end the conflict.

Kerry was back out in the region to drum up enthusiasm for the process in Riyadh. The Israelis had released the third tranche of prisoners on New Year's Eve 2013, so he had something more to work with in the Arab capitals. The Saudi King Abdullah expressed lukewarm support for Kerry's initiative, and did not offer to assist in any material way. Netanyahu was more helpful by postponing any settlement building permit announcements while Kerry was in town. But he blew off steam regarding Abbas's warm welcome to the Palestinian prisoners, who included convicted killers, but whose release was tangible evidence that Abbas could produce results for the resistance. Netanyahu said that Abbas's jubilation raised the question of whether he was a "real partner" for peace. It's not clear what else he thought Abbas could have done.

Discontent, in the meantime, was building on the Israeli side. Defense Minister Ya'alon groused publicly that Kerry should win "his Nobel Prize and leave us alone," adding that Kerry "cannot teach [him] anything about the conflict with the Palestinians."[16] The Israeli mood had become darkly impatient. In the absence of Abbas's preparedness to accept fundamental Israeli requirements for a final status accord, Netanyahu was unwilling to go to the cabinet for its approval of the release of the fourth and final tranche of prisoners. Kerry met with Abbas in Paris on February 19, but the Palestinian leader had already begun to distance himself from Kerry's campaign. To get him to reengage, the White House invited Abbas to Washington. Abbas reluctantly agreed. He dined at Kerry's Georgetown mansion on March 6, where Kerry asked him to accept a delay in the release of the fourth tranche, if only for a few days. Abbas said no.

On the theory that it is harder to say no to the president in the Oval Office, Obama received Abbas and Erekat at the White House the following day. Abbas, however, had not changed his mind overnight. The meeting ended unsatisfactorily, with Erekat defending his president's stubbornness to Susan Rice, saying, "I see we've yet to succeed in making it clear to you that we Palestinians aren't stupid." Evidently irritated by Abbas's ungenerous and presumably unwise response to the president's modest request, she replied, "You Palestinians can never see the fucking big picture."[17]

This awkward encounter triggered a frantic round of meetings to salvage the process. Kerry traveled again to Israel and the West Bank at the end of March. The Palestinians were threatening to join a host of UN organizations if the Israelis failed to release the fourth tranche immediately. The Israelis reacted adversely to this threat, increasing the pressure on Kerry to come up with a stratagem to rescue an increasingly fraught situation. During the next twenty-four hours, Kerry sketched out the terms of a grand bargain: Israel would release the fourth tranche, plus another 400 prisoners of its own choosing and forgo all new announcements of settlement construction throughout the West Bank (excluding Jerusalem). In return, Abbas would agree to a nine-month extension of the talks, during which his UN gambit would be shelved, and the United States would ship Jonathan Pollard to Israel. It looked as though Kerry had found a workable formula, but when it was referred to the White House for approval, Obama was reluctant to approve Pollard's release.[18]

The day, which was unfolding in time zones seven hours apart, was still not over. Abbas announced that if the fourth tranche were not released by 7 P.M., he would convene a ceremony at his headquarters to announce the Palestinian Authority's campaign for accession to fifteen UN conventions and international treaties. Tzipi Livni texted Erekat, "so you had your little show. Now hold back the documents. We have a deal to extend the talks. The prisoners can go out in 48 hours and then we can get to substance; don't destroy this." Whether or not Livni reflected the thinking of the cabinet, let alone the White House, Erekat got back to her the next morning to say that the UN application was "a done deal."[19]

Indyk, heading Kerry's peace team, was not yet ready to concede defeat. During the next three weeks he met repeatedly with Livni, Molho, Erekat, and Faraj to nail down the terms of an extension agreement in writing. According to the American team, an agreement appeared to be within reach on April 23. One can therefore imagine their surprise when Abbas repudiated the deal that evening in the most provocative way possible, by signing a unity agreement with Hamas. The Israeli response was an immediate "suspension" of talks. The denouement was revealing—and not just of the United States' inability to understand what was going on within the Palestinian leadership. It demonstrated that it was too late for a deal on substance.

Whose Fault?

Early that April Kerry testified before the Senate Foreign Relations Committee. He was asked why the talks were collapsing. He answered that Israel's failure to release the fourth tranche of prisoners had been followed three days later by Israel's announcement of 700 new units for settlers in East Jerusalem. "Poof, that was sort of the moment," Kerry said, seeming to indicate that Israel's settlements policy is what killed negotiations.

Israeli commentators and officials reacted with anger, and a Kerry spokeswoman quickly clarified that Israelis and Palestinians had "both taken unhelpful steps."[20] But Kerry's initial statement arguably reflected the strong American view that expansion of settlements was not compatible with a successful peace process. Indyk himself said as much on the eve of Obama's first inauguration in an interview with the ubiquitous Jeffrey Goldberg, who asked Indyk to name "the single thing American negotiators could do differently that might produce a better outcome." Indyk answered:

If you confine me to one thing, I would say they have to hold both sides to their commitments: the Palestinians have to stop the violence and terrorism and dismantle the infrastructure of terrorism; and Israel has to stop the settlement activity (including natural growth) and dismantle the unauthorized settlement outposts. These are not moral equivalents but they are equivalent in the damage they have done to the hope of peace and the viability of a two-state solution. Nothing did more to undermine Clinton's peacemaking efforts so it was no coincidence that at the end of the Clinton Administration George Mitchell made the same recommendations in his report on the origins of the intifada. Those recommendations were incorporated in the Road Map which the Government of Israel and the Palestinian Authority accepted and committed to implement.[21]

These were strong words, coming as they did from a former U.S. ambassador to Tel Aviv with a reputation for being sympathetic toward Israeli perspectives and predicaments. And Indyk's words contained something else: a conviction, shared by many U.S. officials, that Israel's government had already committed itself to stopping settlements well before Obama took office. This was coupled, as he also indicated, with Palestinian Authority commitments to stop terrorism, but Washington was pretty well satisfied with the Authority's effort to do so, albeit with some help from Israel's security barrier. (Hamas-controlled Gaza was another matter entirely.)

Israelis, at least those from right of center, have been angry and incredulous about the United States' fixation on settlements. They point out that Ariel Sharon dismantled settlements in Gaza before Israel's unilateral withdrawal. If there is a peace agreement, they will do the same for those parts of the West Bank that they agree to turn over to Palestinians. They say that most of the building has been in the "settlement blocs" that "everyone agrees" will be part of Israel under a final agreement. And they often add, as a kind of slogan, "Jerusalem is not a settlement."

All of these assertions are problematic. Unlike Gaza, the West Bank is central to those in thrall to a vision of Greater Israel; they call the territory "Judea and Samaria." The notion that building inside the blocs is okay because they will revert to Israel in a final settlement assumes, as one of Simon's former administration colleagues told us, agreement on where new borders will be. The perversity of this position, he added, is that during the months of Kerry's mission, the Israeli side refused at any point to sit down with their Palestinian counterparts over a map. ("Show me the blocs that are going to be part of Israel on a map," he recalls Erekat saying. "Then at least we'd have something to negotiate.")[22] As for "Jerusalem is not a settlement," New York Times columnist Roger Cohen responded correctly, in 2010, when he wrote: "That's not the issue. The issue is that the Israeli annexation of East Jerusalem is rejected by the rest of the world and any peace agreement will involve an inventive deal on its status. To build is therefore to provoke."[23]

The settlements are fundamental because the conflict is over land. And land, the land one calls home, is visceral, emotional, the stuff of nostalgia, passion, and fanaticism. Anyone who has seen the film *Jean de Florette* will understand the epiphany that Peter Beinart says he experienced when watching a video "of a Palestinian man named Fadel Jaber, who was being arrested for stealing water." Jaber's family wanted access to pipes that bring water to a Jewish settlement. But in the occupied West Bank he had no standing to press his claim, so instead he diverted the water on his own.

> In the video, Israeli police drag Fadel toward some kind of paddy wagon. And then the camera pans down, to a five-year-old boy with a striped shirt and short brown hair, Khaled, who is frantically trying to navigate the thicket of adults in order to reach his father. As his father is pulled away, he keeps screaming, "Baba, Baba." . . . As soon as I began watching the video, I wished I had never turned it on.[24]

We can try to drain analysis of emotion, but we should not pretend or imagine that the emotion is not there. This, of course, is true of Jewish settlers as well: They have made Judea and Samaria their home; they have raised children; they have been assaulted and sometimes killed by angry Palestinians—and are their orphaned children to accept that they must now also lose their homes? But that is not a reason to expand settlements, but rather the opposite, because as that attachment to disputed land becomes ever stronger, as the settler lobby and its associated shadow state grows more potent, as "Jerusalem" increases its power over "Tel Aviv" (these are the shorthand terms Israelis use for their divided society)—as all of this happens, the fading prospects of a two-state solution will disappear.

It is very difficult for any Israeli prime minister to stop this disappearance. What we still do not know is whether Benjamin Netanyahu ever intended or intends to try. On our trips to Israel for this book, we found it somewhat astonishing that, after Benjamin Netanyahu had been prime minister for three years in the 1990s, and again for nearly seven years since 2009, with peace-process issues prominently in play for most of that time, we did not meet a single Israeli who could confidently tell us what he or she thought Netanyahu's ultimate intentions were. They did not even agree on why it is that they did not know. Inside the Obama administration there were varying views. Dennis Ross thought there was much to play for. It seemed that Kerry had some faith in Netanyahu's intentions, but by the end of his mission relations had soured. Vice President Biden continued to trust him. Susan Rice, Denis McDonough, and Robert Gates, before he left the administration, were highly skeptical.

Netanyahu's history did not inspire confidence. He had opposed the Oslo Accords, and excoriated Rabin for his apparent willingness to carry them out. (Rabin's widow would accuse him of inciting the hate that led to her husband's murder.) Having replaced Rabin as prime minister, he reinstated subsidies for settlement building and generally obstructed Oslo's implementation. Returning to government in 2009, under American pressure, Netanyahu gave a speech at Tel Aviv's Bar Ilan University in which he for the first time accepted the idea of a Palestinian state. In that same speech, he demanded a reciprocal gesture from the Palestinian leadership:

> We want them to say the simplest things, to our people and to their people. This will then open the door to solving other problems, no matter how difficult. The fundamental condition for ending the conflict is the public, binding and sincere Palestinian recognition of Israel as the national homeland of the Jewish People.[25]

This was tied to an insistence that the Palestinian refugee problem would have to be solved outside of the borders of the state of Israel, which was a reasonable position and fully consonant with American views. But Netanyahu soon added a rather different condition: The Palestinians must formally recognize Israel as a "Jewish state."[26] It is not clear what this was supposed to mean. Israel has peace treaties and diplomatic relations with two Arab states; neither of them contains this statement. The United States, for that matter, has never formulated its recognition of Israel in such terms. It does, of course, broadly support the idea of Israel as a Jewish homeland, but the American idea of Jewish sovereignty is that it should be *de facto* rather than *de jure*. Abbas too conceded *de facto* Jewishness when he stated, "We do not seek either to flood Israel with millions [of refugees] or to change its social composition."[27] A difficulty of official recognition of a "Jewish state" for any Palestinian leader lies in what it implies about the status of Israel's Arab citizens. When Simon first heard Netanyahu's demand, he thought it was a strategem to kill the negotiations. The Obama administration nonetheless did channel it into the set of issues to be part of the negotiations.

At the end of 2014, Netanyahu ejected centrists from his cabinet and called new elections. In March 2015, after polls showed a surging support for the joint list of Isaac Herzog's Labor and Tzipi Livni's "Hatnuah," Likud pulled off a surprise, albeit narrow, victory. In the last week of campaigning, to motivate his right-wing supporters, Netanyahu said three things that frustrated the Obama administration. First, he promised that if he remained prime minister, there would be no Palestinian state. Second, he visited the East Jerusalem settlement of Har Homa and boasted that when he approved the start of construction in 1997, "It was a way of stopping Bethlehem from moving toward Jerusalem. . . . This neighborhood, exactly because it stops the continuation of the Palestinians, I saw the potential was really great." In other words, he was confirming that a strategic purpose of settlements is to prevent the contiguity, and therefore the viability, of a Palestinian state. Finally, on election day itself, he warned about "Arab voters coming out in droves," which Obama officials interpreted as a racist appeal to Jewish fear. After his victory, predictably enough, Netanyahu tried to backtrack on these statements. But Obama himself was unpersuaded; as one of his aides remarked, "You can't unring the bell."[28]

The sorrowful bell is not just the sound of one Israeli politician, or even the right-of-center spectrum of parties. The left in general, and the Israeli peace camp in particular, has been discredited by Palestinian violence, even though the current Palestinian Authority leadership has repudiated it and had considerable success in preventing it. The al Aqsa intifada of 2001–2005 had fundamentally altered Israeli threat perceptions. In that conflict, Palestinian security forces trained by the West took up arms against the IDF, and terrorist and insurgent groups split off from Abbas's party, Fatah, to attack Israelis in ways that were indistinguishable from Hamas. The 2014 Gaza War, during which Hamas fighters tunneled under Israeli territory to emerge—like aliens in a Ridley Scott movie—next to Israeli suburban communities, deepened anxieties.

Yet, as Indyk said at length following the collapse of his and Kerry's latest effort, it is also the Palestinians who have lost faith in the process—and also with reason. He accurately described Abbas's predicament:

> I fear he's lost on the Palestinian side because they see Hamas resisting Israel and they see ISIS [the Islamic State] using violence to establish its Islamic State over in Iraq, and all Abu Mazen [Abbas] has to offer is negotiations as the way to achieve Palestinian statehood. And negotiations don't have any credibility anymore, 20 years after Oslo and with over 300,000 Israeli settlers in the West Bank and settlement growth continuing and the collapse of the latest effort.[29]

This is a perceptive take on the Palestinian attitude, but on the last point—"the collapse of the latest effort"—we should be careful not to confuse cause and effect. The Kerry effort could not succeed because of a preexisting Palestinian posture of skepticism; the skepticism did not result from Kerry's inability to corral Netanyahu. No Palestinian could expect such a colossal reversal of fortune. The Palestinians were perfectly clear about this, both publicly before Simon entered the Obama White House and privately once he was there. Abbas was particularly frank about this in his conversations with the president.

There are some, of course, who say that Obama himself precipitated the crisis between Washington and Jerusalem, and thereby doomed the peace process. These include critics who claim that he is fundamentally hostile to the Jewish state. There is not a shred of evidence for this and, as we have shown, considerable evidence to the contrary. Less feverish criticism points to Obama's essential coolness as a problem: Israel, in this argument, is so insecure and needy that it requires the emotional embrace of a Bill Clinton or George W. Bush to move even tentatively toward peace. It is true that American presidents can be divided, as one scholar has divided them, on a scale of warmth or coolness toward Israel.[30] Clinton, the younger Bush, LBJ, and Truman fit in the first category. Eisenhower, Carter, Bush the elder, and, arguably, JFK fit in the latter. But these categories do not correlate in any obvious way to effectiveness in reconciling U.S. and Israeli interests where they diverge. Carter, to take the most obvious example, was close to Sadat and angry with Begin, and he was an odd duck in any event. But he also brokered the peace treaty that turned Israel's main enemy into a diplomatic partner.

Obama did say, in a meeting with Jewish leaders early in his term, that the policy of "no daylight" between the United States and Israel had failed, and it was time for another approach.[31] He thought that by raising American security assistance to unprecedented levels, he might provide enough reassurance to challenge Israel diplomatically. Israel's security elites recognized and welcomed the administration's extraordinary defense commitment. But politicians of the right believed—or at least acted as though they believed—that the diplomatic challenge invited fundamental threats to their country's security.

THE UNITED STATES under Obama did continue to act as "Israel's lawyers"—that is, mediating on the principle that Israel must be satisfied and the Palestinians convinced. The London process managed by Dennis Ross was in a sense a test case of this logic and of his belief that Israel had to be hugged reassuringly close. He was given running room for this test because, after the failures of the first term, a new approach made sense. However, when White House staffers saw the document that emerged, they were staggered. It contained material that the Arab participant in the process had accepted but which the Palestinian leadership could never sign on to, including the omission of a Palestinian capital in Jerusalem. The document was untenable. Yet its existence limited Kerry's flexibility when he started his peace mission in 2013.[32]

A final criticism of Obama's management of the relationship is that his early fixation on a settlements freeze was a blunder—a tactical but important blunder. The argument is that it had the unintended effect of boxing in the Palestinian leadership; they could not take a softer line on settlements than the president of the United States, but since Israel was not going to stop building in any event, the ultimate consequence was to sabotage the peace process. There is some merit to this criticism, although, as we've argued, the expansion of settlements constitutes an inexorable sabotaging of peace prospects anyway, so Obama's mistake probably was not fatal.

Critics from a different angle say that the fatal error was in not standing firm in his demand that the settlements stop. The White House has leverage, these critics say; Obama's failure to apply it was an act of political coward-ice. But the president of the United States has other priorities, domestic and foreign. The liberal journalist Josh Marshall illustrates this point when he recalls, early in Obama's first term, asking the president a question about Netanyahu's defiance on settlements.

> I don't remember the precise wording of my question but it was some-thing to the effect of, is that it? Can you really say this has to happen and then let it not happen? It's bad for the peace process and (I found some slightly but not very diplomatic way of saying this) it makes you look weak. . . . The gist of his answer was this would be good for peace and it would be good for Israel. It's very important. We've made our position clear. And now the Israelis have to decide whether they are going to do what is in fact in their self-interest. I remember sitting back in my chair, letting someone else ask a question and thinking, wow, I really didn't like that answer. But there was something in that answer that has informed everything that has come after. I think Obama really does care about Is-rael and believes strongly that it is on a bad course that it will have to re-verse. But it's a big world with a lot of problems out there to solve. Israel's just one and it's not the only one.[33]

A Grim Coda

There was a tragic and fitting coda to Kerry's peace mission: The Gaza war that reerupted from July 8 until August 26, 2014, and which served as a dark reminder of all the problems and improbabilities of the peace process.

The problem of Gaza and its Hamas government is very often ignored in peace-process discussions, perhaps because it poses such intractable difficul-ties as to place those discussions in the realm of absurdity. But Gaza's recent history must be understood in order to face three realities: the Palestinians' own bitter disunity; Israel's grim reliance on "punishment" as an overall policy; and, conversely, the reasonable Israeli skepticism that they will ever have a viable Palestinian partner for peace.

Ariel Sharon became Israel's prime minister as the Israeli public was being traumatized by the terrorism wave of 2000–2002. He announced a policy of unilateral "separation" that was to include Israel's withdrawal from Gaza and the construction of a West Bank "separation barrier." Gaza withdrawal in September 2005 required the uprooting of Israeli settlements containing 8,500 settlers. Most left voluntarily, but the IDF had to evict some by force.

Hope for a peaceful departure unraveled the following year. In January 2006 Hamas's victory in Palestinian legislative elections led to the formation of a Hamas-dominated cabinet under Prime Minister Ismail Haniyeh. In late June Palestinians killed two Israeli soldiers and kidnapped another, Gilad Shalit, whose five-year captivity by Hamas became a wrenching *cause célèbre* within Israel. Israel reoccupied parts of Gaza immediately, albeit temporarily.

The eighteen months following Hamas's electoral victory saw street fighting punctuated by short-lived truces between Palestinian Authority security forces, dominated by Fatah, and Hamas militants. In March 2007 the Saudis brokered a Palestinian unity government. In June, Fatah security forces, encouraged by the Bush administration, launched a coup attempt against Hamas, and failed. In the subsequent armed showdown between the two factions, Hamas ejected Fatah from the Gaza Strip.[34]

Since 2007 Israel has faced an intermittent rain of Qassam rocket attacks from Gaza, and Gaza has been sealed off in a punishing blockade from Israel (with the cooperation of Egyptian governments). The impact on Gaza civilians' daily existence has been devastating, even without the occasional incursions and three major wars: Operation Cast Lead (2008–2009), Operation Pillar of Defense (2012), and Operation Protective Edge (2014).

The United States and European governments have joined Israel in a rigid rejection of Hamas's legitimacy, on the reasonable basis that it engages in terrorism and refuses to acknowledge Israel's right to exist. Hamas, for its part, has at times indicated a willingness to negotiate a long-term *hudna* ("truce"), with hints that it could last for decades, during which many things might change. Optimists think that could mean Hamas is changing its attitude. Israelis, more pessimistic, believe it means ending Israel.

Israel is in a genuinely difficult bind. Yet the consequences of its blockade and intermittent military action against Gaza include misery and spiraling deterioration of Gaza society. Israelis bristle at the term "collective punishment." Yet the strategic logic of a "West Bank first" policy—effectively rewarding areas under Fatah control while allowing Hamas-run Gaza to fester in misery—seemed psychologically implausible even when things were going better in the West Bank. It seems unlikely that Gazans will eventually see the light and choose more moderate leadership, even if they are allowed to.

The United States has supported Israel's Gaza policies, at least tacitly. While occasionally, and carefully, criticizing Israel's use of force in the Gaza Strip, President Obama has always hastened to add that Israeli families cannot be expected to live under a rain of rocket fire. But Gaza, at the same time, has been another source of tension, and the tension has worsened over time. Over time there has been a palpable change in American media coverage, and social media coverage, of the Gaza campaigns.[35] With the failure of John Kerry's attempt to revive the peace process and his placing the blame on Israel for the breakdown, Israelis from both left and right were ready to pounce when he seemed to them too eager to end the summer 2014 Gaza War with a cease-fire that would have left Hamas's military infrastructure intact. They accused the American secretary of state of acting, in effect, as a Palestinian terror group's lawyer.[36]

The insults that Israeli government ministers hurled at John Kerry during both efforts conveyed the strong sense that the United States was sticking its nose where it did not belong. The United States was no longer an acceptable partner in resolving crises involving Israel. For many Israelis, the awakening of the United States to this reality will remove a wedge that had been driving the two countries apart. On one level this is obviously true. With the two-state solution dead, the United States can no longer hector Israel about a peace process.

But with the death of the two-state solution, Israeli control over occupied territory will depend increasingly on coercion rather than cooptation and cooperation. The coercion will inevitably be violent. And it will drive a much wider wedge between Israel and the United States.

5

Arab Battles, American Restraint,
Israeli Anxiety

ON SEPTEMBER 9, 2011, a large mob attacked the Israeli embassy in Cairo. It was a time of lingering unrest in the Egyptian capital, after enormous protests earlier in the year that had toppled Husni Mubarak, the country's longtime strongman. On this day the trigger was a soccer defeat. But the anger toward Israel had been building for three weeks, after Arab marauders from Sinai entered Israel undetected and murdered six civilians and two uniformed Israelis on the road to Eilat. The Israeli response led to deaths of five Egyptian soldiers.* So the mood on the street, brittle and surly to begin with, was easily diverted toward Israeli scapegoats. The soccer defeat turned sullen irritation into violent protest.

The Israeli embassy was an easy target. Unlike most of the embassies in Giza or other fashionable districts in Cairo, Israel's did not occupy its own structure, but rather two floors of a high-rise office building. There really was no need for anything more elaborate, since there was not much substance to the relationship. And a big building flying the Israeli flag would have been provocative in a country where Israel remained unpopular. Important matters of state were handled through intelligence channels. When something urgent required discussion, a small Israeli Ministry of Defense and Mossad team would make the short flight to Cairo, typically returning home the same day. But the diplomatic mission was nonetheless an important symbol, to Israel if not to Egypt, of the peace treaty that had transformed

---

* There were conflicting stories about how this happened. Israelis insisted that the Egyptian soldiers were killed by a suicide bomber; the Egyptians claimed that they had been killed by Israeli friendly fire.

Israel from a beleaguered country threatened by massive armies on two fronts to a nation that no longer had to worry about being pushed into the sea. The embassy also represented the somewhat forlorn hope that someday a real people-to-people relationship between Israelis and Egyptians would grow. Israel's Cairo-based diplomats worked hard to cultivate this delicate flower.

On the day the embassy was assaulted, most of the staff were at home. Given the volatility of the street, this was only prudent. The embassy's offices contained six Israelis, mostly armed guards but also the technician who operated the mission's communications equipment. It was late at night when the restless crowd converged. The mob quickly tore down the barrier at street level and proceeded to storm through the undefended lobby and make its way to the twentieth and twenty-first floors. The Israeli staff quickly sought refuge in the safe room, a hardened space hidden behind three separate doors. The invasion happened so quickly that the staff had no time to destroy equipment or official documents, which soon began to float down from the upper windows, like bureaucratic confetti, fueling the rage below.[1]

The Israelis jammed into their bolt-hole were clearly in mortal danger. It was late on Friday afternoon in Washington when Steven Simon received more or less simultaneous calls from Israel and from the Pentagon. The government in Jerusalem had reached out first to Leon Panetta at the Defense Department and then to the White House. White House staff swung into action. This response deserves detailed description, because it showed how the administration mobilized to manage a crisis involving the lives of Israelis. The immediate problem was the apparent indifference of Egyptian officials to the disaster that would envelop them if they were to allow the massacre of Israeli diplomats in the heart of their capital. Field Marshal Mohammad Tantawi, head of the military council in charge of the country's government since Mubarak's imprisonment, was, according to his staff, unreachable. Simon urged the Egyptian ambassador in Washington to get his foreign minister on the case and called the chief of the U.S. Middle East military command, General James Mattis, to ask him to call General al-Sisi—later president of Egypt—and leverage their close relationship to get the general staff in Cairo mobilized. Simon also asked the head of the CIA to call and wake up his counterpart in Cairo. Tom Donilon, the national security advisor, reached out to his opposite number in Cairo as well.

While staff tried to get Tantawi on the phone with Obama, an Israeli official with a voice link to the safe room at the Cairo embassy provided a running commentary on the increasingly desperate situation. The trapped Israelis anticipated their imminent slaughter. The hammering on the last of the three doors separating them from the mob could be heard through the Israeli's cell phone. A dreadful sequence of events was in everyone's imagination. The room would be penetrated, the Israelis would fire in self-defense but run out of ammunition well before the deranged mob could be pushed back, and, finally, they would be fatally overwhelmed.

At this stage, Egyptian authorities had at last flooded the surrounding streets with riot police using dense clouds of tear gas to disperse the crowds. But what the situation required was special forces who could get to the upper floors quickly enough to prevent a massacre.

Netanyahu phoned the president, who took the call in the Oval Office. They reviewed the theoretical options for direct intervention and concluded that none was feasible. The onus, for better or for worse, was on Egyptian authorities. Obama ran through the measures Washington was taking to prod Cairo into action. He said we would keep escalating the pressure until Egyptian commandos intervened. Shortly thereafter, Tantawi made himself available for the call with Obama, who told him that any harm inflicted on the Israeli hostages would be catastrophic for Egypt and for U.S.–Egyptian relations. The message finally registered. Egyptian special forces penetrated the corridor leading to the safe room, bulled the mob out of the area, and extricated the Israelis. U.S. officials worked with the two sides to coordinate the safe transport of eighty-five embassy personnel from locations in the capital to the military side of the Cairo airport, where they were picked up by an Israeli military cargo plane. The Israeli deputy chief of mission could not get out, but he was taken to the U.S. ambassador's residence and sheltered there until he could be safely repatriated.[2]

The Arabs Revolt

Jerusalem was grateful. Netanyahu said of Obama, "He said he would do everything in his power, and he has done that. We owe him a special thank you."[3]

But this drama, with its happy ending, was a rare moment of convergence between two allies for whom the turbulence of the Arab and broader Middle

East was mainly a source of bewilderment and more mutual alienation. There were to be two specific disagreements: first, over the sensible attitude toward the toppling of Mubarak and coming to power of a Muslim Brotherhood government in Egypt; second, and most seriously, over Iran. In broader terms, the Likud government seemed to be in tune, as with so many other things, with the U.S. Republican conviction that Obama was feckless, incompetent, and a congenital appeaser. If one looked deeper into Israeli complaints, however, it became clear that they objected to deeply rooted American attitudes and policies that transcended Obama's allegedly peculiar preferences.

Obama, from his inauguration, was determined to pursue a very different regional policy than his predecessor. He wanted to move away from war and military intervention, engage hostile authoritarian regimes rather than try to isolate them, improve relations with the Muslim world, and jump-start the Middle East peace process. Once elected, he set about implementing his new agenda, beginning to withdraw troops from Iraq, and reaching out diplomatically to Iran and Syria. As we have seen, he called for a "new beginning" in his major address in Cairo, and called on Israel to halt construction of settlements in the occupied territories.

For much of his presidency, however, things didn't work out as hoped. The Iranians and Syrians failed to reciprocate the administration's overtures, and in fact Iran was seized by popular protests that put the administration in an awkward position. On Palestine, the Arab world waited for words to be followed by deeds, and the Israelis bridled rather than buckled under pressure. By the end of 2009, much of the administration's regional policy agenda had stalled, with the exception of the withdrawal from Iraq—which was to be followed in a couple of years, the president announced, by a U.S. withdrawal from Afghanistan as well. The administration decided to pursue the "war on terror" aggressively through drone attacks and raids— including the one that eventually killed Osama bin Laden—but otherwise tried to turn its attention elsewhere. It declared, most notably, its intention to "pivot" to Asia.

Then came the Arab Spring, which fed off a mixture of economic despair, social frustration, and political yearning across the region.

Almost nobody had predicted it. Certainly analysts and activists could speculate, and in many cases hope, that authoritarian regimes would someday fall. But "someday" was not, in practical policy terms, a useful concept; the when and how was a mystery until it happened. The old regimes themselves were taken aback by the force and speed of the uprisings, and even traditional opposition parties were behind the curve, often remaining hesitant well after newer popular protest movements sprang up and seized the moment. The Obama administration was caught by surprise like everyone else, and scrambled to respond.

On the one hand, the United States had long called for democratic reform, and the generally peaceful, idealistic protesters seemed mainly in tune with what Americans believed to be their own most cherished values. On the other hand, many of the authoritarian regimes in question were American allies, or at least clients, and Washington, as the guarantor of regional order, was loath to encourage instability and to leap into the unknown.

So the administration moved cautiously. After Ben Ali fled Tunisia, Washington signaled to Mubarak that it was time to go, and reluctantly stepped in, together with Britain and France, to help the rebels who rose up against Moammar Qadaffi's regime in Libya. At the same time, it mainly looked the other way as Bahrain brutally suppressed its rebellion, did nothing to undermine the other monarchies of the strategically critical Persian Gulf, and watched warily to see what would happen with the uprising in Syria.

The administration's response to the Arab Spring, and the strife and desolation that followed it, wasn't hugely effectual. But neither is it the outright failure so many critics claim, since there were no good policy options for Washington to embrace, and many alternative approaches it wisely rejected would have fared even worse. Given the internal and external constraints under which he has labored, Obama has, on balance, done reasonably well in matching American capabilities and resources to the interests at stake. Much of the messiness in U.S. policy was inevitable, and so, arguably, was the consequent discord between Washington and its Israeli ally.

Egypt and Israel

There is something about Obama that would lead casual observers to assume that he would be an unrestrained advocate of democracy movements wherever they might arise. The truth was more complicated. Certainly it was in his basic *gestalt* to support democrats against authoritarians. But in temperament, and particularly in reaction to the ideological zeal of his predecessor, Obama was also inclined to the view that American interests included other priorities.

The administration as a whole constituted a wide spectrum of views on the proper American role in promoting democracy. Senior staffers who had served in Obama's presidential campaign comprised what might be called a "democracy lobby," pushing the president to put his ideals into practice These advocates, for example Samantha Power, argued that political reform in the Middle East should be a paramount policy goal, displacing more traditional strategic goals. Another faction, led until his departure by national security adviser Tom Donilon, was skeptical about the virtues of democratization as a policy objective and more likely to see U.S. interests in traditional terms. Former deputy national security advisor (now chief of staff) Denis McDonough played the role of swing voter, siding occasionally with each camp. Each side was convinced it reflected the president's innermost impulses—the democratizers his heart, and the realists his head. In the debates over Libya and Egypt, the idealists sometimes gained the upper hand, while policy toward Syria, Israel, and Iran has been shaped more by environmental constraints and the lack of attractive intervention possibilities.

Events in Tunisia moved so quickly and the country was such a minor strategic player that Washington was essentially a bystander to the Arab Spring's first revolt. On Egypt, the next domino, the administration's democracy advocates rather than its regional experts seized the upper hand in internal deliberations, and for them, U.S. interests lay in promoting the revolution. A dramatic shift to popular democracy in Egypt, they argued, would lead to greater stability in the region while laying the foundation for a transformed relationship between Washington and Cairo grounded in shared democratic values. They regarded the Supreme Council of the Armed Forces (SCAF), which was trying somewhat fitfully to shepherd the country to its first truly contested election, as a simple extension of the *ancien régime*. Cooperation with SCAF was derided as "business as usual."

Yet the president's February 11, 2011, decision to declare that the transition in Egypt should begin "now" was not really the consequence of any faction in the White House winning the upper hand. The decision was very likely the one that any mainstream president expressing American traditions and values would have taken. It served the customary U.S. interest in stability, since it seemed to be the only thing that would clear the Egyptian street, while satisfying the American impulse not only to be on the right side of history, but to embody it. In any case, the transition was already under way. The general staff that would shortly take the reins of government had initiated what amounted to a bloodless coup d'état, understanding that Mubarak had become a lightning rod for protest, which could, at the end of the day, undermine the military's economic interests. Obama was essentially calling for a process that was already in motion. Given the undeniably local character of the revolutionary dynamic, the notion that Obama's call for Mubarak to step down had caused, or even accelerated, change was a tribute to both American hubris and the bipolar perception of the United States by its allies that so often sees the United States as simultaneously omnipotent and spent.

Israel, however, together with Saudi Arabia and other Gulf Arab kingdoms, was dismayed. Saudi Arabia was a large country, with a weak military watching rebellions uncoil on every side. As state sponsor of Wahhabi fundamentalism, it was a bitter enemy of the Muslim Brotherhood, competing Sunni fundamentalists who appeared most likely to benefit from open elections in Egypt. The adverse reaction in Jerusalem was perhaps also inevitable, given Egypt's role as the keystone of Israel's regional security architecture. Dennis Ross recalls a conversation in Netanyahu's office in which the Israeli minister Dan Meridor lamented, "Why did the president have to push Mubarak out? Why did he have to say anything publicly?"[4] Israeli liberals were also angry. Shavit, the *Haaretz* correspondent, put it this way:

Obama's betrayal of Hosni Mubarak is not just the betrayal of a moderate Egyptian president who remained loyal to the United States, promoted stability and encouraged moderation. Obama's betrayal of Mubarak symbolizes the betrayal of every strategic ally in the Third World. Throughout Asia, Africa and South America, leaders are now looking at what is going on between Washington and Cairo. . . . Everyone grasps the message: America's word is worthless; an alliance with America is unreliable; American has lost it.[5]

Abundant media reporting indicates that Shavit's dismay reflected broad Israeli government views.[6] Yet such laments betrayed limited understanding of America's responsibilities and real options. They ignored the reality that the United States had actually stuck by Mubarak for at least a decade after his unpopularity and the risks he posed to American interests in the region had become clear. Washington had repeatedly urged Mubarak to implement reforms that might have staved off the revolt. The Bill Clinton and George W.

Bush administrations both tried to persuade Mubarak to reform the electoral process and stop arresting political opponents. But arrests continued,
while reforms were cosmetic. In her own extraordinary Cairo speech of
2005, Bush's then Secretary of State Condoleezza Rice went so far as to finger American complicity in the tyrannies that had inspired 9/11 terrorism:
"For 60 years, my country, the United States, pursued stability at the expense
of democracy in this region here in the Middle East, and we achieved neither," Rice declared. "Now we are taking a different course."[7] But to his final
moments in office, Mubarak had brushed these arguments aside. Obama's
dramatic—if ex post facto—statement therefore was not out of the blue.
There was also the issue of whether alternative courses of action were actually available to the Administration, given that Mubarak's fate had in effect
already been decided by the crowds in Tahrir and the generals in their canton-
ments. There were no real alternatives, except perhaps for silence, but silence
is generally not an option for the United States. And given the ineluctability
of the regime's demise, to undermine U.S. influence preemptively through
silence or approval for whatever measures Mubarak might order to suppress the burgeoning protests would have served no one's interests, including Israel's.

The next stage of discord between Washington and Jerusalem concerned
the likely consequences of democratic elections in Egypt. Most observers of
Egyptian politics forecast a Muslim Brotherhood victory. The Brothers were
well organized, had a large urban constituency, and essentially maintained
a parallel state that delivered social services and medical assistance to Egypt's
preponderantly indigent population. They were clearly a force to be reck-
oned with. The Israelis, like the Saudis, saw the Brothers as an implacable
enemy. There was no question that this secretive, fundamentalist organization opposed the existence of Israel and was committed to the democratic
domination of the regional political order. At that stage, however, it was an
open question how a Brotherhood-led government in Cairo would approach
the peace treaty with Israel. The Brothers, for all the transnationalism baked
into their ideology, were also Egyptian nationalists sensitive to the limits on
Egyptian sovereignty imposed by the Sinai disengagement agreement with
Israel.

Throughout the spring of 2011, there was broad consensus within the U.S.
administration that the course of wisdom regarding the elections was to
avoid appearing to try to pick a winner, and to embrace whatever outcome

emerged from a seemingly legitimate process. Washington had few alternative courses open to it. The United States had no ties with the Muslim Brotherhood and no sympathy for its agenda, and even less for the more radical
Islamists to its right. Other candidates, meanwhile, included a dyspeptic
Nasserist who hated the United States, centrists such as the international
bureaucrat Mohamed el-Baradei, who had vanishingly little support, and
the rump of the old regime. (In the final tally, the latter actually came within
a hair's breadth of tying the Brotherhood, an outcome that would likely have
revived the Tahrir protests, perpetuated instability, and plunged the country into new cycles of rioting and penury.) Washington did try to persuade
the SCAF to put off elections, so as to give the non-Islamist slice of the political spectrum more time to prepare and build support, but the officers were
uninterested. They wanted the swiftest path back to the barracks, which meant
elections as soon as possible. A June 2011 decree giving them some rights to
intervene in the political process later on provided a mechanism to confine
an elected government to rules of the road. Despite the sunset clause included in this writ, they probably judged that they could step in down the
road should the situation become unstable.

In Washington and in the U.S. embassy in Cairo—led by Ann Patterson,
an exceptionally able diplomat who combined steel with finesse—officials
were listening for indications or statements that the Brothers would depart
from Egypt's existing commitment to peace with Israel. Prior to the elections,
the Brothers sent a delegation to the United States, where it met with a
wide range of Washington players including NSC staff. Pushed hard on the
issue of the peace treaty, the envoys assured their hosts that they thought
the treaty needed to be revised but not revoked. From Washington's perspective, this was not the ideal reply, but it was scarcely radical either. U.S. officials told them in any event to forget about revising the treaty, because any
effort to do so would be opposed by Washington and would only invite
countervailing revisions by Israel. If the Brothers were elected, the envoys
were told, they would have more pressing economic problems to worry about
than the a treaty that had, after all, returned every centimeter of Egyptian
territory to Egyptian rule. Left unmentioned was the size of the hammer the
Egyptian military would drop on the Muslim Brotherhood if it took steps
to upend the peace terms.

Once the Brotherhood won, the Obama administration tried to get as
much money to Egypt as soon as possible (to ensure that its government

could deliver basic services and maintain order) while pushing the new leader-ship to cooperate on counterterrorism, maintaining order in Sinai, reestab-lishing military-to-military links with Israel, and keeping the Suez canal open for U.S. warships. Egyptian domestic issues such as protection of minority rights and personal status issues were given a lesser priority, although Wash-ington did oppose initiatives it deemed incompatible with the rule of law.[8]

In the year before the Brothers' victory, and for eight months afterward, Simon met frequently with senior Israeli officials to compare notes.[9] The Is-raeli outlook was grim. It was also remarkably coherent and consistent—all about encirclement. Some thousand miles to the east, Iran's development of a nuclear capability cast an existential shadow over the Jewish state. Imme-diately to the east, there was Jordan. The Hashemite family ruling this small country had been good friends to Israel for decades. The new king's great grandfather met frequently with Golda Meir and other Zionists in the cru-cial years of Israel's state formation. When Syria in 1970 deployed over a hundred tanks into Jordan to support a Palestinian revolt aiming to over-throw the king's father, Henry Kissinger appealed to Israel to mobilize its own forces; the move was successful in convincing the Syrians to withdraw. The current king, Abdullah II, had sustained this pattern of close coopera-tion. But Israel saw danger. The flood tide of regional unrest would almost certainly capsize the Hashemite ship. The Jordanian Muslim Brotherhood was prepared to take command. Continuing northward, the Syrian regime, which was facing the first phase of a swelling rebellion from a largely Sunni population, would fall to the Muslim Brotherhood as well. The Brothers had long been active in Syria, and the Alawite rulers had dealt with them harshly in an escalating cycle of violence that culminated in the 1982 destruction by regime artillery of the city of Hama. Surely the Brotherhood would be back. Swinging westward, there was Lebanon, firmly in Hizballah's grip. Just five years before, Israel had fought a brutal if short war against Lebanese Hizbal-lah, which was seen as having failed to achieve Israel's objectives at great expense. And now, to the west, the prospect of an elected Muslim Brother-hood in Egypt would complete Israel's encirclement. The Muslim Brothers were fundamentalists whose worldview could not encompass a permanent peace between a Muslim Egypt and a Jewish state. This was the most im-mediate and, arguably, the biggest setback and danger. This change alone was enough to ruin Israel's strategic position—raising, for the first time in over thirty years, the specter of a major war.[10]

However, Simon saw no evidence, so far, that Egypt's position on the treaty was shifting. What, Simon asked, was Israel hearing? The Israeli response was that they were not picking up anything either, despite the fact that they too were looking and listening intently. So why were they so confident in their dire forecast? The answer was that the foundational documents of the Muslim Brotherhood movement and the writings of its founder, the fiercely religious and anticolonial Hassan al-Banna, left no room for doubt that Egypt under a Brotherhood government would repudiate the treaty with Israel. Brotherhood doctrine was incompatible with peace.

Simon recalled a lecture he had heard in Israel in the late 1980s. The lecturer was a renowned political scientist and former head of Israel's military intelligence, Yehoshafat Harkabi. Harkabi, a competent Arabist, had been involved in secret talks with Jordanian officials around the time of Israel's War of Independence, and served in the field as an infantry company commander once war broke out. He had made his mark in academia with a book called *Arab Attitudes Towards Israel*, a dark assessment of prospects for peace based on the statements of virtually all Arab leaders and thinkers about the Jewish state.[11] The book had a significant impact. But Sadat's trip to Jerusalem in 1978 had changed Harkabi's thinking. There could not have been clearer evidence of a sea change in Arab mentality. In his lecture, Harkabi emphasized the distinction between a country's "agenda" and its "program." He used the Cold War dynamic of U.S.–Soviet relations to argue, on the basis of each country's ideology, or core beliefs, that their vision of a desirable end-state was a world from which the other had disappeared. This was the Soviet (and indeed American) agenda. Yet their actual program was not destruction of the other, but coexistence, albeit a coexistence that assumed a conflictual relationship. Harkabi clearly intended that his audience substitute Israel for the United States in his analysis, and Arabs for the Soviet Union. So, some twenty-five years later, Simon asked his Israeli interlocutors if Harkabi's distinction could not be applied to Egypt under Muslim Brotherhood rule. The Israelis responded that this was an interesting observation but not really relevant to the Egyptian case.

As it happened, there would be two real-world tests of the Muslim Brotherhood government's approach to foreign policy in general and to Israel in particular. The first came in the Sinai. The security situation in Sinai had never been especially stable. Egyptian military forces were largely deployed to the Nile Delta region, the better to protect the government from rebels, rather than to the Sinai, since Israel was no longer a foe. The military governor in the peninsula had limited resources to maintain order. A modus vivendi therefore evolved between the military administration and the assortment of local brigands, smugglers, and tribal sheikhs, under which they could pursue their various criminal enterprises as long as these did not get out of hand or lead to attacks on Egyptian security forces. In the wake of the revolution in Egypt, however, criminal networks in Sinai were joined by other, ideologically motivated malefactors who targeted Egyptian forces and aimed to carry out cross-border terrorist attacks against Israeli civilians in the southern Negev desert.

As Sinai security unraveled, the Muslim Brotherhood president, Muhammad Morsi, put increasing pressure on the military to get a grip on the situation. They proceeded to deploy tanks, apparently without ammunition, to the central and eastern Sinai in an effort to intimidate troublemakers. The problem with this response was that it violated the military annex to the Camp David Accords, which strictly limited the presence of Egyptian armor in these areas. In their rush to cope with a rapidly deteriorating security situation, the Egyptian army had not abided by the rules. In the moment, however, it was not clear whether this was a function of poor organization in an emergency, or a deliberate step by the Muslim Brotherhood government to test limits in a longer game to dismantle the treaty. It soon became apparent that no such long game was in play. Israeli and Egyptian officers began a series of productive meetings, with the blessing of the Morsi government, leading to Israeli-approved deployments of both armor and attack helicopters into Sinai.

The second test came in Gaza, in mid-November 2012, days after Obama's reelection, as more fighting broke out between Israel and Hamas. The fighting ended quickly without an IDF incursion owing to a cease-fire brokered, with Obama's encouragement, by Morsi. Obama was in Asia at the time for his trip to herald the American "pivot" to Asia-Pacific. Yet he spent an ironic amount of time on the phone with both Morsi and Netanyahu to stop the Gaza fighting before it spun out of control. These calls entailed tutoring Morsi in the art of negotiation and more broadly how international politics worked and diplomacy was conducted. Morsi at least initially was a willing student and quickly abandoned preconceptions and tropes about Israel and how to deal with it productively. It was a fascinating enactment of Pygmalion, with Obama playing Professor Higgins.

Unfortunately, the manipulation of the Egyptian constitutional process and Morsi's November 2012 decree that gave him extrajudicial powers indicated that Morsi was no liberal. For Morsi, everyone else was to blame: the liberals who withdrew from the constitutional process, foreign provocateurs, and conspirators from the old regime. The evident sincerity of Morsi's lamentations contributed to his rigid response to a developing crisis. In the end, he could not have tried harder to alienate a huge, non-Islamist voter bloc that felt, not without reason, disenfranchised and threatened. In an astounding irony, the leader of the Muslim Brotherhood inadvertently handed the country back to the army, which did not want it.

Unwilling or not, however, Egypt's army proceeded to deal with the deposed Muslim Brotherhood according to the only playbook it knew: brutal repression. The SCAF coup against Morsi, to Israel's undisguised relief, took the Muslim Brotherhood off the table as a problem between Washington and Jerusalem. However, it was not possible to ignore the very different U.S. and Israeli attitudes and interests that Egypt's failed democratic experiment revealed. The 2012 runoff election that brought Morsi to power had been accepted by the Obama administration because the process had been free and fair, at least as far as the host of domestic and international observers were concerned. There was not much in the Muslim Brotherhood's program that appealed to American sensibilities, but the feeling was that the United States would have to work with the new government, in part to make the more general point within the region that it was willing in principle to work with Islamists, in part because intensive engagement would be essential to Egypt's economic recovery and political stability, and in part because the long-term consolidation of democratic institutions—including elections and a party system—was more important than the inevitable perturbations of Brotherhood ideology. The Israeli position was, in effect: We don't need some kind of science experiment, because we know already how it ends. They are the Muslim Brotherhood; this will be the last election.

We will never know how it might have ended. Although Morsi had certainly used power in illiberal ways, the coup against him preempted the ultimate question of whether his government could have been voted out of office. But in international policy, Morsi's behavior in Sinai and Gaza constituted two pieces of evidence that ran directly contrary to Israeli predictions. On the international side, Obama's White House was proven right. Between Washington and Jerusalem, however, it was a very divisive moment.

The Sisi military government's crackdown on the Muslim Brotherhood was immediate and massive. Some 1,000 Islamist activists at two protest camps were massacred. Morsi's arrest was followed by the jailing of as many as 40,000 people. In March and April of 2014 1,212 alleged Brotherhood supporters were sentenced to death in mass trials.

Although most of these were later commuted to life imprisonment, further death sentences followed in February, May, and September 2015. The Muslim Brotherhood itself, dissolved by a court injunction in September 2013, was designated a terrorist organization three months later.[12] The head of the Brotherhood's Egypt branch, Mohamed Badie, was arrested in August 2013 and the last member of its senior leadership in November 2014.[13] By August 2015, Badie had accumulated two death and six life imprisonment sentences.[14]

This repression was grimly predictable, and so are the likely consequences. We have seen this movie before. In 2003, Mohammed Hafez, who now teaches at the Naval Postgraduate School in the United States, published a book called *Why Muslims Rebel*, borrowing his title from Ted Gurr's 1970 classic, *Why Men Rebel*.[15] Hafez aimed to apply social movement theory to the Muslim world. His broader argument addressed the question of why and under what circumstances repression can fail. Specifically, he asked why violent resistance had emerged in Egypt and Algeria but not elsewhere in the region.

The answer, he said, lay in the character and form of repression. Where the regime in question repressed dissent in a targeted fashion, and did not go overboard, the repression tended to work. Fence-sitters could be marginalized and radicals would have a hard time recruiting oppositionists to violent action. In 1990s Algeria and Egypt, on the other hand, repression was indiscriminate and policing was brutally aggressive. This left moderate activists thinking: They are going to come after me next, despite my avowed commitment to peaceful protest. Having reached this conclusion, activism would devolve into militancy and, ultimately, war against the machine. In Hafez's view, this was a matter of rational choice. If the other guy is going to come after you no matter what, the prudent course is to pick up a gun.

Israel, with its siege mentality and low expectations of Arab political culture, can live with the repression of democracy in Egypt. America will live with it too, since there is not much it can do, but its discomfort is greater given its strategic responsibilities and its memories of 9/11. Repression of Islamists in Egypt was an essential stage in the emergence of the contemporary jihadism that produced the 9/11 attacks. As splinter groups that were significantly more radical than the Muslim Brotherhood formed, Islamists became more violent. In the 1970s, a charismatic former Brotherhood member, Shukri Mustapha, created al-Tafkir wal-Hijra, one of the early forerunners of al Qaeda. Meanwhile, Muhammad Abd al-Salam Faraj plotted the ideology of al Jihad. The latter group eventually assassinated Sadat, and later provided much of the leadership for al Qaeda, including Ayman al-Zawahri, the successor to bin Laden.

The Egyptian coup was popular, but the military has deluded itself that sufficient brutal repression will bring submission. Criminalizing the Brotherhood, which renounced violence in the 1970s and honored that pledge through Morsi's inept tenure, could prove to be a fateful error.

Civil Wars

Egypt was at the center of U.S.–Israeli disagreements because it was the most populous Arab country and its peace treaty with Israel had become the anchor of Jerusalem's strategic confidence and planning. But after the coup ended Egypt's difficult experiment with democracy, Jerusalem's disagreements with Washington reverted to the more general problem—as many Israelis saw it—of Obama's weakness.

These disagreements revealed very different approaches by the United States and Israel to the maintenance and regulation of international order. To put it in crude terms, military force is very often Israel's solution of first resort, while America is more restrained. That statement may surprise those who consider the United States a kind of imperial bull in the global china shop. But everything is relative, and Obama's was hardly the first U.S. administration to be at odds with Israel over questions of force.

What was different, and possibly unnerving now for Israel, was that the United States was in the midst of ratcheting back its own use of force because it had given overwhelming military power a very serious tryout, without evident success. Obama was an emblem and agent of that ratcheting back. But he was no pacifist. He had come to prominence, while still a state senator from Illinois, in opposition to the Iraq war, but with the important qualification that he did not oppose all wars, just "dumb" ones.[16]

At the end of his first year as president, Obama delivered two statements that expressed contending, coexisting traditions in American foreign policy: the American responsibility to use its vast military power on the one hand, and realist restraint on the other. These statements might be labeled, respectively, his Oslo declaration and his West Point declaration. What's remarkable is that they were delivered within nine days of each other in December 2009. The West Point declaration came first. It had much to do with economic constraints. Obama entered office with a clear conviction that, barely a year after the ruinous financial crisis, domestic economic stability required an acceptance of limits on strategic commitments abroad. Since the primary threat of his early months in office was the possibility of another Great Depression, Obama took many opportunities to draw this connection. When he spoke on December 1, 2009, to U.S. military cadets at West Point, he put it this way: "Over the past few years, [we've] failed to appreciate the connection between our national security and our economy." Obama was announcing an escalation—a "surge"—of 30,000 more troops to fight the war in Afghanistan. But he delivered it at a tricky moment in his relationship with senior military commanders, whom he felt were trying to box him into a more open-ended escalation.[17] And so, in announcing the surge, he took great care at the same time to delineate the limits of America's commitment to that country, dictated by competing interests and limited resources.

> As President, I refuse to set goals that go beyond our responsibility, our means, or our interests. And I must weigh all of the challenges that our nation faces. I don't have the luxury of committing to just one. Indeed, I'm mindful of the words of President Eisenhower, who—in discussing our national security—said, "Each proposal must be weighed in the light of a broader consideration: the need to maintain balance in and among national programs."[18]

Down to its invocation of Eisenhower, this speech was a classic expression of Obama's small-c conservatism, concerned with restoring a balance between international commitments on the one hand, and American capabilities and resources on the other.

The Oslo declaration took a different tack. It was crafted in response to a rather different political problem: the fact that so many considered his Nobel Peace Prize to be some kind of bad joke, awarded as it was in the early months of his presidency before real accomplishments were even possible. Obama signaled that he got the joke, but rather than decline the award he decided to confound the prize-givers by accepting it with a statement on why American exceptionalism is intrinsically tied up with the sometimes greater American understanding of the need for organized violence:

> Make no mistake: Evil does exist in the world. A non-violent movement could not have halted Hitler's armies. Negotiations cannot convince al Qaeda's leaders to lay down their arms. . . . The world must remember that it was not simply international institutions—not just treaties and declarations—that brought stability to a post–World War II world. What-ever mistakes we have made, the plain fact is this: The United States of America has helped underwrite global security for more than six decades with the blood of our citizens and the strength of our arms.[19]

The difficulty of reconciling these two declarations was to be tested by the two civil wars arising from the Arab Spring, in Libya and then Syria. The Libyan uprising against Qadaffi began roughly at the same time as Egypt's against Mubarak, but with very different immediate results. In February 2011 the Libyan dictator fired on protesters, and soon threatened to crush resisters in their stronghold city of Benghazi. Qadaffi promised to hunt the rebels from house to house "like rats." French President Nicolas Sarkozy and UK Prime Minister David Cameron urged action to protect them. In Wash-ington, the liberal interventionist inclinations of White House staff—which in line with Obama's Oslo declaration considered the "responsibility to protect" an important principle—received support from Secretary of State Clinton and UN Ambassador Susan Rice. This lobby, which also included NSC staffer Samantha Power (author of a powerful book on modern geno-cide), overcame the skepticism of Defense Secretary Gates and, it appears, Obama himself. The United States, Britain, and France were able to secure passage of a remarkably robust UN Security Council resolution authorizing member states to use "all necessary measures" to stop the regime's killings. In operational terms, this was to be translated into not just a "no-fly zone" but a "no-drive zone" so that NATO air power was effectively supporting rebels in their efforts to depose Qadaffi. Passage of the resolution was en-abled by arguably constructive abstentions from Russia and China, and it all happened within weeks of the initial crackdown. This was, in the history of UN diplomacy, very fast, and only the fourth time in that history, as Bruce

Jones has noted, that the Security Council had "fully" authorized "force against a member state."

The U.S. military role was meaningful—but carefully limited. The American idea was for France, Britain, other European allies, and some Arab states to fly the bulk of the missions. As the fight wore on and Qadaffi seemed able to survive even as NATO began to run out of planes and ammunition, the White House remained firm that it would not pump more resources into the fight. And when Qadaffi did eventually fall, the president continued to keep his distance, not wanting the United States to become embroiled in the postwar situation.

This whole approach was part of the conscious effort to balance responsibility and restraint, and it seemed successful—for a while. The suggestion from one administration official that there was a doctrine of "leading from behind" was probably meant as a joke, though an impolitic one that drew derision from the president's hawkish critics.[20] But it conveyed the idea that America could support a broader international effort without getting drawn into quagmires. Obama in fact had suggested this model in his Oslo declaration. "American leadership is not simply a matter of going it alone and bearing all of the burden ourselves," he told the Nobel committee. "Real leadership creates the conditions and coalitions for others to step up as well; to work with allies and partners so that they bear their share of the burden and pay their share of the costs."[21]

There were at least two problems, however. First, the American, French, and British determination to use a Security Council resolution of humanitarian protection as a license for regime change—though it made strategic sense in Libya—seriously infuriated the Russians. One could argue, as one of the present authors did argue at the time, that the U.S. insistence on robust terms should have tipped off Moscow as to what the Western powers intended. But it was nonetheless an important stage in the Russian anger and hardening against the Western international agenda. Second, the moment that Qadaffi was found in the drainage pipe where he had sought refuge and summarily slain was a grim harbinger of the chaos soon to engulf Libya. Whatever the man might have deserved for past and intended crimes, the brutality of his execution showed how difficult it is to channel military liberation into rule-based democracy. Both problems would have deep significance for the unfolding of events in Syria.

At first, however, U.S. policy toward Syria was shaped by the quick and—as it appeared at the time—happy course of the uprisings in Tunisia, Egypt, and Libya. When protests broke out in March 2011 in the Syrian city of Deraa, the administration believed that these too would lead to a fairly rapid change of regime, and that whatever followed Assad would be an improvement. On the surface, at least, Assad looked vulnerable. The Assad regime was going down, and Iran was about to lose its only Arab state ally.

As 2011 progressed, demonstrations in Syria gathered pace and the armed opposition began to mobilize, but the conflict had not yet become a full-scale civil war. The White House and State Department used the time to begin working with the exiled political opposition (a surreal experience given its internal rivalries and distance from Syrian realities) and to attempt to isolate the regime by organizing high-profile diplomatic conferences in regional capitals.

At the same time, the administration tried to get the Russians to join—or at least not block—a UN Security Council resolution that would impose multilateral sanctions on the Assad regime if it failed to take steps to release prisoners, allow the media to operate freely, and withdraw its forces from cities. But these maneuvers became entangled in failed attempts at mediation by UN stalwarts Kofi Annan and Lakhdar Brahimi, and in the end, meaningful conversations about Security Council action foundered on Moscow's bitterness and resentment over the ultimate consequences of the UN's legitimation of regime change in Libya.

As the Syrian conflict grew more violent, Obama, his national security adviser, and senior officials at the NSC and the State Department made repeated runs at the Russians, but to no avail. (With Syria descending into hell, Steven Simon flew to Moscow for a meeting with Deputy Foreign Minister Mikhail Bogdanov, who spent an hour and a half in a rant that ranged over exceptionally wide terrain—from the Byzantine empire and Ottoman caliphs, to Lawrence of Arabia and the "deluded" current U.S. administration—without ever allowing for the possibility of cooperation. As a tactic to avoid diplomatic engagement it was weirdly awesome.) U.S. officials tried to convince their Russian counterparts that a long and bloody conflict would stoke the fires of jihad, and so they had their own interests in pulling the plug on their client. The notion that Russia's confidence in Assad's staying power might be more justified than U.S. confidence in the fortunes of his opponents was not taken as seriously, perhaps, it should have been.

Yet, as winter 2011 gave way to spring 2012, there did seem to arise at least the possibility of a negotiated settlement. Quiet meetings between U.S. and Russian officials in Geneva and Moscow led U.S. diplomats to believe that there was enough common ground for the two powers to bring both the opposition and regime to the table. Historians will eventually determine whether this belief reflected wishful thinking, a simple misunderstanding, misleading signals from Moscow, or a combination of all of these. But the result was a confusing whiplash at a summit in Geneva, during which the two sides signed a communiqué mapping a path to a negotiated political transition in Syria, but within minutes publicly accused each other of bad faith, somehow attributing entirely different meanings to an uncommonly straightforward text.

The administration would debate the merits of arming the opposition almost continuously from this point on, coming to different conclusions at different points, partly because the national security principals were themselves divided. Advocates argued that sending weapons would give Washington influence, but had difficulty explaining just how, in practice, such aid would affect the outcome of the war. Opponents framed their arguments in detailed, systematic terms that played to the president's cool and forensic intellectual style: The logical recipients of military aid were not necessarily the most moderate or inclusive factions among the rebels, and critics pointed to risks that U.S. weapons might further split the opposition, end up being used to kill or abuse noncombatants, and give radicals an advantage in the internecine struggles likely to follow the regime's defeat. They also questioned whether it really made sense to commit the United States seriously to a full-scale proxy war with Iran.

During 2012, the president sided with the skeptics. As he put it during an interview at the end of that year,

> as I wrestle with those decisions, I am more mindful probably than most of not only our incredible strengths and capabilities, but also our limitations. In a situation like Syria, I have to ask, can we make a difference in that situation? Would a military intervention have an impact? How would it affect our ability to support troops who are still in Afghanistan? What would be the aftermath of our involvement on the ground? Could it trigger even worse violence or the use of chemical weapons? What offers the best prospect of a stable post-Assad regime? And how do I weigh tens of

thousands who've been killed in Syria versus the tens of thousands who are currently being killed in the Congo?[22]

So the administration focused its attention instead on trying to build a new Syria on a patchwork basis, working with local councils in areas liberated from regime control to help them govern well, deliver services, foster civil society, and care for and feed the populations within their jurisdictions. In essence, this involved putting the administration's plans for the post-Assad era into effect without waiting for Assad to exit the scene fully; Washington hoped this would yield a better return on investment than pouring yet more weapons into a country already inundated with them.

The Red Line

One issue that did grip the West Wing from the early months of the Syria crisis was the prospect of the use or diversion of Syria's significant stockpiles of chemical weapons. In August 2011, the White House asked military commanders for a plan to deal with this challenge, authorized an intensive information sharing effort with Israel, and redoubled its diplomatic effort to focus the attention of Syria's other neighbors, particularly Turkey and Jordan, on the threat to them that the regime's loss of control over these weapons would pose.[23]

This was Netanyahu's worry too. While some Israeli security officials saw an opportunity to damage Iran by toppling its ally Assad, the Israeli prime minister—according to Dennis Ross based on their direct conversations—was more concerned about "what would happen the day after Assad fell." The nightmare scenario, if that happened, was of "Syria's chemical weapons (CW) stocks falling into the hands of jihadis or Hezbollah," who "might not accept the logic of deterrence" that had generally governed Israeli–Syrian state relations. Ross also reports that Netanyahu conveyed these worries to Obama.[24]

This, then, was another of the relatively rare convergences between Netanyahu's government and Obama's White House. Obama took the problem very seriously. On more than one occasion he drew a distinction between America's limited interests in the Syrian civil war, and its significant interest in keeping a lid on Syrian CW. And during an August 20, 2012, press conference, he said—with specific reference to "our close allies, including Israel"—the following:

We have put together a range of contingency plans. We have communicated in no uncertain terms with every player in the region that that's a red line for us and that there would be enormous consequences if we start seeing movement on the chemical weapons front or the use of chemical weapons. That would change my calculations significantly.[25]

Syrian regime forces proceeded to use chemical weapons. There were reports of this use in the spring of 2013, but verification took several months. The U.S. response, when it came, was incremental: an announcement that some lethal weaponry would be supplied to Syrian rebels. Then, on August 21, Syrian forces used chemical weapons to kill 1,400 people, including 400 children, in the Damascus suburb of Ghouta. The United States had to do something, and started to plan military action in the form of air strikes against regime targets. But the ensuing sequence of events opened another chasm between America and its regional allies—Israel included—about what "doing something" should mean.

It was a principle of Obama statecraft that the American use of military power to enforce international rules, as opposed to pure self-defense, required international partners. Washington had seemed to find ready partners in Britain and France. In Britain, however, a tragicomic debacle ensued. Prime Minister Cameron put the motion for joining air strikes to a vote in the House of Commons. He, and much of the country's political class, were astonished to see it voted down. It was an awkward moment for the UK, revealing how laden with subterranean bitterness was the supposed "special relationship" with America. Britons of all parties and all stations had really hated their participation in the Iraq war and, Lady Macbeth–like, they were still trying to wash off the stain. As Cameron himself had acknowledged during the Commons debate, "the well of public opinion has been well and truly poisoned by the Iraq episode."

France was ready to go ahead, but the loss of one ally through a parliamentary vote gave Obama constitutional pause. He surprised his staff with a decision to seek congressional approval for the action. Cameron's defeat might have seemed an inauspicious example for the U.S. president to follow. Yet Obama apparently decided that the withdrawal of Britain left him in a diminished coalition, and that the legitimacy of his intended action needed bolstering through democratic procedure. Obama maintained, as have all post–Second World War presidents, that such a procedure is not a constitutional necessity for ordering military attacks. The War Powers Act, passed over Richard Nixon's veto in 1973, instructs the president to consult Congress before committing military forces "in every possible instance," calls on him to "report to Congress" within forty-eight hours of such deployment, and requires him to withdraw forces within sixty days unless Congress has approved the action. (If the president claims "unavoidable military necessity," he has an automatic extension to ninety days.) This legislation, arising out of the bitterness of the Vietnam War, most clearly pertains to extended deployments involving ground troops. The administration was proposing missile strikes lasting less than a week, and it was fairly quiet on the subject of what it would do if Congress voted no.

The U.S. Senate would probably have voted yes. But the House of Representatives was a huge unknown. Since 2011, that chamber has been a vessel of right-wing animus against Obama. This animus is a minority emotion in the country at large, but it is a significant minority with raw feelings undiminished, and possibly intensified, by the president's reelection. There were, in other words, a sizable number of House Republicans who would vote against anything the president proposed. This is not to say that all opposition was driven by blind animus. There was also on the political right a new— or at least newly invigorated—current of opposition to U.S. military activism abroad. They were joined by some on the left, where a part of Obama's base remains deeply averse to the use of military force. In this setting, it is unlikely that Obama was able to take an accurate mental vote count before his decision to seek congressional backing. But he may have decided it was time to test whether Washington could unite around anything at all.

Into this somewhat antic succession of policy twists there came a truly surprising development—Syria's agreement to join the chemical weapons convention and to cooperate in the removal and destruction of its CW stockpile. There remains some confusion about where the idea originated: Moscow, Washington, or even Jerusalem. But while Congress was considering its vote, Secretary Kerry and Russian Foreign Minister Sergei Lavrov discussed the idea and turned it into a plan.

It was a big undertaking. Syria had a lot of CW, and though its storage had been partly consolidated since the beginning of civil war, it was still relatively dispersed through western Syria. Its removal or the imposition of safeguards to destroy it on site was going to require a large and pervasive presence from the Organization for the Prohibition of Chemical Weapons

(OPCW) with security forces to protect them. Yet the project was agreed and completed. Within a little more than a year, the OPCW announced that 98 percent of Syria's declared stockpile of 1,308 metric tons of mustard agent and precursors had been destroyed at sites in four countries and aboard the *Cape Ray*, a U.S. merchant marine ship refitted for the purposes of neutralizing a large part of the stockpile.[26]

This was a significant accomplishment, and it could happen only in the shadow of U.S. military intervention. Political commentators may have concluded that Obama had checkmated himself by referring the matter to Congress, but Russia and Syria obviously were not entirely sanguine about what might emerge from that process. In Senate testimony to enlist support, Secretary Kerry made the arguably unwise promise that the air strikes would be "incredibly small"—yet neither Syria nor Russia could be confident that the effect wouldn't be incredibly big. As Lawrence Freedman once said of "surgical" air strikes, patients die on the operating table all the time.

In response to the agreement and removal of Syrian CW, Israel did two things. It stopped distributing gas masks to its citizens, because it recognized that the strategic threat of poison gas had been eliminated. And it joined in the cries of dismay from Saudis, Emirates, and other Arab partners that Obama, having set a red line and then failed to bomb Syria, had brought American reputation and credibility to a new low. "We are stunned," a senior Israeli official told Ross by telephone, according to Ross's account. "This is a terrible day for all America's friends in the Middle East."[27] Those who traveled in the Middle East over subsequent months frequently heard similar judgments and from many sources, and the verdict was well known, for example, to be shared by the Saudi king.[28] The Saudi ambassador to Britain, Mohammed bin Nawaf bin Abdulaziz al Saud, wrote a few months later in the *New York Times*, "for all their talk of 'red lines,' when it counted, our partners have seemed all too ready to concede our safety and risk our region's stability."[29]

If superpower reputation is measured through the eyes of countries that depend on it—and that is certainly one way it must be measured—then it is tautologically true that Obama's decisions damaged America's reputation. Before accepting that final verdict, however, it is necessary to consider the costs of the different decisions that his critics in Israel and elsewhere say they wanted from him. The critics believe, presumably, that limited air strikes would have demonstrated the price to be paid for crossing the red line. As noted, it is possible that the strikes would have done more—the patient might have died on the operating table. (The consequences of regime death could have been good or bad, as Netanyahu had seemed to appreciate.) But it is equally possible—in fact, more likely—that the Assad regime would have absorbed the attack and then desisted from the precise behavior that provoked it, while carrying out equally deadly massacres with high-powered conventional explosives. Limited air strikes against Muammar Qadaffi in 1987, Bosnian Serb forces in the early 1990s, Saddam Hussein throughout the 1990s, and the Sudan government in 1998 did varying degrees of damage, but it was not always clear whose reputation suffered more, the attacked or the attacker.

More certain, however, is what the Syrian air strikes would *not* have accomplished. They would not have solved the problem of Syrian CW. U.S. intelligence probably knew where much but not all of the stocks were held. Some were in populated areas where hitting them could have dispersed clouds of poison gas to deadly effect. And post-bombardment chaos might have created conditions under which the chemical agents would have been more likely to fall into the hands of anti-Assad jihadists (as indeed could have happened in the chaos of post-invasion Iraq, had Saddam Hussein actually possessed chemical and biological weapons when he was toppled). Given these dangers and uncertainties, U.S. airstrikes would not have been conducted against all known or suspected CW sites. Much CW, therefore, would have remained in Syria.

Even without these unintended consequences, the intended consequences would have included the gruesome and painful deaths of Syrian soldiers, possibly many of them. There would have been a concrete moral cost, among other costs of military action, in preserving credibility that cannot be blithely discounted.

America has had these arguments many times before. In April 1961, for example, the new President John F. Kennedy allowed 1,303 CIA-trained Cuban exiles to be killed or captured at Cuba's Bay of Pigs, rather than provide them with U.S. air support. General Lyman Lemnitzer, chairman of the Joint Chiefs, was to voice the near consensus of military commanders and intelligence chiefs when he called Kennedy's passivity "unbelievable ... absolutely reprehensible, almost criminal." But the president later promised Arthur Schlesinger Jr. that he would never again allow himself to be "overawed by military advice," and he had more to say on the concept of credibility and prestige:

> What is prestige? Is it the shadow of power or the substance of power? We are going to work on the substance of power. No doubt we will be kicked in the ass for the next couple of weeks, but that won't affect the main business.[30]

The important, fascinating, and never-to-be-fully-answered question is whether JFK would have maintained that determined restraint as the demands of reputation and credibility seemed to require ever-deeper engagement of U.S. ground troops in Vietnam.[31]

Half a century later, the claims on behalf of credibility remained strident. After Russian president Vladimir Putin responded to the winter 2014 Ukraine crisis by annexing Crimea and destabilizing eastern Ukraine, critics of U.S. policy pointed back to the transgressed red line in Syria. Even before Putin's reaction, David Kramer, a deputy assistant secretary of state in the George W. Bush administration, wrote that Ukrainian authorities had "used gruesome force against protestors" because President Obama failed to bomb Syria after its use of chemical weapons.[32] The *Washington Post* itself, in an editorial, said that "while the United States has been retrenching, the tide of democracy in the world, which once seemed inexorable, has been receding"— without even pretending to put forward a theory of connection between the two.[33] The same week, Senator John McCain told delegates to the annual AIPAC conference that Russia's seizure of Crimea was "the ultimate result of a feckless foreign policy in which nobody believes in America's strength anymore."[34]

The striking thing is that such critics gave this game away at the start by conceding that there were no conceivable circumstances under which the United States should engage the Russians in military conflict over Ukraine. McCain said as much to AIPAC, as did the *Post* in its editorial. These were reassuring nods to realism, but they also pinpointed America's real credibility problem in facing down Russia on the Crimean peninsula. It is plausible that foreign antagonists will, at the margins, calculate a likely American response by assessing such intangibles as presidential character and resolve. But academic literature and common sense both tell us that a far more important measure is the perceived respective national interest in the outcome.[35] In Ukraine, the respective American and Russian interests at stake were gapingly asymmetrical. Ukraine borders Russia; Crimea is the home base of Russia's Black Sea Fleet; it is economically intertwined with Russia; it has a large Russian-speaking minority with special affinities for Russia; and—on the more emotional realm—it is the birthplace of the Russian nation and the Orthodox Church. U.S. interests are real but far less direct. The United States has a general commitment to Ukraine's territorial integrity stemming from Kiev's 1994 agreement to surrender Soviet nuclear weapons that were based on its soil. It also has a general interest in European security and stability, and that stability is diminished if Russia can carve up a neighboring country under any pretext.

What connected Syria and Ukraine was not that American restraint in the former had somehow triggered bad Russian behavior on a separate continent. What connected them was that they both entailed local fights involving countries and groups whose stake in the outcome was disproportionately, even existentially, greater than America's. Putin's unquestionably thuggish assertion of Russian claims beyond its border would not have been deterred by U.S. air strikes against Syria, because, to state the obvious, such strikes would have indicated absolutely nothing about American readiness to launch air strikes against Russia.

The Israeli government and foreign policy elites did not care much about Crimea and Ukraine, and were not even overwhelmingly sure that they wanted to see Syria's Assad regime toppled. Like neighboring Arab governments, however, these Israelis were convinced that Washington's restraint in Syria, added to its refusal to stand by Mubarak, had ruined American credibility, and thereby devalued its overall deterrence.

Yet the question of America's actual stake in the Syrian civil war was one the Obama administration rightly asked from the start. Where the administration has gotten into trouble is where its rhetoric has once or twice slipped the bounds of its actual policy, raising hopes of intervention in the face of the clear U.S. determination not to over-engage in the conflict. Obama's redline statement was the most obvious example.

Russia violated the sovereignty of Ukraine, and it was appropriate that the United States and its allies made sure that Moscow paid a price. But we need to be honest, first and foremost with ourselves, about the price *we* are willing to pay. This argument extends likewise to the awful humanitarian catastrophe in Syria. We should do what we can to alleviate it, but we should never promise more than we can do. If a gap opens up between our rhetoric and our real interests, then we will either overextend ourselves in a course of action that we cannot sustain, or fail to match our rhetoric with our actions. In either case, American credibility will truly suffer.

6

Iran

IN THE FINAL YEARS of the George W. Bush administration, and during the first term of Obama's, the most urgent question about Israel was whether it was planning to launch air strikes against Iran's nuclear facilities.

Successive Israeli governments have maintained that any nuclear weapons capability in the Middle East, other than Israel's own, poses an intolerable threat. Their planes have flown to destroy such threats in the past. In 1981, Israeli planes destroyed the Iraqi reactor at Osirak. In 2007, they destroyed a nuclear facility in Syria. In both cases, Washington was uneasy, and some of its officials were quite angry. Although Ronald Reagan's immediate response upon hearing about Osirak was a jocular "boys will be boys," many on Reagan's team were less than amused, and the United States backed a UN Security Council resolution condemning the attack.[1] The Syria attack in 2007 was not entirely a surprise to the Bush administration, and White House hawks such as Vice President Dick Cheney and NSC senior director Elliott Abrams argued beforehand that the United States should destroy the site itself, or at least get out of the way and let Israel do it. But a sizable opposing faction, led by Defense Secretary Robert Gates and Secretary of State Condoleezza Rice, argued strongly that it was time to give international diplomacy a chance and to use force only as a last resort. Gates in his memoirs writes about this with evident emotion. In another intelligence failure, U.S. agencies had failed to detect what was going on in Syria, so the White House was relying solely on Israeli evidence of a reactor built with North Korean help. This evidence of a facility like the North Korean reactor at Yongbyon that could produce plutonium for nuclear weapons was, however, strong. Israel was pressing for action, and Prime Minister Olmert extracted a promise from President Bush not to publicize the discovery—the preferred course of the administration faction that wanted a diplomatic solution—to preserve the element of surprise for an attack. Bush agreed. Gates recalls being "furious." He had urged the president to "tell Olmert very directly that if Israel went forward on its own militarily, he would be putting Israel's entire relationship with the United States at risk." In a later meeting, according to his own account, he told Bush's assembled national security team that "Olmert was asking for our help on the reactor but giving us only one option: to destroy it. If we didn't do exactly what he wanted, Israel would act and we could do nothing about it. The United States was being held hostage to Israeli decision making." Gates was never sure what Bush himself really thought, but he concluded that, by "not confronting Olmert, Bush effectively came down on Cheney's side. By not giving the Israelis a red light, he gave them a green one."[2] On September 6, Israel destroyed the reactor.

Both attacks were operational successes and have gone down in conventional history as strategic successes as well. For Osirak, the conventional view is that the Israeli action significantly delayed Saddam Hussein's nuclear ambitions, so that when America led a coalition ten years later driving Iraqi forces from Kuwait, it could thank Israel that it did not face a nuclear-armed opponent. There is a counterargument that the Osirak raid, having destroyed the Iraqis' plutonium reactor, simply pushed them to massively increase money and manpower for a more promising, highly enriched uranium route.[3] But this does not change the view of many Israelis that it was their country's action that bought the world extra time to deal with the threat from Saddam. The Syrian accomplishment was even cleaner, in Israeli eyes. Contrary to the expressed fears of Gates and others, there was no regional blowback. In fact, to hide their embarrassment the Syrians kept quiet about the whole affair, removing the debris and cleaning the site in the dark or under cover of tarpaulins. But Gates and Rice were still unhappy about the course of events, because they believed there had been scope for a campaign of publicizing, shaming, and organizing an international diplomatic coalition for nonproliferation purposes using nonmilitary means, albeit with the military option remaining in the background as one crucial source of pressure.[4]

The argument over the Israeli air strike on Syria was most important as a proxy for the bigger problem of what to do about Iran's nuclear program. Again, Israelis' inclination toward direct action against a threat that they considered existential confronted an American faction that was weary of wars and wary of a new one. And again, Washington was divided between the fierce hawks led by Cheney and the advocates of restraint led by Gates and Rice. The problem for the advocates of restraint was that, as retired U.S. Air Force colonel Sam Gardiner put it memorably at the time, an "excess demand for military action" was being generated by a convergence of factors: the steady advance of Iran's nuclear program; the Holocaust denial and promises of Israel's destruction from Iran's reactionary president, Mahmoud Ahmadinejad; the killing and maiming of American soldiers by Shia militias, especially by improvised explosive devices introduced by Iranian agents in Iraq; confrontations in the Persian Gulf where Iranian speedboats were harassing and potentially threatening U.S. Navy ships; and on top of this, the rhetorical warnings from Israeli and U.S. officials that had the effect of boxing both countries in to limited options.[5]

The restraint faction in Washington nonetheless prevailed by persuading President Bush that military action would be unwise. This was no doubt a disappointment to Prime Minister Olmert and Saudi King Abdullah, who both hoped that a president who had proved his forcefulness in Iraq would also take care of the Iranian problem before he left office. In fact, it was another example of how going to war, far from bolstering "credibility" for the next military threat, severely limits a country's future options. "When you find yourself in a hole, the first thing is to stop digging," is how Gates expressed the American predicament as it appeared to him in 2007. "Between Iraq and Afghanistan, I thought the United States was in a pretty deep hole."[6] As much as Iranian actions against U.S. soldiers in Iraq aroused desire for retaliation, the awkward truth was that Iran was in a position to do much more damage. At a decisive White House meeting on May 12, 2007, national security principals including President Bush discussed Israel's request for U.S. military deliveries that would improve their ability to attack nuclear installations by themselves. Again, Gates squared off against Cheney, and this time the president sided with Gates, who believed his most winning argument was about the potential consequences for U.S. troops in Iraq. The gains of the administration's vaunted surge, Gates warned, could be erased; in a worst case, U.S. troops might be forced out of the country.[7] Instead of the equipment they asked for, Israelis this time received a solid red light from Washington.

Whether they would stop at it remained an open question. The following month, Israel conducted a military exercise in which a hundred F-15 and F-16 fighters flew out over the eastern Mediterranean using refueling tankers and followed by rescue helicopters. They flew two nautical miles further than the distance between the airfield from which they took off and the Natanz uranium enrichment facility in Iran.[8] They were advertising their readiness for unilateral action. But they held fire.

Iran's Ambiguities

In late 2007 the U.S. National Intelligence Council released a declassified version of the "key findings" of their latest National Intelligence Estimate (NIE) regarding Iran's nuclear program. The release caused controversy and confusion. Both stemmed from this passage:

> We judge with high confidence that in fall 2003, Tehran halted its nuclear weapons program; we also assess with moderate-to-high confidence that Tehran at a minimum is keeping open the option to develop nuclear weapons. We judge with high confidence that the halt, and Tehran's announcement of its decision to suspend its declared uranium enrichment program and sign an Additional Protocol to its Nuclear Non-Proliferation Treaty Safeguards Agreement, was directed primarily in response to increasing international scrutiny and pressure resulting from exposure of Iran's previously undeclared nuclear work.[9]

The document was a headache for the Bush administration, inspiring speculation that intelligence analysts had forced its release in continued anger over the misuse of intelligence about WMD on the eve of the Iraq War. This was not true. It was President Bush who decided that the finding should be made public, though no doubt motivated at least partly by the realization that some version of it was likely to leak. Critics also claimed that it undermined American and Israeli claims about the threat that Iran's activities posed. This was only partly true. Like a previous version, this NIE in fact confirmed that Iran had a nuclear weapons program, and suggested it had been suspended only in the face of "scrutiny and pressure." An important source of pressure was the American invasion of Iraq, at least until that undertaking turned into a disaster. Moreover, the NIE assessment of "moderate-to-high confidence that Tehran at a minimum is keeping open the option to develop nuclear weapons" was critical, because R&D work on actual weaponization—constructing warheads—was arguably the least challenging of three main tasks for a would-be nuclear weapons state. The other two were the development of delivery vehicles—in Iran's case, long-range missiles—and mastering the nuclear fuel cycle by learning to spin thousands of industrial centrifuges at the supersonic speeds required to enrich uranium. This enriched uranium is the fissile material of a nuclear weapon (which can also use plutonium), and it is the hardest-to-obtain element of a weapons program.

And so to say that Iran was hedging—"keeping open the option"—did not significantly discount the threat. "Everyone thinks their goal is a nuclear weapon," a senior U.S. intelligence analyst associated with the NIE told one of us in late 2009, referring to his colleagues in the intelligence community. "But Iran is playing a long game."[10] The supposed sovereign right to nuclear power was the vehicle of Iran's hedging; it said it needed the nuclear fuel for reactors to generate electricity, even though the effort and expense of industrial-scale enrichment would make sense only if Iran was building nuclear power stations in the double digits, of which there are still no signs as this book goes to press. (The single Russian-built reactor at Bushehr uses Russian-supplied fuel, which is promised for the life of the plant.) In fact, the international consensus that Iran was up to no good was surprisingly strong—surprisingly because one might have expected that the debacle of false claims about Saddam's WMD would have cast a shadow. It did not. France, the leader of the coalition against Bush's invasion, took if anything a consistently harder line against Iran's nuclear activities than the United States. Russia, even with the emergence of what resembled a new Cold War, continued to play a constructive role in international diplomacy to stop Tehran from developing a bomb. The strength of this consensus, which the Obama administration was to nurture wisely and exploit successfully, attests to the strength of the evidence about Iran's nuclear intentions.

Yet, if the ambiguity of Iran's hedging did not significantly affect consensus about what Iran was up to, it had a huge effect on the debate over how to respond. The problem with Iran's progress toward nuclear latency— sometimes described as being a screwdriver turn away from a nuclear weapon—is that it is virtually impossible to reverse this condition by military means short of outright invasion and occupation. Enrichment facilities can be bombed, but they can also be rebuilt. Scientific knowledge and technical know-how, once learned, cannot be unlearned short of a wave of assassinations that would be unfeasible on a sufficient scale, even leaving moral considerations aside. Key officials in both the Bush and Obama administrations were convinced that an attack by Israel or the United States would be counterproductive in the narrowest of terms. It would rally a disaffected population behind the regime, it would invite retaliation that could escalate into another regional war, and it would make the regime determined to go well beyond the strategy of hedging, withdraw from the NPT, and actually assemble nuclear weapons.[11]

This line of logic did not mean ruling out military action under any conditions. But for those American analysts and officials who subscribed to the thinking, it meant that military force had to be reserved for the moment when Iran crossed the threshold from latency to actually developing nuclear weapons. The threat of attack could be at least a partial deterrent against Iran's crossing that threshold, whereas an earlier preventive attack would actually propel them toward it. As our colleague Mark Fitzpatrick, a former senior State Department official, now a nonproliferation expert at the International Institute for Strategic Studies, has put it:

> A pre-emptive strike at a time when Iran is not on the verge of crossing the threshold and might still be dissuaded from doing so would surely create an Iranian determination to build nuclear weapons, and this time in secret. This problem of counter-productivity would no longer prevail if Iran had already decided to cross the line.[12]

This was to become the American approach: Deter actual weaponization, apply pressure in the form of sanctions and other forms of international isolation, conduct sabotage by cyber and other means to slow down the program, and offer the regime negotiations as a way out of the impasse.

The approach depended on a certain view of Iranian politics and its regime as not monolithic, with goals beyond the bloodthirsty ones of expanding revolution and ending Israel, and open to tactical and perhaps even strategic compromise with the West. In other words, a view of Iran as becoming, thirty years after its revolution, something more like a normal country. The offer that Obama made in his first inaugural address, January 21, 2009, was hedged but based on at least the hope of Iranian normality. "To those who cling to power through corruption and deceit and the silencing of dissent, know that you are on the wrong side of history, but that we will extend a hand if you are willing to unclench your fist."[13] This was well understood to be directed in the first instance toward the Iranian regime.

From the perspective of many Israelis, the new U.S. president was offering his hand to radical anti-Semites. Its clerical supreme leader, documented in his disdain for Jews, had also called Israel a "cancerous tumor" that had to be "removed from the region." The hardline president, Mahmoud Ahmadinejad, had called the Jewish state a "dried up and rotten tree which will be annihilated with one storm." Most famously, Ahmadinejad, who convened a farcical academic conference in Tehran to determine the "truth" of whether there was a Holocaust, also repeated the conviction of the Islamic Republic's founding Ayatollah Khomeini that Israel must and will be wiped off the map.[14]

American advocates of engagement and restraint have argued that a more accurate translation of Ahmadinejad's remarks would be that Israel will "disappear from the pages of history," just as the Soviet Union disappeared.[15] They also point out that Iran has a Jewish community of some 25,000—the largest in the Middle East outside of Israel—and that it is relatively unmolested and able to worship. Distinguishing between agenda and program was going to be difficult for Israel, however, because through its thirty-year history the Islamic Republic was almost never content to be a passive witness to historical process. Having suffered stalemate if not defeat in its decade-long war with Iraq, Iran's Khomeini decided that revolutionary spirit had to be revived with the execution of thousands of political dissidents, many of whom had already served their full prison sentences. He issued his fatwa against British writer Salman Rushdie, who was to be assassinated for the crime of writing an impious book. Iranian exiles in Europe were already assassination targets. Iran backed anti-Israeli terrorism while its IRCG Quds force organized terrorist murders of foreign Jews who had no connection to Israel (as though that would be an excuse in any event). Iran continues to execute homosexuals. Israeli fear of such a country developing a nuclear capability was hardly irrational.

Nor was it irrational, however, for a new American administration to think that it was worth an effort to see if thirty years of bitter enmity might be unwound. For a medium-sized power, revolutionary Iran played an outsized and oddly fixed role in the American consciousness. The humiliation of the U.S. embassy hostage crisis at the end of Carter's presidency lingered. Bombings of the U.S. embassy and marine-barracks compounds in Beirut, followed by Hizballah's taking of hostages and a scandal-ridden scheme to get them released, were the central foreign-policy traumas of the Reagan administration. There was clear evidence that Iranian operatives were behind the 1996 truck bomb attack on Khobar Towers, a complex near the Saudi coast that housed U.S. military personnel. Nineteen died, and the Clinton administration came close to attacking Iran in response. And, of course, after the George W. Bush administration removed Iran's most dangerous enemy, the regime of Saddam Hussein, the Iranians repaid this inadvertent strategic favor by harassing and killing American soldiers in Iraq.

Very bad memories worked both ways, however, which is something that must be understood to grasp the full array of factors that could motivate Iran to develop a nuclear capability. The most bitter of these memories was American support for Iraq in its brutal war with Iran, a foundational experience for the Islamic Republic that lasted nearly a decade and cost possibly hundreds of thousands of Iranian lives.[16] Saddam Hussein hoped to take advantage of Iran's postrevolutionary turmoil to exploit the demoralization of the regular army and perhaps inspire a popular revolt. But after Iraq's initial battlefield successes, Iran mounted ferocious counteroffensives, human-wave assaults with seemingly unlimited supplies of Iranian youths. Iraq then escalated with chemical weapons assaults against not only Iranian troops, but also Iraqi Kurds in Halabja. Steven Simon, monitoring the war as a relatively junior U.S. government official, has never forgotten the chilling words in Iraq's communiqué around the time of the Second Battle of al-Faw: "For every insect there is the proper insecticide."

Any Reagan administration qualms about Iraq's strategically significant use of chemical weapons were balanced if not outweighed by Washington's stated "interests in 1) preventing an Iranian victory and 2) continuing to improve bilateral relations with Iraq," as outlined in a State Department cable from Secretary of State George P. Schultz containing "briefing notes" for then presidential envoy Donald Rumsfeld, who was traveling to Baghdad for a second visit in 1984.[17] U.S. companies sold Iraq chemical precursors suitable for chemical weapons, while Washington helped find third-country sources for weaponry, including cluster bombs, that America legally could not provide, and transmitted satellite intelligence on the disposition of Iranian forces. The U.S. Navy, in support of a Gulf Arab effort to finance Iraq's war, protected Kuwaiti oil tankers against Iranian Revolutionary Guards' attacks. These operations brought U.S. ships into skirmishes with small Iranian gunboats, and in July 1988 one of those skirmishes involved the United States in an immense tragedy. The USS *Vincennes* launched two missiles at an Iranian commercial airliner that had just taken off from Bandar Abbas on its way to Dubai. The plane was destroyed and all 290 passengers, including 66 children, were killed.

It was an accident. The *Vincennes* captain believed his radar showed an attacking military plane. But Iran's leadership believed it was deliberate, and the shooting down of Iran Air Flight 655, according to Iran expert Ray Takeyh, "appears to have been the catalyst that convinced Khomeini that it was time to end the war." Iraq was attacking Iranian cities with ballistic missiles. The next step was to combine those missiles with chemical weapons. America was on Iraq's side and, with the attack on a commercial airliner, had apparently "decided to finish the job itself."[18] From our perspective, the U.S. tilt toward Iraq was strategically and perhaps even morally defensible. But it should surprise no one that Iranians will never see it that way, and might even feel justified in seeking nuclear insurance, at least as a hedging strategy.

This history of mutual grievance was inhospitable terrain for any kind of engagement. There had been attempts, however. Iran-Contra, as noted, ended in failure and embarrassment for the Reagan administration. A more promising opportunity came with the election in 1997 of the liberal cleric Mohammad Khatami to Iran's presidency. A leader of the Islamic Republic's first serious reform movement, Khatami proposed a "dialogue of civilizations." After the 9/11 attacks, Khatami expressed "deep sympathy to the American nation," while thousands of Iranians joined candlelight vigils. There followed real strategic cooperation against the Taliban, the common U.S.–Iranian enemy in Afghanistan, and diplomatic cooperation to assemble a new Afghan government at an international conference in Bonn.[19] The convergence did not last, however.

Washington became convinced that Iran was sheltering al Qaeda fugitives, and it caught Tehran in covert shipments of weapons and explosives to Palestinians during the second intifada. Soon thereafter President Bush, who had been briefed on intelligence about Iran's still-secret nuclear program, delivered his famous speech designating the country, along with Iraq and North Korea, as comprising an "axis of evil." Bush then launched the invasion of Iraq, which probably motivated the Khatami government's final bid for talks to normalize U.S.–Iranian relations. In May 2003 the Swiss ambassador in Tehran, Tim Guldimann, who represented U.S. interests there, passed on a memo proposing talks aimed at a grand bargain under which Iran would restrain its nuclear ambitions, end support for terrorism, cooperate in Iraq, and endorse a two-state solution for Israel and Palestine. In exchange America would lift sanctions and make concessions to Iran's regional security interests. The overture was genuine, authorized by Khatami, and it may have had the approval of Khamenei. That is not to say that Iran's government could have delivered on such a bargain. In any event, though Secretary of State Colin Powell and his deputy Richard Armitage were strongly in favor of pursuing the possibility, it was shot down by Vice President Cheney and Defense Secretary Rumsfeld. Flush with seeming victory in Iraq, just days after President Bush had landed in full flight suit on the aircraft carrier USS *Abraham Lincoln* to deliver a speech in front of the banner "Mission Accomplished," the administration as a whole was in no mood for compromise.[20]

Six years later, following Obama's inauguration and his outreach to Tehran, Iran was roiled by an extraordinary election campaign. Ahmadinejad's 2005 election had been part of a right-wing restoration organized against the liberalism of Khatami. Now, in the spring of 2009, there was hope of another liberal opening as candidates such as Hossein Mousavian, Mehdi Karroubi, and even establishment stalwart Hashemi Rafsanjani engaged in an open and lively debate, with very public complaints about the damage that Ahmadinejad's Holocaust denial and other posturing had inflicted on Iran's international reputation.

It is highly possible that Ahmadinejad nonetheless won a majority of votes for his 2009 reelection. But the margin of his official victory and the haste of its announcement were highly suspicious, showing that the supreme leader and other conservatives were taking no chances. The weeks of Green Movement protests that followed, and their thuggish repression by IRGC and Basij paramilitaries, indicated the complex and fractured composition of Iranian society and politics. To speak of an ongoing struggle between moderates and hardliners oversimplifies, but it is closer to reality than the picture presented by U.S. and Israeli hawks whereby Iran's "liberals" are just decorative decoys for a ruthless and determined regime. This analytical debate was reminiscent of the arguments about whether to take seriously Gorbachev reformism in the Soviet Union, or to deride it as a trick. Ronald Reagan, against the advice of many of his aides, did take it seriously and he was right to do so. This did not mean, however, that Soviet and Russian reformers could be expected to swallow American narratives or perspectives regarding fundamental Russian interests. It would be a comparable mistake to confuse Iranian reformers with Westerners.

Year of Engagement, Rumors of War

Early in his first term, Obama told Netanyahu that he needed a year to try engagement with Iran. After that, the United States would revert to pressure.[21]

The year of engagement failed, but the pressure, when it came, was effective. Europe's cooperation was key. The EU is often derided as congenitally divided and toothless. The reputation is sometimes deserved, but not always and certainly not in this case. Ahmadinejad's anti-Semitic bluster helped create a consensus of revulsion through much of Europe. Strong leadership from France, Germany, and the UK produced mandatory sanctions for the entire union, a massive economy of twenty-eight countries and 503 million people. By summer 2011, the EU, which had been Iran's second-largest oil market at 600,000 b/d, was not importing a drop of Iranian crude. The European boycott was hugely significant since the United States had very limited economic relations with Iran anyway, so there was not much American trade to cut off. The United States did find its own source of pressure, however, in the fact that American financial institutions are central and unavoidable because global transactions are conducted in dollars. The U.S. Treasury was able to impose a series of secondary financial penalties that made global companies, including oil shipping companies, wary of doing any business with Iran, lest they incur penalties cutting them off from the far more lucrative U.S. market. Severing Iran from the Belgium-based SWIFT payments system worsened its isolation. If not crippling, the sanctions against Iran were severe and produced real pain.

This success could not alleviate the suspicions between Jerusalem and Washington. Jerusalem did not trust the United States to take military action if needed, and was sure it would be needed. Washington strongly suspected that Israel would act on its own, starting a war that would pull

America in. The president promised Israel's government that "all options were on the table," and he directed the Pentagon to make sure it had real options ready. The resulting plans and capabilities were serious and significant. These included the procurement of specialized munitions, such as the Massive Ordnance Penetrator (MOP), which is capable of destroying deeply buried installations, as well as the customized tactics to make best use of such weapons while evading air defenses and minimizing collateral damage.[22]

At the political level, this profound American effort to prepare for military action was disregarded by Israel. To be fair, the Israelis were listening in part to what uniformed and civilian Defense Department officials were saying. The chairman of the Joint Chiefs, Admiral Mike Mullen, had given congressional testimony warning of the consequences of military action, and Defense Secretary Gates's private counsel against another war were well known in Jerusalem, even if he was less outspoken in public.

Mainly, however, Israelis believed they had taken the U.S. president's measure and found him inadequate. This led, perversely, to the hugely counterstrategic behavior of Israeli officials frequently and very publicly questioning the resolve of their key ally. Simon, back working at the White House in the third year of Obama's first term, found the Israeli rhetoric mystifying. To Tehran, it must have seemed as if the Israelis knew their closest ally's real intentions. If Israelis were saying that Iran was safe from American military attack, it must be true. Israel's government was significantly undermining U.S. deterrence.

Such was the backdrop to a tense first term and mandate for Obama and Netanyahu, respectively. On the subject of Iran, they eyed each other warily, as did their respective governments. The present coauthors traveled to Israel in July 2009 and encountered palpable contempt toward the new U.S. president. The then deputy prime minister and Intelligence Minister Dan Meridor, who spoke to a small dinner meeting that we attended in Tel Aviv, stands out in memory as especially derisive. (It should be noted that this was a mere five months into Obama's presidency, so the derisory judgments came from someplace other than analysis of Obama's performance.) For our part, the overriding question, which we posed to everyone we met, was a simple one: Would Israel attack? No one really knew. "The Israeli leader of the moment would agonize over his historical duty," Ariel Levite, former Israeli deputy national security adviser and former deputy director general in Israel's

Atomic Energy Commission told us. "For Begin [regarding the 1981 attack on Osirak] it was between him and God. There is strong evidence that that's how Bibi [Netanyahu] defines his historical mission."[23] When we voiced the American concern that an attack would delay Iran's program by perhaps three years at most, and make the Iranians hell-bent on developing a weapon, the common Israeli response revealed that the two allies were operating on very different time scales. For Israel, two or three years was considerable. And the uncertain prospects for success did not faze Israeli strategists. Retired IDF brigadier general and former deputy national security adviser Shlomo Brom, who was no great advocate of military action, nonetheless put the Israeli perspective to us in aphoristic terms. "There is a difference in the way the world looks when you are looking through the sight of a weapon and when you are looking into the barrel of a weapon," he told us. "When you are looking through the sight you ask, 'What if I miss?'" When looking through the barrel, the main question is, "What will happen if he hits me?" It was true, Brom said, that Israel could not be confident about the possibility of unknown facilities or rebuilding the program. "But on the Iranian side, they can't be certain that [the attacker] doesn't know all these things, and won't bomb them over and over."[24] Bombing "over and over" would be a task that some Israeli officials likened to "mowing the lawn" (a phrase borrowed from counterterrorism officials). As Iran rebuilt, it would be hit again. For Israel, this looked like grim necessity. For America, it looked like endless war.

The American alternative, to be fair, did not look very promising to Israel. Many American strategists argued that a nuclear-armed Iran, though unnerving and destabilizing to the global nonproliferation regime, could be deterred and contained like other nuclear adversaries. There was no reason to believe that Iran's regime was less rational or amenable to deterrence than Stalinist Russia or Maoist China. Veteran U.S. diplomat James Dobbins, who had negotiated with Iranians over Afghanistan's government at the 2001 Bonn Conference, put it in these terms: "The [Iranian] leadership doesn't compare to Mao and Stalin. Both were psychopaths by the time they had developed nuclear weapons."*[25]

---

* We ourselves laid out these arguments for containment, acknowledging their problems and flaws, in a previous book that was published in late 2010, just before Simon joined the Obama administration. Dana H. Allin and Steven Simon, *The Sixth Crisis: Iran, Israel, America, and the Rumors of War* (New York: Oxford University Press, 2010). For an assessment along similar lines,

Less than two years later, however, President Obama committed the United States to a significantly different policy. In a March 2012 interview with Jeffrey Goldberg of the *Atlantic,* he took deterrence and containment off the table as a way of dealing with an Iranian nuclear weapon.

[A]s president of the United States, I don't bluff. I also don't, as a matter of sound policy, go around advertising exactly what our intentions are. But I think both the Iranian and the Israeli governments recognize that when the United States says it is unacceptable for Iran to have a nuclear weapon, we mean what we say.[26]

A few days later at the annual AIPAC meeting, he repeated the message. "Iran's leaders should understand that I do not have a policy of containment; I have a policy to prevent Iran from obtaining a nuclear weapon," Obama declared, and added, "I will not hesitate to use force when it is necessary to defend the United States and its interests."[27]

Since one of us participated in discussions leading up to these statements, we can write with confidence that the determination to prevent an Iranian nuclear weapon was grounded in a considered view of American national interest. At the same time, the timing and venue of these statements was directed at reassuring Israel and preempting an Israeli attack, rumors of which were spiking at the time. Defense Minister Ehud Barak was warning that Iran was approaching a "zone of immunity."[28] Israeli officials that summer again approached Washington with requests for hardware, including the Massive Ordnance Penetrator, a 30,000 pound bunker-destroying bomb, and V-22 Ospreys, fixed-wing aircraft that take off and land like helicopters, and so are well suited for landing commandos at nuclear sites. They could not have been too surprised to be turned down.[29] The White House was open and explicit about not wanting an Israeli attack. "Already," Obama said in his AIPAC speech, "there is too much loose talk of war."

The president's statements, and administration consultations with Israel, served the purpose. Netanyahu guardedly conceded that the time left to deal with the threat could be measured "not in weeks, but also not in years."[30] He

---

see also Kenneth M. Pollack, *Unthinkable: Iran, the Bomb, and American Strategy* (New York: Simon & Schuster, 2013).

gave the United States more time for diplomacy. But he was not to be happy with the results.

Diplomacy, Agreement, Acrimony

Negotiations with Iran to curb its nuclear program started soon after its existence became public in 2003. France, Britain, and Germany formed a group called the "EU-3" to prove, against the backdrop of dissension over Iraq, that "effective multilateralism" worked better than war. Under the European Union's imprimatur, the three powers engaged Iran in talks that led to its temporary suspension of uranium enrichment. But Iran insisted on its "sovereign right" to fuel-cycle technology. Permanent or even long-term suspension, Tehran insisted, was not on the table.

These initial talks broke down and Iran returned to building and spinning centrifuges. Subsequently, from summer 2006, Russia and China joined with the Americans and Europeans to pass a series of UN Security Council resolutions demanding suspension of Iran's nuclear activities. The Security Council cited Chapter VII of the UN Charter, which amounted to a declaration that Iran's nuclear program was a "threat to international peace and security." The Security Council unity was a significant accomplishment, and it indicated that Russia and China were seriously concerned about the consequences of a nuclear Iran, though they viewed the matter less gravely than did the Americans or Europeans. Subsequent negotiations were conducted under the rubric of the "P5+1"—that is, the permanent members of the Security Council (Russia, China, the United States, France, and the UK), plus Germany by virtue of its leadership in Europe and economic relations with Iran. Later, the High Representative for EU foreign policy was added. Iran's nuclear effort was a gradual and steady effort, never a crash program, and it occasionally demonstrated some restraint for the purposes of diplomacy. However, the negotiations had no discernible effect in slowing the program, which expanded between 2003 and 2013 from a few thousand centrifuges to nearly 20,000. What did slow the program for a time were acts of sabotage and cyber attack, notably the Stuxnet virus, which made centrifuges spin out of control, but also escaped to spread across the Internet. There were also assassinations of Iraqi physicists, presumed by news organizations to be directed by Israel, which stopped after Secretary of State Clinton criticized them publicly in January 2012.

In July, Puneet Talwar from the White House national security staff and Jake Sullivan, a top aide to Secretary Clinton, traveled secretly to Oman, where they met a delegation from Iran.[31] The Iranians said that any progress in the nuclear negotiations would require an American acknowledgment of Iran's right to enrich uranium. The Americans were not ready to offer that concession. But this was the beginning of a series of secret meetings—the first sustained bilateral talks since the 1979 Iranian revolution—that would eventually lead to an agreement.

Obama won reelection four months later. Half a year after that came the real game changer. Iran elected a new president, cleric Hassan Rouhani, who had campaigned on a promise to end Iran's international isolation and repair its sanctions-hobbled economy. Here was another anomaly of Iran's hybrid political system, both a clerical dictatorship and a semi-democracy. The Islamic Republic operates under the doctrine of *velayat e-faqih*, which accords the clerical supreme leader final say over foreign and domestic policy. But the dictatorship has practical limits, and the office of the elected presidency has grown more powerful over time. The electoral system itself is partly but not entirely rigged. Iran's Guardian Council decides who can be on the ballot. In 2013, the Green Movement heroes of the previous election were exiled, in jail, or under house arrest. Rouhani was allowed on the ballot, but this did not seem like a huge concession. He was a former nuclear negotiator associated with the revolutionary establishment, and he was in any event expected to lose to the supreme leader's hardline protégé, Saeed Jalili.

But Rouhani won because he attracted the hopes and votes of Green Movement supporters. He took their mandate seriously, assembling a team of diplomats educated in the United States and prepared to talk seriously to their American counterparts. Ali Akbar Salehi, a physicist trained at MIT, became head of Iran's Atomic Energy Organization. Mohammad Jafad Zarif, former ambassador to the UN with a Ph.D. from the University of Denver, became foreign minister. The secret talks were energized. In August, at the third session in Oman, U.S. Deputy Secretary of State Bill Burns conceded for the first time that an arrangement of strict inspections and limits on Iran's nuclear program could also entail some ongoing enrichment. For the Iranians, this was a crucial concession that they had demanded for many years. Most outside analysts knew it had to happen. The following month, at the UN General Assembly meeting in New York, a staged handshake turned into a half-hour meeting after John Kerry pulled Zarif into a side room. Later that week, Obama placed a phone call to Rouhani, who was riding to the airport for his return flight to Tehran. Two months later, the P5+1 and Iran announced an interim agreement. In exchange for limited sanctions relief, Iran would freeze—which is to say, stop expanding—its nuclear program for six months.[32]

According to then State Department official Robert Einhorn, the Israelis when consulted about the Iran negotiations were never willing to indicate what kind of agreement they could accept. "It made us feel like nothing was going to be good enough for them."[33] The Oman talks were kept as secret from Israel as from everyone else. Obama only told Netanyahu about them on September 30. But three days earlier—on the same day as Obama's historic phone call to Rouhani—Netanyahu's National Security Advisor Yaakov Amidror told White House officials that Israel knew something was up because it had identified tail numbers of American planes landing in Oman. It was insulting, Amidror is reported to have said, for U.S. officials to think "they could go to Oman without taking our intelligence capabilities into account."[34] The surprise of the interim agreement, combined with the Oman secrecy, made for more bad blood. Some American officials, including Einhorn and Gary Samore, Obama's chief nuclear advisor, have argued that the American secrecy unnecessarily heightened suspicions in Jerusalem. Yet later events would validate the belief of Susan Rice and others that, if Israel had known too much about the talks, it would have tried to derail them.[35]

It would take the negotiators not six but twenty months to reach a final agreement. They announced success on July 15, 2015, after two final all-nighters in Vienna. The diametrically opposite reactions in Jerusalem and Washington spoke volumes about the gap that had opened between Israel and the United States. For the U.S. administration, and American strategic experts, the agreement was gratifying indeed. For a period of ten years, Iran's operating centrifuges would be limited to 5,000 first-generation—which is to say, relatively inefficient—machines. This was just a quarter of the centrifuges in operation when the deal was reached. Its stockpile of low-enriched uranium would be reduced by 98 percent, and was not to exceed 300 kg for fifteen years. These two measures produced Obama's bottom line: a "breakout time" of more than a year. This was the period it would take for Iran, if it abrogated the agreement and went full tilt, to accumulate enough highly enriched uranium for a nuclear bomb. And one year, by American calculations, was enough time for the United States to reassemble an international coalition and, if necessary, take military action. Moreover, Iran in the agreement signed on permanently to the toughest nuclear inspections regime ever negotiated.*

From Israel's perspective, the agreement allowed what Iran was never supposed to have: industrial-scale nuclear enrichment after the limits come off. At least in theory, Iran's program could then be unlimited in size. Iran would be the virtual nuclear power that Israelis had been saying they would never tolerate. Meanwhile, the lifting of sanctions and the release of frozen assets could finance Iran's military and IRCG terrorism against Israel.

These complaints were at the center of the combined Israeli–U.S. Republican campaign against the agreement. They were more or less true, but also completely at odds with the reality of plausible alternatives. Israel's government and its American political allies understandably preferred that there be no Iranian nuclear program whatsoever. Yet the baffling part was how they proposed that the world they lived in could be transported to this alternative universe. As Graham Allison, a professor and director of the Belfer Center at Harvard's Kennedy School, wrote,

> Beyond poisonous partisanship, the primary reason for discomfort with the current deal is that it surfaces ugly realities that most Americans who have not been following the Iranian nuclear story have never internalized. During the Bush administration, Iran mastered the technologies and know-how for manufacturing centrifuges and enriching uranium, thus overcoming the only high hurdle to building a bomb. This know-how is ingrained in the heads of thousands of Iranian scientists and engineers. Before 2003, Iran developed plans and tested explosives for a nuclear weapon. Over the past decade, Iran's nuclear program advanced to the point at which it stands today: just two months away from one bomb's worth of nuclear material. These are brute facts that no agreement, airstrike, or

---

* The Arak heavy-water reactor and underground facility at Fordo were to be converted so they could not produce fissile material, but kept open for other purposes as a face-saving concession to Iran. The most astonishing provision, arguably, was a mechanism for sanctions "snap-back": If Iran was caught cheating, a single permanent member could bring demands for reimposition of sanctions to the Security Council, and they would be reinstated automatically unless the Security Council decided otherwise. But since Security Council decisions are subject to a veto by any permanent member, this meant in practice that the United States, for example, could single-handedly require all UN sanctions to be reinstated.

alternative anyone has proposed can erase. In other words, it is impossible to "solve" the Iranian problem through this agreement or any feasible alternative. Iran's nuclear ambitions will long remain a cardinal challenge for the United States and its allies—a challenge that will demand constant vigilance and a demonstrable readiness to do whatever is required to prevent Iran from acquiring nuclear weapons.[36]

Israel's campaign to kill the agreement started months before it was signed. In January 2015, as Obama was about to deliver a triumphant (because of good economic news) State of the Union Address, the Republican leaders of both houses of Congress were in discussions with Israeli U.S. ambassador Ron Dermer, an American native who had worked as a Republican operative before he moved to Israel in 1996. They arranged for Netanyahu to speak again to a joint session of Congress on March 3, where he would do his best to rally Congress against the as-yet-unreached deal. This gambit inspired anger in the administration, a generalized head-shaking from Democrats, and even some incredulity from pro-Republican commentators at Fox News. For weeks to follow, it became Washington's central drama, with dueling interviews, daily front-page headlines, and feverish gossip in both Israel and the United States. The theater was compelling because Netanyahu's speech was in fact unprecedented. No foreign leader had delivered an address to Congress for the unambiguous purpose of rallying the opposition party to torpedo a diplomatic negotiation that the president of the United States considered vitally important to American security and foreign policy.

Some Democratic lawmakers say that Netanyahu lost the battle right there, by aligning himself so directly with the Republican Party against a Democratic president. In the course of the campaign, he also tripped himself up with some overblown rhetoric, as when he told a Jerusalem audience that Iran's aggression "has the ultimate true aim of taking over the world."[37] There were complaints about the heavy-handed lobbying by Dermer. And there was some wonderment that AIPAC, which spearheaded a negative campaign costing $30 million, failed so decisively.[38]

The Iran deal was not a treaty requiring Senate ratification, but under pressure from Democratic lawmakers, the administration had agreed to a process whereby it would be subject to congressional review. A resolution of disapproval by both houses was virtually guaranteed, since the Republicans held majorities in both houses and were sure to oppose it uniformly. But the president could veto the resolution, and opponents would then need a two-thirds majority to override the veto. This would have been possible only with a significant number of Democratic votes. For Israel and its U.S. lobby, the optimistic scenario involved moral and political pressure on the disproportionate number of Jewish Democrats in Congress. But, with the notable exceptions of New York Senator Charles Schumer and a few others, Jewish Democrats sided with the president. The failure of the "no" campaign was so complete that the resolution of disapproval never reached Obama's desk. There were enough Democratic supporters in the Senate to filibuster it, keeping it from coming to a vote.

Forced to choose between Israel's campaign and one of the most significant achievements of a Democratic president, Democrats were always likely to choose the latter. But the main reason for this victory was that the agreement was manifestly in the American interest. Obama was harshly criticized for claiming that the alternative to the deal was war, but he was right. If the deal had been torn up, international unity would have dissolved along with the sanctions regime. Iran would have gone back to an unrestrained nuclear program. The pressure to use the only tool left—military force—would have been immense, in Israel if not America. The pressure might have been resisted for a time, but as Iran was seen to come closer to a bomb, conflict would have been very likely.

Israeli critics of Netanyahu's performance were incredulous. "I've never seen such an effort, almost in broad daylight, to involve ourselves in internal American politics, to work on the ground to try to effect a political outcome," former Mossad director Ephraim Halevy told the *Wall Street Journal*. His successor, Meir Dagan, said: "Friendly countries are not supposed to do this to each other."[39] The critics were right: Netanyahu once again had misread and misplayed American politics. The episode might be dismissed as another example of the Obama–Netanyahu psychodrama that has filled these pages. But the problem was deeper. The battle over Iran's nuclear program really did reveal that the two countries had diverging interests—or at least radically different priorities, which, in a world requiring choices, can amount to the same thing.

First, it has long been a central tenet of Israeli security policy not to put Israel's fate in the hands of any other country, the United States included. This might derive from Israel's haunted history, but it is really a central tenet of realist international relations theory. States can only trust themselves. What's more, Israel was being asked to trust America fifteen years in the future when—as we will show in the next chapter—both countries are likely to be in very different places.

Second, Washington was ready to work within the apparent fractures in Iran's body politic, the terrain of reformers and hardliners that had proven possible and rewarding to navigate in the Soviet case. But fractured can also mean unpredictable. Iran as a whole doesn't need to be virulently anti-Semitic for IRGC and other hardliners to support Hizballah and other anti-Israeli groups. And although it would appear irrational and suicidal to provide terrorists with nuclear weapons or technology, Israel does need to worry about the scenario of rogue elements in a fractured regime doing so.

Finally, Israelis were not crazy to worry that the lifting of sanctions would strengthen an implacable enemy. With some 5,000 IRGC troops in Syria, some were going to end up on the Golan border. Israel in early 2015 had already accidentally killed an Iranian general, Mohammad Allahdadi, who was reconnoitring the Syrian side of the Golan Heights with Hizballah officers.[40] Jerusalem could not be sanguine about the possibility of a second front against Israel, the equivalent of south Lebanon on the Golan. So Israel would prefer to see Iran kept poor and weak.

The American interest was different. It had experienced the baleful consequences of a long-term sanctions regime against Iraq that eviscerated the Iraqi middle class, empowered rather than weakened the dictatorship, and did nothing to prevent an eventual war. Iran's regime may be hostile, but the society is relatively advanced, middle class, intrinsically pro-Western, and even pro-American. Building on areas of cooperation could eventually transform the relationship. This might not happen until the old guard leaves the scene, but—as Soviet developments proved—it certainly could happen.

Israelis have joined Sunni states such as Saudi Arabia in defining Shia Iran as the most potent danger to stability in the Middle East. America certainly did not want to find itself allied with the Shiite power in a widening sectarian conflict. Nonetheless, since the beginning of this century it has been Sunni, not Shia, extremism that has tormented the United States. And just as the Iran deal was being negotiated, moreover, a new and shockingly virulent form of Sunni extremism appeared.

ISIS and the Confusion of Alliance

"Whence come these wars against us? Whence multiply barbarian invasions?" So lamented Patriarch Sophronius of Jerusalem in 637 C.E. as fierce Muslim invaders seemed to come from everywhere out of nowhere. Sophronius was to be reassured, however, by the actual behavior of the caliph who conquered Jerusalem that year. Omar ibn Al-Khattāb negotiated a protected status for Christians, and—according to Muslim sources—declined Sophronius' invitation to pray in the Church of the Holy Sepulchre, so as not to endanger its Christian sanctity.[41] Omar also welcomed Jews back to Jerusalem and allowed them to pray on the Temple Mount.[42]

Fourteen centuries later another kind of barbarian invasion swept across expanses of Middle Eastern desert. This time, there was no victor's magnanimity. In the summer of 2014, the jihadists' vicious catalog of beheadings, crucifixions, immolation, rape, enslavement, and genocidal war against religious minorities posed a new challenge to American identity and purpose, and frustrated the administration's hopes for turning the page on the wars of the Bush era. As ISIS overran much of Iraq, Iraq's American-trained army fled. Videos depicting the grisly beheadings of two Americans were enough to shift U.S. public opinion dramatically, if temporarily, on whether it was in the American interest and responsibility to seek out more war with the Sunni extremists.[43] All of a sudden, Vice President Joe Biden, hardly the most jingoistic among America's current crop of politicians, was vowing to follow the perpetrators "to the gates of hell."[44]

And so Obama became the fourth American president in succession to order military action in Iraq. The United States launched a campaign of air strikes against ISIS in Iraq and Syria, and another effort to train, equip, and advise Iraq's army. But the administration remained determined to limit the U.S. role, supporting local forces with air power but avoiding ground war. It articulated, more broadly, a doctrine of "strategic patience."[45] The government of Israel was, by this point, nervous about the meaning of American strategic patience. Mainly, however, Jerusalem feared that, insofar as Washington was ready to fight, it had chosen the wrong enemy. Iran was a much bigger threat than ISIS, Netanyahu said repeatedly, and he was supported in this warning by politicians and security officials from across Israel's political spectrum. A senior MOD official told one of us that the

United States did not have "the bandwidth" to deal with both Syria and Iran. Since Iran was the greater strategic threat, he argued, Washington should focus on that and leave Israel to deal with both Syria and terrorism in general.[46]

But Shiite Iran and Sunni ISIS were also each other's fierce enemies. Alongside Kurdish *peshmerga*, Iranian-backed Shiite militias and Iran's own Revolutionary Guard Corps units were by far the most effective forces fighting the Islamic State. For the United States, the temptations of a tacit alliance were undeniable—even if those same Iranian-backed militias had killed and maimed many U.S. troops during the Iraq War, and even if Washington and its military commanders knew very well that the image of America in league with Shia domination of Iraq would drive more disaffected and fearful Sunnis to the ISIS cause.[47] Israel's anxiety turned to anger and alarm as it became evident that some administration officials even entertained tentative hopes that the nuclear agreement could lead to a broader détente. That détente might, in turn, help calm the killing fields of the Middle East. In Washington, there was not huge confidence in this proposition, but it seemed worth a try—whereas, to Jerusalem, it seemed like dangerous nonsense.

As a global superpower, the United States has always had a "choice of enemies," to borrow from the title of Lawrence Freedman's history of America and the Middle East since the Carter administration. It happens, though, that the Obama administration came to power at a moment when the frustrating and ultimately failed war of choice against Iraq necessitated a reassessment of America's overall strategic posture and priorities. This was a global reassessment, and it is our contention that the Obama priorities were not peculiar to his presidency. Rather, they reflect an objective ranking of American interests in the first half of the twenty-first century, likely to guide his successor of either party. The United States is not withdrawing from the Middle East. Its strategic presence remains massive and, in certain respects, is even growing. However, it needs to set limits on the blood and treasure that it invests in the region: first, because it has lost faith in military action as a way of changing things for the better; second, because, simply put, it has other global priorities.

The Obama administration's concept of a pivot or rebalance to Asia was intended to emphasize the overwhelming importance of the Asia–Pacific region to the American interest.[48] China is the only country with the economic potential to become a peer competitor, as the Defense Department puts it, of the United States. Another way of saying this is that China is the one country that could in the foreseeable future fight a major war with the United States, and the consequences would be catastrophic even if war stayed below the nuclear threshold. As important, China and the United States are also the two indispensable countries for international diplomacy to avert catastrophic climate change—which is arguably one of the two or three gravest threats to human security in the impending future.

Second in order of importance for the United States is the East–West struggle in Europe that has reemerged violently in the Ukraine conflict. To rank Europe below Asia–Pacific is in some ways an anomaly. America's most important allies and partners are and will remain European. Europe's successes after World War II and after the Cold War were the most significant successes of American international policy. (Obviously they were successes for the Europeans, but America deserves credit too.) Europe's disintegration would undo much of what has been accomplished, and would threaten American security. Yet, from America's perspective, the struggle with Putin's Russia in Europe is a secondary struggle for the simple reason that it is being contested on Russia's borders. That does not mean that it is unimportant for the United States, or that there are no important principles at stake, or that the fight over Ukraine couldn't contain seeds of a larger disorder in Europe. But Russia's stake in the fight is much greater than America's. This becomes obvious if we compare this current crisis to the classic Cold War, when the military front line was the inter-German border, and the ideological front line was in Germany, Italy, France, and even, at times, Britain. Russia in Ukraine has been nasty and aggressive, but in strategic terms it is on the defensive. The corollary, however, is that on its own borders it has much greater leverage and its interests cannot be ignored. "They have overwhelming tactical military superiority in eastern Ukraine and there's nothing we can do about it," as former Reagan administration official Richard Burt put it in April 2015. "If the Russians wanted to fight us on the Rio Grande . . . in Texas they would face a similar scenario."[49]

It is the Middle East that for the past fifteen years has been the theater of greatest tragedy, the focus of the greatest American military and nation-building effort, and the place where the United States exhausted itself morally, economically, and politically. President Obama's most fundamental judgment, perhaps, has been that most of this effort was wasted. The Arab

Spring offered some temporary hope that the tragedy could be redeemed, and some of the investment recovered, if not by the United States then by the mobilized youth within the region. That wave of hope, change, and then chaos should be understood, however, as only one episode in a still larger process of modernization and development. The Middle East, as the economist Alan Richards has observed, is still making the transition from a largely rural, illiterate society ruled by urban notables to a mass-educated, highly urbanized world. Such transitions have been brutal wherever else they have occurred, and they were ultimately responsible for much of the twentieth century's extraordinary violence and turmoil. This is a structural process that outsiders can affect only on the margins. The dislocations and insecurities imposed by this process have transformed the longstanding Sunni–Shia divide. America's invasion of Iraq certainly accelerated, whether or not it caused, the turning of that divide into a region-wide sectarian conflict. Iran and Saudi Arabia have been avatars of, respectively, the Shia and Sunni sides of that conflict. These two powers have superimposed on the conflict their geopolitical cold war, arising from the opportunity that regime change in Iraq offered for the expansion of Iran's regional power, and the fear that this expansion provoked in Saudi and other Sunni states.

For Riyadh, the greatest source of anger has been Obama's determined refusal to engage effectively in the Syrian civil war, which is the central proxy war between Saudi Arabia and Iran.[50] Obama said on repeated occasions that Iran's principal client, Bashar Assad, needs to go, but he has not willed the means to match that stated end. The United States did arm and train rebels against Assad, but the results have been meager—almost laughably so in the case of the overt program. And since the rise of ISIS, which happens to be Assad's most formidable enemy, the United States has been even less willing to consider regime change in Damascus its core interest. Critics of this restraint, both in the Arab world and in the United States, have made two claims about the consequences: First, they blame Washington's restraint for the awful humanitarian consequences of the civil war: some 200,000 dead; millions of refugees in Lebanon and Jordan; and, at the time of this writing, a flood of refugees into Europe causing political disorder in the European Union. The human cost has indeed been heartrending. Yet the serious flaw in this attribution of blame is that it is historically illiterate. For the United States is hardly a stranger to the fighting of proxy wars: A partial list during the Cold War against the Soviet Union includes the wars in Korea,

Congo, Vietnam, Cambodia, Angola, El Salvador, Nicaragua, and Afghanistan. Some of those wars made strategic and, arguably, even moral sense. But in none of them—with the possible, partial exception of Korea—was the American decision to fight or give support to the fighters a benefit to the local population. On the contrary, the civilian death toll of these wars was many millions. The critics' second claim is that, even if the Assad regime's most effective opponents are unpalatable, the United States could have avoided this Hobson's choice with an early decision to arm and train a moderate, secular, and democratic opposition. This claim is impossible to refute but also hard to believe.

Such fatalism may not be very inspiring, but it too is supported by history. The United States has a lot of experience arming and training surrogates, but its success rate is not impressive.[51] One spectacular recent failure is the Iraqi army, trained and equipped at a U.S. taxpayer cost of many billions, which fled at its first encounter with ISIS, leaving its weapons behind. A notable success, on the other hand, was the program to arm mujahedeen in Afghanistan who drove out the Soviets and, arguably, helped destroy the Soviet Union. But the arming of jihadists had some unforeseen and unwelcome consequences. And one thing the record makes clear is that arms from the outside are only decisive under certain conditions: The donors have to pool resources and agree on the recipients, the rebels need to be unified, and the United States needs to have troops on the ground. In the crucial period when critics say the transfer of weapons would have had a determinative impact, the donors were at each other's throats over the Muslim Brothers and Iran, the recipients were more fragmented than ever, and no one in the U.S. Congress would tolerate the deployment of troops to Syria. It was a nonstarter. America's big problem in Syria is that it is strategically incoherent to seek the defeat of both sides in a civil war. When Moscow in late 2015 sent troops and launched air strikes against ISIS and other anti-Assad rebels, it could be seen in part as an act of desperation to preserve its one Arab ally and its single naval base on the Mediterranean. Putin did have one great advantage, however, in that he knew which side he was on.[52]

For Israel, the main source of consternation is not so much this strategic confusion in Syria, for—as we have seen—the Israeli government has also been ambivalent about the consequences of toppling Assad. Israelis must understand, as well, that the United States is hardly about to leave the Middle East: In comparison to Russia's single base in Syria, the United States has an array of ships and airbases and other military installations throughout the region, and no intention of removing them. In this regard, the idea of a pivot to Asia was not quite accurate. But Israel's government became convinced that Obama's instinct of restraint regarding military force was a central character flaw, a loss of confidence, even cowardice. It is a judgment we believe to be utterly unwarranted. But it unquestionably poisoned the dialogue between Washington and Jerusalem.

AT THE CENTER of that poisoned dialogue was Iran. And it would be prudent for both the Israeli and American governments to consider the long-term implications of Obama's victory and Netanyahu's defeat on the Iran nuclear deal. One lesson is that, when the White House defines a paramount American interest, it is able to pursue that interest without too much concern for the American Israel lobby. The record of historical evidence for this proposition is a long one. From 1950 until the early 1960s, the United States effectively imposed an arms embargo on Israel. In 1956, it forced Israel's withdrawal from the Sinai. In 1967, it refused to honor its commitment to keep open the Strait of Tiran to Israeli shipping. In the early 1970s, it forced Israel to cease attacks into Egypt during the so-called war of attrition. In 1973, it prevented Israel from destroying the Egyptian Third Army. The Reagan administration in 1982 effectively broke Israel's siege of Beirut and saved the PLO leadership from destruction. Reagan also sold AWACS radar planes to Saudi Arabia against the fierce opposition of Israel and the Israel lobby. The George H. W. Bush administration prevented Israel from lashing back to destroy Iraqi Scud missile sites even as the missiles were raining down on Israeli territory. Both the Clinton and George W. Bush administrations pressured Israel, successfully, to stop high-tech arms sales to China. The George W. Bush and Obama administrations prevented Israel from attacking Iran, and the Obama administration then proceeded to negotiate the JCPOA behind Israel's back.

This pattern, it should be noted, has worked the other way as well. When Israel is convinced that its national interest is at stake, it is unlikely to bow to American wishes or even demands. It ignored President Truman's demand that it permit the return of Arab refugees from its war of independence. It defied one of John F. Kennedy's paramount foreign-policy priorities, the campaign against nuclear proliferation.[53] It attacked Iraqi and Syrian reactors against the wishes of the United States. And, of course, it has defied the stated position of every U.S. administration since LBJ's that Jewish settlements in occupied territories were corrosive to prospects for peace.

This record is in some ways unremarkable. Sovereign nations define and defend their national interests. But both countries should be concerned about how this plays out in the future. One important lesson for Israel is that its powerful influence in the U.S. Congress can yield disappointing dividends. (When the Israeli government refused to meet with John Kerry as he shuttled between Cairo and Jerusalem during the last Gaza conflict, Israeli officials explained for the record to a *Wall Street Journal* reporter their casual contempt for him personally and his diplomatic efforts by pointing out that Israel did not need the White House because it effectively controlled the Congress.[54]) Congress is a reliable provider of funding. But foreign and national security policy is made with considerable autonomy by the White House, and a disaffected White House is by definition a problem for Israel. Regarding the plight of the Palestinians, Israel has been able to defy the wishes of successive administrations mainly because their plight was seen as an important but not paramount American interest. This truth is perfectly illustrated by the fates of two Obama initiatives: his demand for a settlements freeze, and his determination to reach and safeguard a nuclear agreement with Iran. Both were important to Obama, but only one was paramount.

This leaves open the question, however, of whether a two-state solution might be seen by a successor president as a paramount American interest. The viability of the U.S.–Israeli strategic alliance is strained when the two countries disagree fundamentally about how to deal with the key strategic issues—Iran and the Palestinians—that concern them both. If these disagreements continue, then the relationship will require the continued effective shock absorber of mutual political and cultural affinity between the two societies. But that affinity is severely threatened.

PART III

The Future

7

The Growing Divide

ISRAEL IS MOVING RIGHT while America moves gently but percepti-bly left. These trends are neither linear nor uncomplicated, and the Ameri-can case is more ambiguous than the Israeli. Israel's transformation is in part demographic and in part the grimly logical response to its tragic pre-dicament and formation over a century of war.

During the first thirty years of Israeli independence, the nation's politics were dominated by a combination of Labor Zionist parties. Their control over the machinery of government as well as cultural expression was so comprehensive that it is often referred to as the Labor hegemony. This hege-mony was established by the leading role socialists had played in the Yishuv, the pre-statehood administration of Palestine. Many of these leaders came from Eastern Europe and were favorably disposed to the left and a commu-nitarian approach to social organization. They tended to disdain the reli-gious component of Jewish identity and to associate the oppressive Jewish existence in the ghettoes and rural towns of Eastern Europe with the reli-giously observant way of life prevailing there. Abandonment of a degrading diaspora went hand in hand with rejecting Jewish liturgical tradition and the strictures of Halakhah. Ethnically, the Labor movement was largely Ashkenazic. It radiated an aura of entitlement and cultural superiority cou-pled with a corresponding condescension toward Sephardim, the many Is-raeli Jews who hailed from the Middle East and North Africa. Successive Labor governments chalked up some tremendous achievements, including Israeli independence, safeguarding it through a series of violent wars, and providing a home for a shattered population of Holocaust survivors as well as impoverished Jews from the Arab world. But their long stretch of unchallenged rule bred complacency, a reputation for corruption, and discrimination against "Oriental" Jewish immigrants. And Labor was blamed for the terrible losses incurred by Israel in the Yom Kippur War of 1973. The economic stagflation that plagued Western economies also damaged Israel's and further discredited Labor rule.

Labor leaders were aware of their diminishing grip on popular support and worked to unify the cluster of small, separate parties that comprised the movement. But such measures could only go so far. In 1977, the Labor alignment suffered a staggering reversal. The right wing of Israeli politics had also consolidated in the 1970s and, helmed by Menachem Begin, rode to power on cumulative Sephardic resentment of the Ashkenazic left. A centrist party emerging from within Labor, the Movement for Democratic Change, won fifteen seats and then opted to partner with Likud, ensuring Labor's defeat. This pivot in Israeli politics came to be known as the upheaval, a term coined on the evening of election day 1977, when Channel 1 news anchor Haim Yavin—after reading the first ever televised exit polls in Israel—announced "Gvirotai U'Rabotai—Mahapach!" ("Ladies and Gentlemen—an upheaval!") The new majority was ethnically distinct from the Ashkenazic community. It emerged from Arab homelands and was therefore militantly anti-Arab, having tasted the bitter cup of discrimination by Muslim neighbors in their countries of origin. The new majority was also more religious than its Ashkenazic predecessors and more open to right-wing rhetoric about a territorially greater Israel, a staple of Begin's party, Herut. Begin's worldview, which combined religion and nationalism, was eloquently summed up in his first speech to the Knesset after his election:

> The government of Israel shall not ask any nation, near or far, great or small, to recognize our right to exist. We received our right to exist from the God of our forefathers at the dawn of civilization nearly four thousand years ago, and for that right, which has been sanctified by the blood of Jews from generation to generation, we have paid a price unheard of in the history of nations.[1]

Begin's premiership began triumphantly with the visit of Egyptian president Anwar Sadat to Jerusalem. This astonishing event paved the way for the 1979 peace treaty and the yearly multibillion-dollar program of U.S. aid for Israel's economy and military. Freed from concern about the security of

Israel's southern flank, and flush with cash, Begin turned his attention to Israel's northern front, particularly the Palestinian attacks emanating from southern Lebanon. Lebanon was then the home of the Palestine Liberation Organization. The country was still roiled by civil war, a conflict engendered in part by the destabilizing presence of a Palestinian army in an already highly factionalized society. Heedless of Lebanese interests, Palestinian militants invited Israeli retaliation on their hapless host country. In August 1982, as Israeli forces entered Beirut, Begin wrote to President Reagan that Arafat was like Hitler in his Berlin bunker in the last days of the Third Reich. Begin imparted to his inner circle that he intended to kill him there.

Israel's ill-fated invasion of Lebanon was to be followed by a nearly two-decade occupation of its southern districts. The U.S. embassy in Tel Aviv presciently dubbed this military adventure "Vietnamowitz." The tensions that the adventure caused in Israel's relations with America were, at times, acute. The Reagan administration became exasperated as the incursion became a full-scale siege of Beirut intended to destroy the PLO; finally Reagan demanded of Begin that the IDF cease its bombardment of the city, or Israel would face "grave consequences."[2] (In fact, the US–Israeli acrimony over this war could have been much worse; at one point in August 1982 after Ariel Sharon interrupted the evacuation of Palestinians from Beirut harbor, the Pentagon ordered ships of the U.S. Sixth Fleet to escort Palestinian-laden vessels to safety, and to be ready to fire upon Israeli forces if necessary.[3]) The culminating events of the initial phase of the war—the U.S.-engineered transfer of the PLO leadership to Tunis and the massacre of Palestinians by Israel's Lebanese Christian allies—appeared to break Begin's will. The death of his wife at this time probably contributed to the decline that led to his resignation in 1983.[4] Yitzhak Shamir, an old comrade in arms, replaced him as Likud leader.

But Shamir's government was burdened by high inflation and the consequences of the botched invasion. Both spurred his enemies within Likud to try to unseat him. On the eve of the 1984 elections, public opinion surveys presaged a Labor landslide. However, the two parties crossed the line with nearly equal numbers of seats: 61 for Likud, 59 for Labor. With the disqualification of a single-seat Likud coalition partner because of its avowedly racist platform, the opposing coalitions were forced into a series of national unity governments and rotating premierships. The pattern finally broke when the outbreak of the first Palestinian uprising, or intifada, undermined the credibility of Likud's security policy and gave the edge to Labor, led at the time by Yitzhak Rabin, a famous former IDF chief of staff and ambassador to the United States.

Rabin, in other words, was a Labor politician with impeccable security credentials. This center-left interregnum provided the space for the Oslo Accords, a bilateral Israeli–Palestinian agreement that led to the establishment of the Palestinian Authority. Neither side met its commitments, however, and the assassination of Rabin by a nationalist religious fanatic arguably destroyed Oslo. In an elegiac assessment on the twentieth anniversary of Rabin's death, veteran American negotiator Aaron David Miller concluded that Israel might well have evolved along different lines had Rabin lived. He concedes that Rabin was "a cautious peacemaker, an incrementalist," and that at "the time of Rabin's death, the Oslo process was already in serious trouble." It was unclear that Rabin would have been able to shepherd a centrist constituency to back his basic approach, especially in the storm of Hamas and jihadist bombs and bullets that killed sixty Israelis in March 1996. Nonetheless, Miller contends that

> Even had Rabin not been able to bring his peace initiatives to fruition, he would still have remained critical to Israel's political life, a repository of authority and wisdom in helping his nation sort through the challenges it faced. A strong champion of reciprocity and respect in the U.S.–Israeli relationship, Rabin would have done everything he could have done to keep that bond from fraying at both the personal and policy level.[5]

It was not to be. Shimon Peres, who succeeded Rabin, had contributed mightily to Israel's defenses, but not in uniform on the battlefield. And he had a reputation for slippery, even unscrupulous political dealings. As Palestinian extremists thwarted the modest progress of the Oslo Accords with a series of vicious attacks on Israeli civilians, Peres simply lacked the capacity to continue Rabin's work. Likud returned to power in 1996. But Likud's leader, Netanyahu, was caught between pressure from Washington to comply with the Oslo Accords and countervailing pressure from a galvanized right that perceived the accords as a fundamental threat to Israel's claim on the West Bank. He failed to strike a convincing balance and lost the support of voters on both the right and left. He was unseated by Labor under its new leader, Ehud Barak, another former IDF chief of staff and war hero. President Bill Clinton saw Barak as the key to a final status accord. Clinton built a renewed peace process around him that stretched from Camp David in Maryland to Taba in Sinai. But, in truth, Barak lacked the broad public support he would have needed to meet Arafat halfway—just as Arafat had no mandate to meet the Israelis halfway. The outbreak of the second intifada, following Barak's controversial withdrawal of Israeli troops from southern Lebanon, again undermined Labor's claims to security expertise and moral resolve.

The nation shifted back to the right in the 2001 elections. Likud returned under the leadership of Sharon, another of Israel's great warriors. Israelis are frequently mocked, even or perhaps especially by their admirers, for having a tactical genius that tends to undercut strategic objectives. Sharon's command of the Lebanon misadventure might be cited as an example. He was, however, capable of strategic vision, and he was daring enough to act on it. He came to clearly understand the risk posed to Israel's future by continued occupation. In December 2003, Sharon gave a major speech in which he declared that Israel must sever its connection to occupied territory, except for settlements that were widely acknowledged to be part of Israel in the context of a final status accord. The key part of this declaration was his assessment that continued occupation was untenable and that Israel needed to act boldly, before it was too late. By 2005 he had withdrawn Israel from Gaza, but without adequately coordinating the move with either the Palestinian Authority or the United States, thereby creating the space in which Hamas could—and did—flourish. There were hints that he intended to pursue this basic course on the West Bank; his split from Likud and formation of a new centrist party, Kadimah, seemed to support this interpretation. But his incapacitation by a massive stroke in December 2005, and his replacement by Ehud Olmert, will forever conceal the truth of the matter. Olmert was regrettably scandal prone, however, and traded his political future literally for trinkets. In 2009, Likud, led by Netanyahu, returned to power.

Hegemony of the Right

In the 2015 election, right-wing parties won every district apart from Tel Aviv and Haifa, which has a large Arab population. Their natural constituency—religious, less wealthy, skeptical about democracy, and hostile to Arabs—is growing as a result of long-term social and economic changes.

Israeli society, in contrast to the United States, is becoming more religious. Longstanding subsidies for the ultra-Orthodox, combined with the belief that reproduction is a religious duty,[6] are driving rapid demographic growth among ultra-Orthodox Israelis. The fertility rates among ultra-Orthodox women are between two and three times the rates among secular Israeli Jews and Arabs. The ability of right-wing parties to dominate the majority of Israeli electoral districts is due in part to this demographic dynamic. Secular right-wing parties have consistently been more capable of outbidding left-wing parties for ultra-Orthodox collaboration in the coalition formation process that follows national elections.* In the last Knesset session, even Naftali Bennett's moderately Orthodox right-wing party had to give up on a legislative measure that would have compelled ultra-Orthodox males to serve in the army.

There have been other profound changes to the country's demographic profile. The last one was triggered by the arrival of hundreds of thousands of Jews from the Soviet Union in a fairly short space of time following the Soviet collapse. The shift now underway is toward a society that will incorporate not only a large ethnically Arab population, but also a correspondingly large group of ultra-Orthodox citizens. The Haredi share of Israel's population is about 11 percent. In fifteen years, it will be edging toward 20 percent. This startling increase has several implications. The first is economic: Haredi men don't participate in the work force at the same rate as non-Haredi men. The burgeoning Haredi population therefore presages a drag on an already decelerating economy.

The Haredi surge is also important because religious beliefs tend to correlate with attitudes that could change Israel's approach to democracy. When asked, for example, whether there should be full equality of rights between Jews and Arabs, about one-third of the secular respondents disagreed; a little over half of the "traditional" Jewish respondents disagreed; approximately two-thirds of "religious" Jewish Israelis disagreed; and 72 percent of Haredim disagreed.[7] On the question of whether foreign-born Jews should be accorded citizenship if they were not born of a Jewish mother or were converted by an Orthodox rabbi, half of secular Jews were opposed, while 88 percent of Haredi Jews were opposed. When asked whether Jewish com-

---

* The bidding process included government subsidies, separate education, and army service exemptions.

munities should get more resources than Israeli Arab communities, only 18 percent of secular Jews agreed, while a bit over half the Haredi respondents felt this way.

The Haredim are also inclined toward the settlement life. There are eight large Haredi settlements in the West Bank, outside of Jerusalem, which together house about 116,000 residents, roughly one-third of the overall settler population.[8] The settler population of all stripes has been growing faster than an otherwise fairly rapid nationwide increase. Between 1991 and 2012, the Israeli population grew by around 60 percent, from five to eight million. The distribution of this population growth was geographically skewed, with the number of people living in settlements ballooning by 240 percent.[9] The remarkable aspect to this disproportionate increase is that it took place mostly in the Haredi settlements. Growth in the Haredi settlements alone was a staggering 376 percent.[10] These are rough estimates, because ways of determining whether settlements are Haredi vary; some demographers look at voting patterns, others at self-identification in census surveys, still others at the high school attended. But the trend is clear. When Netanyahu boasts of the extraordinary 120,000 increase in the settler population on his watch, he is not referring to construction, which actually has fallen since 2009, but to the sum of an overall fertility rate of 5.1 on the West Bank and a very low death rate owing to the youthful profile of the settler communities.[11]

The significance of the trend lies in the intersection of attitudes and geography. When Haredi views about intercommunal relations are considered against the realities of Haredi demographic growth, the possibility of Israeli withdrawal from the West Bank appears remote. In a survey released in 2014, between 55 and 58 percent of the Haredi and other Orthodox respondents said that soldiers ordered to evacuate settlements have a duty to disobey.

The Haredis are the farthest right wing of Israel's Jewish society. Overlapping with them is the big tent of the religious nationalists, a technical term used by the Israeli Central Bureau of Statistics to categorize the religious affiliations and practices of the population. As the census experts well understand, the categories are not hard and fast. A person's identity, after all, is really a shifting, elastic self-conception. The boundaries between religious nationalist and Haredi, for example, are blurry depending on what a particular respondent is asked on a questionnaire. The distinguishing characteristic of the religious nationalist group is that on important issues—the role of religion in public policy, the nature of the state and the place of Arabs in it, the legitimacy of the settlement enterprise, the privileging of Israel's Jewish identity over its democratic political legacy, and the superiority of parties to the right of the political spectrum—it enfolds many Israelis who would otherwise be counted in different categories. There are many who don't consider themselves particularly religious but who support the national religious camp, as well as many whose patterns of religious observance are far more punctilious than the religious nationalists but who nonetheless identify with that camp.[12] It is not surprising therefore that religious nationalists represent the fastest growing and youngest segment of Israeli societies and look destined to dominate Israel's political space for some time to come.[13] A recent survey assessed that about 45 percent of Israeli Jews have some degree of affiliation with this camp.[14] Religious nationalists are almost twice as likely to be on the right of the political spectrum as the Israeli Jewish population as a whole. Israeli analysts compare the religious nationalists to the kibbutz movement of decades past. Just as the kibbutzniks embodied the national ethos and were widely admired by the vast majority of Israelis who had never set foot in a kibbutz or would consider a collectivist lifestyle for themselves, the religious nationalists command broad respect for their principled insistence on the Jewish character of the state, unified Jerusalem as a Jewish capital, and the widest possible territorial sweep.[15] And just as the kibbutzniks dominated the IDF officer corps in that earlier era, the religious nationalists are following in their footsteps. In 1990, 2.5 percent of graduates identified as religious, compared to 26 percent in 2008.[16]

Education and Economics

The rightward swing is accompanied by another trend. Israeli schoolchildren, both Jewish and Arab, are increasingly maleducated. The proximate cause is long-term underfunding of public education. Starved of resources, the school system also struggles with a poor distribution of the resources that are available: Jewish schools are decidedly better funded than Arab ones and, on the Jewish side, schools catering to the ultra-Orthodox do not fund the secular subjects needed to prepare students for participation in the local and global economies. Given that in 2015 fully half of all children starting their first year of school were ultra-Orthodox or Arab, this does not bode well for Israel's economic future. Even now, in international rankings, Israeli students are near the bottom of the list of OECD countries, hovering between Hungary and Croatia. Israel's educational achievement in core subjects is near the bottom of developed world. As of 2012, the average achievement level of Israeli children in math, science, and reading is below twenty-four of twenty-five most relevant OECD countries. In these surveys, one out of three Israeli students tested at or below "level 2," which, according to the OECD, means that "at best, they can only handle the simplest and most obvious tasks."[17] In a 2014 OECD survey designed to measure "the ability of 15-year-olds to solve problems that they haven't encountered before and for which a routine solution has not been learned," Israeli students came in thirty-fifth out of forty-four countries. Of those tested, nearly 40 percent were at level 2; 22 percent could not get past the level 1 threshold.[18] Had the ultra-Orthodox Jewish children been included, Israel's national average would have been even lower. As it is, over half the Haredi male population in Israel, a group destined to grow considerably in the decades to come, has no education beyond the eighth grade. Arabic-speaking children achieved results below many developing countries, including neighboring Jordan.

This shortfall affects political attitudes. In 2011, the Friedrich Ebert Stiftung, a distinguished German research organization, joined with the Dahaf Institute, Israel's version of the Pew survey organization, in their third poll of young Jewish and Arab Israelis between 15–18 and 21–24.[19] The resulting report registered a sharp decline in support of Israel's identity as a democratic state, from 26.1 percent in 1998 to 14.3 percent. Among the 15–18 year old group, 60 percent assessed a "strong leader" as more desirable than "rule of law," while 70 percent averred that security should trump democracy where the two conflict. Those stressing the importance of keeping Israel a Jewish state rose from 18.1 to 33.3 percent. At the same, belief in the possibility of peaceful relations with Israel's neighbors plummeted from 28.4 percent in 1998 to 18.2 percent in 2011. These attitudes aligned with a sharp drop in support for left-wing parties among the Jewish respondents. Between 1998 and 2011, approval of Labor parties dove from 32 to 12 percent, as the favorability of parties to the right on the political spectrum rose from 48 to 62 percent.[20] It is possible that the views of these young men and women will shift over time. Under some conditions, voters mellow as they age. But in the United States, for example, party affiliation tends to remain constant over a voter's lifetime. And it is true, according to the Israel's Democracy

Institute, that already in 2010, 60 percent of adult survey respondents registered the view that authoritarian government and strong leadership would
be more likely to solve the country's problems efficiently. A slight majority
of the respondents in that survey also thought that the Israeli government
should be entitled to encourage Arab emigration. (At the same time, a plurality back in 2010 still believed that it was equally important for Israel to be
both Jewish and democratic.)[21]

Higher education in Israel has not escaped the challenges that have undermined primary and secondary education. This is especially disconcert-
ing. Israel's universities have long been at the global forefront of learning in
both the humanities and sciences, an impressive achievement for an embattled nation. In policy terms, the cultivation of higher education in Israel for
so many years, especially in the bleak decades following the establishment
of the state, was wise as well as courageous. As the right wing gained ascendancy, however, the resources allocated to research universities began to
shrink. Most countries of Israel's size, population, and economic clout establish new research universities periodically. Israel, however, is an exception. Since 1969, when Ben-Gurion University of the Negev was founded, no
new research universities have opened.[22] This was not due to a considered
decision to increase investment in existing research universities. During this
period, the budgets have not kept pace with enrollment in Israel's two leading universities—Hebrew University and Tel Aviv University. Between 1973
and 2012, Israel's population grew by 142 percent and students in research
universities grew by 240 percent, while senior faculty in research universities
grew only by 14 percent. Even when non-research colleges are factored in,
the number of students grew by 525 percent, while the total number of senior faculty grew by 40 percent.[23]

At the same time, a host of private colleges have sprung up. Although the
proliferation of these schools has probably given access to higher education
for those less well prepared for entry into a major university, they cannot
produce the top-tier research that will sustain a strong economy. The ero-
sion of higher education in Israel has accelerated a serious brain drain
because young Israeli doctoral students have little hope of finding teaching
jobs in their own country. A truly astonishing percentage of tenure-track
physics professors in the United States are Israeli. This is great news for
America, but a disturbing bellwether for Israel—and not just because of the
economic implications. Long-term polling shows that center-left voters tend

to be better educated than their right-wing counterparts. Attrition in the education sector is therefore likely to reinforce the imbalance between the main players in Israel's political system, locking in the dominant position of the right and slowly squeezing the left.

This trend could be worsened by the long-term decline in Israel labor productivity and in the role of technology as a factor in production. This is a shocking assessment, especially if one's knowledge of Israel's economic performance is drawn from the pages of books like *Start-Up Nation*, a recent bestseller coauthored by an American Republican operative, which extols Israel's economy in terms most professional economists think are fantasy.[24] Israel does have startups, and a thriving high-tech industry. The problem is that these are only a very small part of the overall economy and getting smaller.[25]

The gap between Israel's labor productivity and that of the EU has widened alarmingly over the past twenty years. If the gap continues to grow, Israelis will both be paid less and work longer to produce goods and services. Economic growth will slow. Unemployment would also rise. When the employment picture reflects the entire working-age population, which includes the burgeoning number of men who are simply not part of the actual labor market because they've given up looking for work, the situation is bleak. Over the next ten or fifteen years, the ratio of retirees will increase sharply, from 16 percent in 2015 to 23 percent in 2030.[26] In this interval, the retiree population will shift from one that is largely Ashkenazi and tends to be relatively well off to Sephardim who never were able to accumulate comparable property, savings, and job pensions. And the aging Arabs won't have the benefit of family support, which, like other attributes of their traditional lifestyle, is fading among youth. The burden of social security and medical care for this substantial share of the population will fall on a shrinking base of employed citizens. Ironically, this problem will be compounded by the expected high level of births during this period, which will necessitate greater expenditures on infrastructure, such as classroom space, and government employees, including many teachers.

If the gap between employment and productivity rates among Haredim and Arab Israelis on the one hand, and the rest of Israeli society on the other, is not narrowed, the ratio of government tax revenues to GDP will drop, while the ratio of government expenditures to GDP climbs. The Israeli Finance Ministry forecasts a fourfold increase in the government deficit as a share of GDP.[27] Government economists do not believe that even the con-siderable income from Mediterranean gas fields that Israel is now beginning to exploit will bridge this gap. With government income falling and expen-ditures rising under the scenario in which employment and productivity rates among Haredim and Arab Israelis do not converge to those of the rest of society, Israel's debt will rise precipitously, which in turn will hurt its standing in the capital markets. Nor is Israel's future growth picture under scenarios devised by the Bank of Israel especially inspiring. According to the BOI, the rate of growth in Israel's standard of living (GDP per capita) is ex-pected to drop from the current 1.4 percent over the past decade and a half to 0.5 or 0.8 percent a year.[28]

These trends will make it more difficult to slow Israel's brain drain. If you are well educated, feel at home in the wider world, have high aspirations for career—and the usual middle-class aptitude for consumption—in other words, if you are the archetypal urban Labor voter, then you have the op-tion of emigration. Many will take it. Over time, this process would facili-tate the right-wing grip on electoral politics, not only by decreasing the pool of potential left-wing constituents but by increasing the societal load of eco-nomically disenfranchised voters, who, like their American counterparts, may be more attracted to right-wing policies.

It is important to stipulate: Demography is not destiny. Wise policy can sometimes restore economic vitality; projected cultural, religious, and po-litical futures do not unfold according to some iron law of determinism. To take one salient example, Haredi birth rates are tied to deep religious com-mitment, yet even deeply religious communities are not completely isolated from the influence of modernity. Birth rates can change.

And yet, the trends we have described look considerably more plausible than a reversal leading to a Labor comeback. And it is such a reversal of for-tune that optimists anticipate. Chuck Freilich, a former Israeli National Se-curity Council official, wrote in October 2015 a sharply critical assessment of Netanyahu's handling of the Israeli–U.S. relationship, but took comfort in the expectation that a center-left government would return to change course.[29] Similarly, Bernard Avishai, the *New Yorker* columnist and gener-ally perceptive analyst of Israeli politics, sees a restoration of a long-lost lib-eral dominance, perhaps once Israelis grasp the implications of what he sees as a disastrous turn away from the West. Even essentially conservative ob-servers of Israel's volatile parliamentary system fret about the viability of a

Likud-led coalition government that as of the fall of 2015 had a one-vote majority.

All of this could happen. But the evidence laid out in preceding pages make it look less likely than a right-wing future.

Another complicating factor might be the role of Arab voters and parties in Israeli politics. The 2015 elections saw this fractious segment form a surprisingly united list, raising hopes that a tactical alliance between the Israeli Arab parties and the left-wing secular Jewish parties could upend right-wing dominance. But this did not happen in 2015, and seems unlikely for the foreseeable future. One reason is that collusion with non-Zionist parties would invite accusations of treasonous behavior, or at least defeatist pandering to an Arab fifth column. The success of Netanyahu's pre-election ploy in 2015, whereby he got out the vote by warning that Arab Israelis were turning out "in droves" and had to be countered as a matter of urgent necessity, shows just how radioactive Jewish parties would become if aligned overtly with Arab parties. Not that the Arab parties would be keen to link their fortunes to the left-wing parties that maintained discriminatory policies against Arabs for decades. In September 2015, an Arab legislator on the floor of the Knesset put this reluctance into words:

> The Labor Party is the father and mother of racism. Even Yisrael Beiteinu is better. Even the extreme right is better. You guys invented the term "racism." Those who took our lands, who expelled us, are not those who chant "death to the Arabs," but those who claim to "bring peace upon us." You should be ashamed of yourselves, you racists! Is this "left"? You elitist white Ashkenazi Jews. Give us back our lands! You stand on the land that you stole from me and take a piss on me from above, under the banner of universal values. Who hurt us [Arabs] more? Likud or the Labor? Labor, of course! The Likud built settlements next to the Arab villages. You guys built your socialist kibbutzim on top of the Arab villages, after you destroyed them. Then you come to talk to me about social justice and liberalism. You nationalists! Look at yourselves! You should be ashamed of yourselves![30]

This was obviously a theatrical performance. One can assume that the speaker understands well enough that Arabs would be better off under a Labor government than under a right-wing coalition. Still, it would not be unreasonable to assume that the underlying resentment applies to Jewish Israelis across the political spectrum. Although a tactical alliance might yet be forged between the left-wing Zionist parties and the non-Zionist Arab ones, the emotional hurdles, quite apart from the practical obstacles, will be hard to surmount.

The Cauldron of Conflict

There is little mystery in the rightward turn of Israeli society and politics. Protracted conflict distorts politics. The torment of civil war led Lincoln to suspend habeas corpus and declare martial law. In World War II, the Roosevelt administration confined Japanese Americans to concentration camps and gave military tribunals jurisdiction over civilians. In the war on terror, the Bush administration authorized torture, targeted U.S. citizens overseas, and approved massive surveillance of Americans at home. These departures from our tradition of civil liberties were triggered by relatively brief, if terribly violent, conflicts. Israel, and the Jews who settled the land beginning in the 1880s, have been at war not for five or ten years, but for nearly a century and a half. Arguments that Israel missed opportunities to resolve the underlying disputes might well be true, but most observers agree that the Arab penchant for missing opportunities was also consistent. The fact remains that the state of Israel emerged from the Holocaust, which was preceded and followed by nearly constant violent conflict within Palestine prior to 1948 and subsequently on the borders of the state as well as within it. That Israel's politics and even its self-conception have evolved in a way that emphasizes Israel's Jewish character and disdains institutions and parties that are seen to foster weakness should therefore come as no surprise. This might not be the direction that sentimental American Zionists, nurtured by images of folk-singing kibbutzniks decked out in sandals and *kova tembels*, wish to see, but it was perhaps inevitable.

Social scientists have found that it is easier to protect minority rights in circumstances where the majority greatly outnumbers the minority. Hence, Israeli Arab citizens constituting roughly 20 percent of the population within the Green Line enjoy a modicum of civil liberty despite their somewhat checkered relationship with the state. Where the two sides are more evenly matched, as with Palestinians and Israeli Jews on both sides of the Green Line, rights will be fiercely contested. The result is a volatile arrangement that can erupt into civil war.[31] The 2012 wave of violence in Jerusalem, the one place where Arabs and Jews are jammed together in a microcosm of a mixed society, speaks eloquently to what might happen if Israelis tried to establish a single state between the River Jordan and the Mediterranean. They would be unlikely, in any event, to seek such a one-state solution based on equal rights for Palestinians and Jews—as this would remove the protection of Jewish sovereignty that Israel was founded to preserve.

In 2015 George Washington University Professor Michael Barnett made the uncomfortable observation that in the debate about Israel's future, our imagination seems to be limited by some wishful assumptions. "Discussions of 'solutions' always presuppose the existence of a problem and a limited universe of permissible outcomes," Barnett writes. Hence, the two-state solution is posited as inevitable because it is the only solution that allows Israel to remain a democracy. However, that does not really mean that it is the only solution.

> As the two-state solution fades into history, its alternatives become increasingly likely: civil war, ethnic cleansing or a non-democratic state. Although all three are possible, the third is rising on the horizon. Whether it goes by the name of an apartheid state, an illiberal democracy, a less than free society or a competitive authoritarianism, the dominant theme will be a Jewish minority ruling over a non-Jewish majority. Although such an outcome would be an emotional blow to those who favor the two-state solution as a way to maintain Israel's democratic and Jewish character, it looks quite familiar in a world where liberal democracy not only remains the exception but has actually lost ground over the last decade.[32]

If Barnett is right, can Israel and the United States remain close allies? The answer depends in part on what we mean by "allies."

American Transformations

As the magnitude of Obama's victory on the Iran deal became evident, former Democratic congressman Robert Wexler assessed why the Israeli government campaign against the deal had failed so dramatically: "The unfortunate problem with Prime Minister Netanyahu is that he prides himself on being the Israeli that knows America the best," Wexler, who runs an Israel-friendly think tank, told the *Washington Post*. "Where he's mistaken is, Prime Minister Netanyahu knows the America that elected Ronald Reagan president. He's completely unfamiliar with the America that elected Barack Obama president. And they are in fact very different Americas."[33]

America has indeed changed dramatically, and Obama's election and then reelection were both consequences and, because of the color of his skin, emblems of that change. In contrast to the Israeli developments outlined above, we cannot be quite so confident about the future consequences of America's transformation for U.S. politics, foreign policy, and relations with Israel. But it does seem likely that the dissonant trajectories of Israeli and American societies will threaten the moral and emotional core of the alliance.

At the time of his first inauguration, President Obama was assembling a team that naturally contained a number of advisers from the last Democratic administration of Bill Clinton. Many carried bad memories of their last encounter with Netanyahu as prime minister, and were loaded for bear when he came back into office just weeks after Obama. But leaving personalities aside, there was a distinct sense of sea change in the attitudes of the American foreign-policy community regarding the alliance with Israel. The controversy over *The Israel Lobby*, a book by Harvard and University of Chicago Professors Steven Walt and John Mearsheimer, published in 2007, had left a bitter taste in many mouths, with charges of anti-Semitism against the authors raising painful questions about the boundaries of criticizing Israeli conduct and American support.

There was an associated development among senior U.S. military officers. Their responsibilities for American troops under fire in Iraq and Afghanistan made them increasingly vocal in speculating about the role of Israel–Palestine in broader Middle East conflict. Early in Obama's first term, for example, General David Petraeus, commander of Centcom, presented to the Senate Armed Services Committee testimony including the following statement:

> Israeli–Palestinian tensions often flare into violence and large-scale armed confrontations. The conflict foments anti-American sentiments due to a perception of U.S. favoritism for Israel. Arab anger over the Palestinian question limits the strength and depth of U.S. partnerships with governments and peoples in the AOR [area of responsibility] and weakens the

legitimacy of moderate regimes in the Arab world. Meanwhile, al-Qaeda and other militant groups exploit that anger to mobilize support.[34]

A retired IDF officer who strongly favors Israeli concessions for peace with the Palestinians, nonetheless derided this analysis as the "Centcom" view of the Middle East.[35] Dennis Ross also derides it as "the view embedded in every administration that our problems with the Arabs and Muslims were largely connected to the Palestinian issue." Ross says that Obama came into office with this mentality, but suggests that he was disabused of it over the course of his presidency.[36]

It is certainly true that, over the course of Obama's presidency, the multivectored conflicts in Syria, Yemen, Iraq, and Libya, along with turmoil in Egypt and elsewhere, had gathered a momentum and viciousness that has nothing to do with Israel or the Palestinians. But just as obviously, the Palestine question has enduring resonance and potential to cause further instability in neighboring countries such as Jordan. And it cannot be discounted as a continuing cause of terrorism.

What is interesting for our present purposes is that, as Ross observes, the idea that the relationship with Israel creates strategic problems for the United States is an old one, "embedded," as he puts it, in every U.S. administration since Israel was created. The sense that the relationship is unbalanced is also an old one. To underscore this point, Ross juxtaposes statements separated by half a century, from Robert Komer, an NSC official in the Kennedy administration, and from Obama's Defense Secretary Gates. In 1962 Komer wrote in a memo to President Kennedy:

> We have promised the Israelis Hawks, reassured them on the Jordan waters, given a higher level of economic aid (to permit extensive arms), and given various security assurances. In return we have gotten nothing from our efforts. . . . The score is 4-0.[37]

In 2010, according to Ross, Secretary Gates lamented in a White House meeting: "With Israel, it is all give and no get. We give and give and give and we get nothing. It is a one-way street."[38]

If this lament is such a consistent theme, and yet American support for Israel has remained solid and in fact grown more generous, one could argue, as Ross argues, that the crisis of the Obama–Netanyahu years has little long-term significance, and the alliance is indeed "doomed to succeed"—hence the title of Ross's book. One experienced American diplomat offered a structural explanation for this durability. The relationship, he agreed, has always caused significant frustration and even anger in the American foreign-policy community. But the concern is asymmetric: Whereas frustrated diplomats have many concerns and frustrations, supporters of Israel are highly focused on the single issue in their campaign contributions and voting behavior.[39]

Yet there are structural changes in American society and politics that are likely to disrupt this stasis too. Though it is too early to predict, we would be surprised if the Democratic senators, congresswomen, and congressmen who supported Obama's Iran deal suffer for it at the polls. As American politics become more polarized, there are more and more ideologically safe districts. Republican politicians worry more about challenges from the right, while Democratic politicians worry more about challenges from the left. The left, moreover, appears to be growing stronger.

An Emerging Liberal Majority?

In the late 1960s, Nixon strategist Kevin Phillips wrote a seminal book, *The Emerging Republican Majority*, which in effect predicted and strategized the "conservative years" of Chapter 2. This was part of a broader shift to the right among most Western democracies—tied to the end of cheap oil and built-up inflationary pressures in neo-Keynesian welfare states—but the Nixon–Reagan realignment also drew strength from distinctively American traumas of Vietnam, rising crime, and, above all, race.

In 2002, John B. Judis and Ruy Teixeira published their own mirror analysis, *The Emerging Democratic Majority*. In the book's introduction, they stated: "A longer trend . . . is leading American politics from the conservative Republican majority of the 1980s to a new Democratic majority. Democrats aren't there yet, but barring the unforeseen, they should arrive by the decade's end."[40] Like Phillips thirty-four years earlier, Judis and Teixeira were writing in the face of considerable intuition and street-level evidence to the contrary. George W. Bush's election in 2000 may have been disputed, but 2002 was the year that Republicans, after a brief hiatus, retook control of the Senate, thus placing the White House and both houses of Congress in conservative hands for the first time since the 1950s. Following the terrorist attacks of September 11, 2001, Republicans were well placed to exploit the advantages that they had traditionally enjoyed in voters' minds regarding national security, and Bush indeed took advantage, winning reelection in 2004 on his strengths as a "war president" even though the main war in question—in Iraq—was going badly. Moreover, there was a case to be made that Bill Clinton's two terms in office had manifested rather than repudiated the thesis of a conservative ascendancy. Clinton used decidedly centrist language—for example, declaring the "era of big government" to be over.

And yet, like Phillips in 1968, the theorists in 2002 of an emerging Democratic majority could point to what they regarded as inexorable socio-political trends favoring their argument. Obama's triumph in 2008 could be interpreted as a singular event—a consequence of voters' deep disaffection with the Bush administration, of the effects of a traumatic financial crisis, and of the excitement of transcending America's longstanding racial divide. His win in 2012, however, may indicate something more lasting. Its ingredients were precisely those that Judis and Teixeira had predicted would lead to a realignment by the end of the last decade. One should be cautious about sweeping predictions: Mitt Romney in 2012 won just under half the votes cast, and there are no permanent realignments in American politics. But Republicans now have a problem based on a pattern. Every four years the electorate is likely to be even younger and browner than the last time.

Demography is not destiny, and the Republican Party should be able to adapt, but as this book goes to press, a year away from a presidential election, the Republican Party's boisterous base is driving it further and further to the right.[41]

And yet America remains a closely divided two-party system. The Senate may be up for grabs, but Republicans will almost certainly hold onto the House of Representatives. They have their own structural advantage insofar as many Democratic voters are "wasted" with lopsided majorities in urban districts, whereas Republican voters are more evenly deployed with thinner majorities in suburban and rural districts. This advantage is compounded by success in midterm elections, when poorer minority voters—a crucial part of the Democratic constituency—are relatively less likely to turn up at the polls. Republican voters, by contrast, have been angry and agitated in recent midterm elections, driving a fierce reaction against Obama and his policies—with consequent high conservative turnout. Another consequence is a very strong Republican position in statehouses and governors' mansions, giving them an important strategic advantage.

If Democrats have an advantage, though certainly not a lock, on the presidency, this will be important for matters involving Israel.

Israel and a Polarized America

For most of its history, Israel has enjoyed real bipartisan support from Americans. Its most enthusiastic American supporters at the outset were liberals, among whom American Jews were crucial promoters and validators of a Jewish state that matched more or less comfortably with the liberal ethos.

The American Jewish community no longer plays this role in the same way, and Jews' nearly uniform support for Israel is fading. Peter Beinart, among the most astute observers of changes in American Jewish support for Israel, writes that liberal Jews used to make an exception for Israel, conferring on it a kind of asterisk regarding expected standards of liberal behavior and universal civil and political rights. This was understandable in purely human terms, and also because they knew the Israeli situation well enough to know in granular terms that the Jewish state was really in a difficult position, that resort to force and imperfect treatment of Arabs under its control were not completely, or even mainly, Israel's fault. Beinart's key point is that younger American Jews no longer confer the asterisk. This is partly because they are less connected to and knowledgeable about Israel, so they judge it like any other country. It is also because Israel's policies and behavior look less attractive and understandable after fifty years of occupation, especially as its politics move further rightward. Meanwhile, mainline Jewish organizations lobbying for Israel, notably AIPAC, themselves have moved to the right since the 1980s, and are less able to help Jewish liberals resolve their cognitive dissonance. "For several decades," Beinart writes, "the Jewish establishment has asked American Jews to check their liberalism at Zionism's door, and now, to their horror, they are finding than many young Jews have checked their Zionism instead."[42]

Beyond politics, there are broader sociological developments causing younger Jews to drift away from Israel. These include the alluvial effect of generations of intermarriage. As Steven Cohen, the dean of American sociologists who study the Jewish community, points out, 70 percent of the children of intermarried parents intermarry. And the rate of intermarriage has been accelerating. Before 1970, about one in six American Jews intermarried; in the following generation, the rate had climbed to four in ten.[43] Mixed marriages tend to transmit religious values and customs less diligently than marriages within the faith. With each generation, by and large, the connection to Israel and the strength of affiliation with the Jewish community tends to weaken. It is not unlikely that a religious connection to Jewish identity would have faded in any case. American Jews reflect a broader trend toward "no religion." Among U.S. Jewish millennials, disaffiliation characterizes about one-third of the age cohort. According to Pew polling, two-thirds of Jews of "no religion" do not raise their children to be Jewish, either in religious or in cultural terms. Among younger "no religions," the number who consider an attachment to Israel an essential part of being Jewish is about one out of five, about half the number of religious Jews who feel that way. This large segment of only loosely affiliated American Jewry will be less likely to vote on the basis of their feelings for Israel and somewhat more likely to object to Israeli policies that don't align with their generally liberal worldview.

There is, of course, a community of conservative—in some cases very conservative—American Jews, many but not all of whom favor Orthodox practice. There is evidence that the birthrate among Orthodox Jews is on the rise and, at some point, might offset the high rate of loss that this part of the American Jewish community has experienced in recent decades. The debate about the Iran deal in significant measure pitted conservative Jews against more numerous liberal Jews, and it was imbued with a bitterness commensurate with the perceived stakes, but also with a sense of betrayal that can characterize divided communities. American Jews are increasingly split into two camps: a liberal camp that is less concerned with Israel, and a more religious and political conservative camp that includes many American Jews who will be no less fervent in their support of a strong U.S.–Israel relationship. They will also inherit a robust lobbying infrastructure increasingly funded by like-minded men and women of wealth, including most famously the casino magnate Sheldon Adelson.

The billionaire Adelson is important mainly for his role in Republican politics. The Jewish population of the United States is small and the Jewish vote is limited. It was more important in national elections in the past when states such as New York were genuinely contested. Now their patterns of geographic concentration place American Jews largely in, or in the suburbs of, big cities in blue states. In the realm of national politics, they will be aligned with or subsumed by larger trends. Where the depth of concern for Israel as a dimension of Jewish identity will be important is in congressional elections. This clearly matters in the realm of foreign policy, as the opposition to the Iran nuclear deal showed clearly; but it is not decisive, as the outcome of the deal also showed clearly.

But Jews could matter as bellwethers. Like Jewish millennials, American youth generally are characterized as experiencing eroding religious affiliation. This could be important because of a strong correlation between religiosity and support for Israel.[44] Extending the Beinart thesis: Just as younger American Jews no longer confer an asterisk exempting Israel from liberal standards, so too American youth in general will be decreasingly patient.

The neoconservative principles of military force and moral certainty are again paramount in Republican circles; they preclude any ambivalence toward the Jewish state. Meanwhile, despite the emergence of a progressive cohort of young Evangelicals organized under the *Sojourner* banner, Evangelical support for Israel will likely be undimmed. Evangelical numbers, unlike those of Catholics and mainstream Protestants, have diminished only slightly in the past decade. Moreover, there are hardly any Evangelical Democrats—as a statistical matter, U.S. Evangelicals who vote, vote Republican. As we have seen, unquestioning support for Israeli policies is now a defining feature of the Republican foreign-policy platform. The combination of this posture with high levels of anti-Islamic sentiment among both Evangelicals and Republicans virtually guarantees sustained backing for tough Israeli policies. Eschatology might still play a role in the fervent Evangelical support for Israel, but at this stage political preference would be enough to sustain it.

The situation on the left will be harder to predict. The Democrats' projected growing strength has much to do with the demographic advance of minorities, and especially Hispanic minorities. While there is some evidence that Hispanics lack affinity for the Jewish state, or even the philo-Semitic impulses of their Anglo white compatriots, these factors could be too diffuse to substantially affect voting habits.[45] The asymmetry of interest might continue to operate in Israel's favor. There is, however, a subjective reality deriving from minorities' cultural and racial experience that should not be discounted—even if it relies on some speculation.

A life on the receiving end of racial or other discrimination makes people naturally more conscious of its various manifestations. In the decades-long discourse, both American and European, about Israel, there has been evident a sharp difference between "liberal" and "leftist" views. Liberals, though situated on the left of the spectrum, have been devoted to civil and individual liberties, and have been profoundly allergic to any hint of anti-Semitism. Leftists, in their anticolonial and antiracist zeal, have been more focused on matters of "justice" and redressing oppression. And on matters regarding Israel, they have been less careful about avoiding anti-Semitic tropes or associations. The left, in this and other respects, is sometimes illiberal.

We are not suggesting that the emergence of a Democratic majority based on demographic growth of Hispanic and other minorities will push the American center-left in an illiberal direction. The Democratic Party is a liberal party with traditions and principles that will continue to shape minority discourse. What we are suggesting, however, is that the growth of minorities in a party that already contains most of them will inform its discourse on an Israeli ally that is moving further in the direction of Jewish nationalism and away from the idea of equal rights for Arabs under its control.

Obama is a liberal, not a leftist, but his liberalism is certainly informed by a black man's perspective on civil rights. Recall from Chapter 3 that Condoleezza Rice, obviously no leftist, referred to her own childhood in the segregated South in articulating sympathy for the plight of Palestinians. As America becomes a majority-minority country, this sensibility will become more important.

And it will inflame the left–right divide in America. It has been a theme of this chapter that predictions are hard; even as Democrats' supporters increase as a share of the population, factors of polarization and Republican hegemony in the House of Representatives will continue. In a closely divided country there will also obviously be Republican presidents. But Israel should worry about becoming a left–right issue in American politics.

A Broken Mirror

The emotional dimension of the American connection to Israel is complex. But the cognitive process that has sustained it is the fairly simple one of mirror imaging. Americans who looked at Israel saw themselves.

Otto Preminger, director of *Exodus*, the 1961 blockbuster that chronicled the birth of the new state a mere thirteen years after the event, understood this well. There is a moment in the movie when Paul Newman, playing the Zionist hero Ari ben Canaan, brings his paramour, played by Eva Marie Saint, to the collective farm where his parents worked the land. As they approach the cabin that was Ari's childhood home, we see his father driving stakes, and then his mother emerging from the interior darkness of the house into the glare of the Mediterranean sun, squinting and shielding her eyes, dressed and coiffed like a sodbuster in a John Ford western. Viewers of a certain age would almost expect her call out, "Shane!"

Two and a half decades later, as the U.S.–Israeli relationship took on a strategic character, Americans looked to Israel and saw the fortitude and unblinking realism that they feared had been lost in the jungles of Vietnam and on decadent college campuses at home. In the 1977 film *Black Sunday*, a joint Palestinian–German revolutionary plot to massacre the spectators at a Super Bowl game nearly succeeds but for the intervention of a grimly tough Mossad agent who sidelines the timid, handwringing FBI agent in charge of the investigation. Robert Shaw, who played the Israeli, had one of the squarer jaws in Hollywood; Fritz Weaver, in the FBI role, had one of the pointier chins, coupled with eyebrows in a perpetual upside down V.[46]

It has been quite a while since these films were screened. Neither has been transferred to Blu-ray, which suggests that they are no longer much in demand. But of course much has changed. While it was once possible to project Manifest Destiny and the settlement of the frontier onto border kibbutzim, overlooking orange groves on one side and hostile states on the other, it is much harder to see Haredi settlements on the occupied West Bank in this light. The sustaining image of Israel as a democracy like that of the United States—an image that was essentially accurate even if it was excessively flattering to both sides—will become less compelling over time as Israeli skepticism about democracy grows in tandem with Palestinian pressure for civil rights. And Israel's Supreme Court, which has served as a powerful brake on illiberal government initiatives, will not be able to prop up the country's democratic traditions forever. As former Israeli Chief Justice Aharon Barak told one of us, "If my fellow Israelis do not want democracy, what can the court do?"[47]

The longstanding if self-congratulatory image of the United States and Israel as egalitarian societies where opportunity and socioeconomic mobility were guaranteed, a perception shaped by lingering if oddly juxtaposed images of kibbutzim and successful high-tech business sector, will also be hard to maintain. As Nobel Prize–winning economist Paul Krugman notes, 20.5 percent of the Israeli population is living on less than half the median income. Twenty years ago, the proportion of the population living in poverty was half that number. The ratio is higher for children; between one-quarter and one-third of Israeli children are living in poverty. "Both numbers," says Krugman, "are the worst in the advanced world, by a large margin."[48] At the same time, a handful of families, who benefited from the crony economy of the 1980s when state enterprises were privatized, control half the value of Israel's stock market through a maze of shell corporations.[49]

Another mirror image threatened by the evolution of Israeli politics, and by the difficult strategic environment in which those politics are practiced, is called by the Israelis "purity of arms" (*tohar haneshek*). The gist of the concept is that Israel's army is used to fight only defensive or preemptive wars of "no choice" (*ein breira*) and that it does so with the aim of protecting enemy noncombatants from harm. This was both possible and largely true until 1982, when Menachem Begin launched the Lebanon invasion explicitly as a war of choice, which could not as a practical matter avoid collateral damage. Avoiding such damage is no longer even conceivable. Israeli combat operations are no longer confined to the vast desert space of the Sinai Peninsula or the windswept plateau of the Golan. Israel's wars are now fought in cities and other densely populated and built-up areas, where enemy soldiers are necessarily embedded within a civilian population and infrastructure. Like the U.S. military, and for good reason, the IDF is casualty averse. In an urban environment, however, this means shifting the burden to the other side through the use of firepower that can never be sufficiently discriminating to avoid killing civilians. The resulting images of advanced American aircraft and missiles striking the teeming slums of Gaza will undermine the IDF's reputation among Americans who admired Israel precisely for its restraint. Unless Israel can reach an accommodation with the Palestinians, the adverse effects on public opinion will not be susceptible to better messaging.

THE GROWING DIVIDE between the two countries was illustrated in the 2015 publication of a book, with associated interviews and short articles, from newly elected Israeli Knesset member Michael Oren—the same Oren who had been Israel's ambassador to Washington and who had engaged in the published email exchange with David Rothkopf quoted in Chapter 1. Oren, in his book, scoured Barak Obama's biography for an explanation of why US–Israeli relations had been so troubled during the Obama presidency. The answer, Oren claimed, must be in Obama's unfulfilled relations with two Muslim fathers—his actual Kenyan father who left his white mother when Obama was an infant, and the Indonesian stepfather whose marriage with his mother also did not last—as well as his exposure to anti-Zionist claptrap at the elite universities that he attended. All of this, in Oren's view, made Obama vulnerable to the lure of the minaret and therefore determined to improve America's relations with "the Muslim world." Oren also psycho-analyzed American Jewry, suggesting that some liberal American Jews have criticized Israel out of resentment, because the Jewish state has "further complicat[ed] their already-conflicted identity." He added: "Pondering these questions, I could not help questioning whether American Jews really felt as secure as they claimed."[50] He further pondered the religious development of this book's Jewish coauthor, calling him an "apostate" and a "WASP"[51]—a rather hilarious idea for Simon's friends and colleagues who see his over-the-top *fun dem shtetl*—straight from the Eastern European ghetto—demeanor and enthusiastic embrace of Jewish identity, which includes ritual practice.

For someone with the background (born in New Jersey, educated at Princeton and Columbia) and with the official responsibility to understand America, this was toweringly inane.[52] And there were echoes of the inanity in early 2016, when Netanyahu's former spokesperson and chief of staff called the U.S. ambassador Dan Shapiro an Uncle Tom for publicly stating the U.S. government's view on legal arrangements prevailing in the West Bank.[53] (The epithet *yehudon* is typically rendered "Jewboy," but in context it carries the sense of Uncle Tom, or perhaps, "Court Jew.") It was not the first time that current or former Israeli officials have stigmatized U.S. officials who were Jewish. When Daniel Kurtzer was the U.S. ambassador to Israel, he was referred to publicly as a *yehudon* at least twice. And when one of the U.S. Defense Department's most senior officials, Dov Zakheim, called into question the wisdom of using all of Israel's U.S. assistance money to build a fighter plane aimed for the export market, he was referred to as a *bahur yehudi nehmad*, a nastily sarcastic appropriation of the English term, "nice Jewish boy." Such vilifications are important because they reveal a view of the Jewish diaspora as illegitimate, or perhaps simply of no consequence, meaning, or integrity as a community of Jews. In the process, they raise issues about dual loyalty among Jewish-American officials that Americans themselves put to rest a long time ago (to their everlasting credit), while perpetuating a mercifully obsolete vision of the place of the Jew in American society—the notion that to secure their livelihoods, Jews had to deny their Jewishness.

The overall message from the Israeli government, in any event, is that the United States is not a very good ally. To many Americans, especially on the Republican side of the political divide, this message is pure catnip. To many others, it is puzzling at best and, at its worst, alienating—as when Israeli officials are quoted for the record saying that the secretary of state is idiotic when he proposes that Israel and the Palestinians take cautious and commonsensical measures to tamp down violence in Jerusalem.[54] Israeli officials in conversations with U.S. journalists display a powerful resentment against the United States.[55] In conducting off-the-record interviews with former Israeli security officials for an academic study that preceded this book, the authors were astounded by the vituperative language directed at the Obama administration over the peace process and more broadly the U.S. approach to the Arab Spring. This tone is generally puzzling for those Americans who believe that their country has remained Israel's most faithful supporter. The consequent cognitive dissonance cannot be healthy for the most important image of all: that the United States and Israel have each other's back.

8

The Struggle to Save an Alliance

IN LATE 2011, Avigdor Lieberman, then Israel's foreign minister, received a high-level U.S. delegation in Jerusalem. In a series of careful and upbeat presentations, Lieberman and his team made the case that Israel could forge a new alliance framework involving Russia, China, India, and other countries. The United States would remain important to Israel both strategically and culturally, of course, but many of the benefits of Israel's American alliance would be available from these other powers with no strings attached. The Israelis' tone was friendly, but their sobering presentation conveyed deep disdain for the encumbrances, especially regarding the Palestinians, that Washington attaches to its support. Simon, who was among the visiting Americans, left wondering what would happen if Israel found itself in real peril, yet the ties of interest and affection between the United States and Israel had become too weak to sustain an American rescue.

Lieberman is a controversial figure, at least in America, where even passionate Zionists have castigated him for anti-Arab racism.[1] But he is not the only important Israeli who has been thinking about strategic alternatives to the United States. After countless American votes and vetoes against UN resolutions that Israel didn't like, the Israeli ambassador to the UN, Ron Prosor, was notably absent when U.S. envoy Samantha Power rounded up votes for a General Assembly resolution condemning Russia's annexation of Ukraine. There were probably multiple reasons for his abstention—including a desire to avoid establishing yet another predicate for UN condemnation of territorial annexation—but one motive was surely the ties to Russia that Jerusalem has worked to strengthen since at least the 1990s. Israeli officials were delighted when India's government declined to support a UN report accusing Israel of war crimes in Gaza.[2] And Chinese social media, as Martin Indyk has observed, ran strongly in Israel's favor during the same war. "I think there's a sense in Israel, particularly on the right, that they can afford to be defiant of the United States," Indyk continued, adding:

> Now some politicians on the right feel that standing up to the United States is a cheap way to assert their independence and patriotism. I don't remember a situation before where right-wing Israeli politicians could disparage the United States' leadership and yet gain popularity. And maybe it's because they don't seem to pay any price for it. But I suspect that it's something deeper. There's a sense that Israel has become a power in its own right, and it doesn't need the United States as much. It's a kind of hubris.[3]

That hubris might stem also from the rhetoric of permanence that recent U.S. presidents have used to describe the American commitment to Israel. There have been frequent assertions of unbreakable devotion from the last three American presidents, including Obama. This ritual is so familiar that it may not be understood how new it is; the speeches and other public remarks of George H. W. Bush, Richard Nixon, or even Ronald Reagan did not contain anything approaching this steady stream of endearments.

What Kind of Alliance?

The partnership between Israel and the United States is unique. The small country certainly takes up a large bandwidth of American political discourse and policymakers' attention, as the debate about it oscillates between emphasis on the alliance as a strategic partnership and stress on the relationship as a moral bond. There have been times when the strategic value to the United States was clear. Israel's 1967 occupation of Egyptian territory gave the Nixon, Ford, and Carter administrations leverage to pull Cairo away from the Soviet Union and into the American camp. The Reagan administration recognized that, in case of conflict with the Soviets, Israel could provide an important base of operations in the eastern Mediterranean. Israel's invasion of Lebanon imposed moral and political costs for the United States. But Israel's deft use of American aircraft—to shoot down dozens of Syrian-piloted MIG fighters and to demolish Syria's network of Soviet-supplied missiles in the Beka'a Valley—probably enhanced the credibility of American conventional deterrence in the final years of the Cold War.[4] With the end of the Cold War, George H. W. Bush's administration's strategic assessment was more ambivalent. In the war to repel Iraq's invasion of Kuwait, Washington considered the link with Israel to be mainly a diplomatic complication, albeit a manageable one. And it was manageable as well in relation to America's broader interests in the Middle East—both during and after the Cold War—because autocratic Arab states made hardheaded calculations about their need for American protection and rarely, if ever, had to worry about popular sentiment in real elections.

Is Israel a strategic asset for the United States now and in the future? The answer, in cold and narrow terms, and considering the broader context of American interests in a Middle East in convulsive turmoil, is that the value of the asset is real but limited. Israel in its region possesses unparalleled intelligence capabilities, but it does not always have the right answer; in any event, America's tactical and strategic difficulties will only be marginally eased with better intelligence. Israel, despite its serious economic and educational problems, remains a fountainhead of innovation and high technology. But the fountainhead is relatively small, a "miracle on the margin" in the words of one American high-tech executive, and America, for all its problems, is not really short on technology and innovation. Israel, finally, and despite its profound conflict with the Palestinians, is a small island of stability in a region of violent and worsening instability. Its internal stability, however, does not project stability to its neighbors.

It is difficult to conjure the scenarios in which Israel would facilitate the projection of American power or the pursuit of American purposes in the region. The reason, of course, is political. As this book goes to press, the United States is conducting air strikes against ISIS targets in Iraq and Syria, but the realities of Arab politics preclude using Israeli airfields for those missions. And those politics would become irrelevant to America's broader purposes and strategy only in a situation of such dire chaos and threat that the overriding purpose of America's alliance with Israel would be to protect Israel.

Protecting Israel is in fact a solemn obligation of American power. It is a moral obligation that derives from the two countries' long association, from their shared democratic heritage, from their common cultures, including religious cultures and, above all, from the circumstances of Israel's birth in the

Nazi Holocaust—an event of vast scale in the history of human suffering and evil. The Jewish people warrant the protection of their own state, because history taught them in the vilest terms that there is no other sure protection.

The centrality of the obligation suggests that it would be absolute and eternal. Yet absolute moral obligations are logically problematic if they entail harm to others, including stateless Palestinians. What's more, even if the obligation *should* last forever, that does not mean, in practical terms, that it *will* last forever. Even in the course of reaffirming her own genuine commitment to Israel, presidential candidate Hillary Clinton has very specifically acknowledged the threats to the relationship that we have laid out in this book. "Because there is a new generation in both countries today," Clinton writes,

> that does not remember our shared past; young Americans who didn't see Israel in a fight for survival again and again, and young Israelis who didn't see the United States broker peace at Camp David or kindle hope at Oslo or stand behind Israel when it was attacked. They are growing up in a different world.[5]

Israel has become another cause of partisan contention in the United States. Republican and Democratic politicians continue to express bipartisan support for the country, but the polls clearly show a divergence among the parties' polarized bases. Perhaps unconditional support for Israel can be carried forward by Republican conviction and the ability of Republican politicians to frighten their opponents with accusations of anti-Israel animus, such as have been directed against President Obama. But for Israel to count on this polarized basis of American support into the indefinite future would be a huge gamble.

Isolation and Legitimacy

Many Israelis recognize these trends, and characterize them as the "Europeanization" of America. They do not mean it as a compliment. They tie it to what they perceive as a global campaign to "delegitimize" Israel, a campaign that they believe many Europeans have joined with great enthusiasm.

Israelis point frequently to the selectivity of European human rights concerns. Israel, they say, is singled out for its injustices against Palestinians amidst much greater abuses in the Arab Middle East, in Iran, and in the world at large. The European Union's promulgation of regulations for the labeling of Israeli products produced in the West Bank, presumably to make them easier to be boycotted by consumers, reminds Israelis of historical boycotts of "Jewish" businesses, and blurs into the broader BDS ("Boycott, Divest, Sanction") movement, whose promoters are, at best, vague about accepting the idea of a Jewish state. Then there are the periodic university campaigns for academic isolation of Israeli scholars—a truly insidious assault on liberal discourse and values.

For many Israelis, and some of their American supporters, the reason for singling out Israel is obvious. It is because Israel is populated by Jews. This conviction that European, and some American, criticism of Israel derives from eternal anti-Semitism should not be advanced carelessly—but neither can it be discounted entirely. It is difficult to accurately poll attitudes that are widely understood to be uncivilized. We should also be wary of fitting isolated events into preexisting narratives; for example, the April 13, 2014, shootings, with three dead, at the Kansas City Jewish Center by a professed neo-Nazi, would have resonated differently if they had occurred in Germany or France. With these caveats, we would assert that, in our experience, one encounters casual anti-Semitism in Europe—among white Europeans of Christian heritage—that that one does not encounter so readily in the United States.[6]

The main and most virulent source of anti-Semitism in Europe, however, is among radicalized Arabs, as well as other radicalized Muslims, in France and other European countries. It happens that France also has the largest remaining Jewish community in Europe, and it is objectively under threat. The January 2015 terror rampage that started with killings at the offices of the satirical magazine *Charlie Hebdo* ended with hostage-taking and killings in a kosher grocery in Paris. Terrorists in Europe have chosen numerous other Jewish targets and victims in recent years. France's Prime Minister Manuel Valls said after *Charlie Hebdo* that the real prospect of a Jewish exodus from his country posed a threat of historic national defeat. "If 100,000 French people of Spanish origin were to leave, I would never say that France is not France anymore," said Valls, whose parents were Spanish immigrants. "But if 100,000 Jews leave, France will no longer be France. The French Republic will be judged a failure."[7] In guarding against this threat, France and the rest of Europe must also somehow accommodate its Muslim citizens.

This is a huge challenge, a continuing historical legacy from the age of colonization and the traumas of decolonization.

Israeli suspicions of European motives are understandable, just as their vigilance against delegitimization is justified. Yet while it is problematic to selectively target the flaws of Israeli democracy, it is also problematic to wilfully ignore Israel's undemocratic direction. Moreover, nonviolent struggle for human rights requires—to some extent, at least—a strategy of "delegitimizing" the denial of those rights. Palestinians have the inherent right to say that their status is illegitimate, and to seek foreign support in changing that status. Martin Luther King Jr. led marchers at Selma and elsewhere to delegitimize the Jim Crow system of racial oppression. Yet the strategic and moral genius of his campaign was to ground it in the traditions and principles of America's founding documents: the Declaration of Independence and the U.S. Constitution. He challenged the illegitimacy of racial subjugation with reference to the fundamental legitimacy of the American system and the "inalienable" human rights enshrined in those documents.

A problem with the Palestinians is that too few of them may be capable of the generosity of understanding contained in Martin Luther King's appeal to white America. Many, perhaps most, Palestinians are trapped in their own competing narrative of *al Nakba*, suffering, and the imperative of justice. To be clear, this narrative is not altogether false, but Israelis of good will are understandably skeptical of how it could be the basis of genuine reconciliation.

This is where America remains so important. America, of all nations in the world, is not only Israel's most powerful protector; it is also the one powerful country that emotionally intuits the legitimacy of the Zionist project. It understands, as Beinart put it, that while there is a tension, there is no insoluble contradiction between a Jewish state for a historically stateless and persecuted people, and a democratic state of equal rights for Jewish and Arab citizens.[8] America's acceptance of this compatibility is grounded in a bipartisan tradition that combines conservative and liberal values. Conservatives bring to their support for Israel their regard for tradition, for religious values, and for national security. Liberals bring an emphasis on sympathy for the oppressed and downtrodden; sensitivity to racial, religious, and ethnic discrimination; and an emphasis on rights, diversity, and economic security. American friendship with Israel helps to legitimize its unique tensions—between a religious state and a modern secular state; and between its humane values and its military necessities. But America's legitimizing role is threatened, both by the American polarization in which conservatives and liberals no longer recognize the other side's values, and by trends in Israel that could make it unrecognizable to its American friends.

Even if they deny that they are culpable in causing it, many Israelis worry about their growing international isolation. If Israel's illiberal evolution can be stopped, America could play a useful role in ending that isolation, first by reconciling Israel and Europe. The history is unbelievably dark, but there are also good memories. Israel started as a European outpost; Ashkenazi settlers, however traumatized, brought with them a cherished European culture; in the 1950s and 1960s there was a fashionable ideological interchange among sister socialist parties, as well as a stylish buzz about the Israeli experiment in modernism (the buzz included the "boatloads of Swedish au pairs" that one of our middle-aged Israeli interlocutors remembered fondly). And whatever the extent of anti-Semitism in their diverse and troubled populations, most European leaders have made a good-faith effort to exercise their responsibilities as inheritors of the continent where the Holocaust occurred, and they have understood that these responsibilities include maintaining a special relationship with Israel. But those leaders, who include Germany's Angela Merkel, are becoming more critical as Israeli policies make the relationship harder to sustain politically.

A Grand Bargain

"If something cannot go on forever, it will stop." This truism, famously codified as "Stein's Law," was Nixon administration economist Herbert Stein's acerbic argument against the lazy extrapolation of unsustainable economic trends (as though their very unsustainability would not at some point affect their trajectory). The economic principle has some relevance to political and strategic relations between peoples and states.

We fear that a different set of unsustainable trends threaten the sustainability of the U.S.–Israeli alliance. There are, however, plausible scenarios that would disrupt such an outcome. To begin with, the Republican candidate might win the presidential election in November 2016, or in 2020. While past Republican presidents have adhered to an international consensus against Israeli settlements and favored some kind of two-state solution (and have, in fact, tended to prefer center-left Israeli governments), future Republican control over both Congress and the White House could consolidate the growing alliance between Likud and the Republican Party. Worsening domestic terrorism in both countries could sustain the electoral hegemony of both parties, as they promise a hard response and deride the flabbiness of center-left alternatives. In a worst case, the United States and Israel could be joined darkly in a kind of shared Trumpismo.[9]

Israel could also complicate things by announcing and implementing a unilateral withdrawal from much of the West Bank. The government would likely include in this announcement language to the effect that while decades of fruitless negotiations had shown that there was no genuine Palestinian partner for peace, Israel remained ready to negotiate further. But it would also announce that most if not all current Jewish settlements—that is, most of "Area C" as stipulated in the Oslo Accords—would be annexed to the Jewish state. The security barrier would be extended accordingly. The rump Palestine after this move would be neither economically nor politically viable. Yet even a Democratic White House might be hard pressed to effectively challenge the Israeli move. And if it bred worsening Palestinian conditions, then an Israel flanked by a second Gaza might enjoy the sympathy, or at least the grudging acquiescence, of a U.S. government that by this point could offer no credible advice for improving the situation.

But the more likely scenario is a continuation of current policies, with continued building of settlements creating more facts on the ground, a piecemeal Palestinian territory lacking contiguity and therefore viability, a weakened and ineffective Palestinian Authority with limited real authority, and the strengthening of illiberal forces in Israeli politics. Among those illiberal forces there are voices that today call for a "Jordanian solution"—a solution that Ariel Sharon advocated in his more right-wing days—entailing tacit or more coercive pressure on Palestinians to move across the Jordan River. A more liberal America—the scenario we consider more likely—would find this very hard to swallow (as would any Democratic administration or Republican administration resembling those of the past). But even short of this troubling scenario, the danger to a U.S.–Israeli alliance is real and present.

It is serious enough to require the exploration of initiatives within the capacity of the United States that might alter Israeli behavior in ways that strengthen the moral bond while also injecting it with renewed strategic vigor. The initiatives would have to be dramatic enough to change the direction of

Israeli policy. Some eminent retired American diplomats have suggested that the United States should stop vetoing UN resolutions and introduce its own with a detailed American plan for peace. In their anger and frustration following Netanyahu's behavior in his 2015 campaign, White House officials suggested that this might happen, or that they would work with French diplomats to shape and then support a Security Council resolution that Paris would table in the fall of 2015. But 2015 is over. It is unlikely that the Obama administration would make any such move during a presidential election campaign in which it fervently hopes to see a Democratic mandate to preserve the achievements of the Obama presidency. And Hillary Clinton has already signaled an aversion to involving the UN on questions related to the peace process. The likelihood of a Republican president doing so appears vanishingly small. Moreover, although such a move might bring greater consistency and credibility to U.S. diplomacy, it could risk counterproductive consequences in Israel itself. It is possible that it would have a salutary effect on those elites who would be desperate to avoid a breach with the United States. But it is also possible that it would empower those who are already looking for one.

The United States should table its peace plan. But it should do so in the context of a grand bargain that would offer the Israelis otherwise unattainable benefits. The form could be a defense treaty that would bring Israel under formal American protection and that would extend the U.S. nuclear umbrella explicitly and formally. The United States could offer to reinforce the deterrent power of this commitment and enhance Israel's defenses by deploying a tripwire in the shape of a U.S.-manned ABM system, although one could imagine other kinds of tripwire deployments. An attack against Israel would therefore be an attack against the United States and, given the tripwire presence, put U.S. troops at risk. Such an attack would automatically warrant a strong U.S. response. This arrangement would be codified as a treaty alliance requiring painstaking negotiation and ratification by a two-thirds majority of the U.S. Senate.

The negotiations would require precision about the borders of the country that the United States was committing itself to defend, and the negotiations could only be opened on the basis of a full and complete freeze of settlement activities. It would be understood that successful completion of negotiations would entail the dismantlement of many settlements. The goal would be to stage the treaty negotiations simultaneously with final status negotiations between Israel and the Palestinians. The final status accord might not be reached; perhaps the Palestinians would prove that they were not genuine partners for peace. But Israel would have to demonstrate that it was such a partner, by committing itself to the arrangements that Prime Ministers Ehud Barak and Ehud Olmert accepted at Taba and Annapolis—effectively the Clinton parameters. This means the borders referenced in President Obama's May 2011 speech—June 1967 lines adjusted through mutually agreed land swaps. It means a refugee settlement entailing, at most, symbolic returns to Israel proper and compensation for both Arab refugees and Jews forced to flee Arab countries in the postwar era. It means shared sovereignty of an undivided Jerusalem (yes, these are weasel words, but not beyond the capacity of diplomats to actualize), with a special status for the Holy Basin.

The idea of a formal defense treaty is not new. In 1954 Israel raised the idea of either joining NATO or reaching a bilateral defense pact with the United States. Ben-Gurion, as we have seen, pushed for ever closer and more formalized relations. After the 1967 Six Day War, it was American diplomats and scholars who proposed a defense pact in exchange for Israel's withdrawal from occupied territories. Now Israelis became suspicious of the idea, because they saw clearly the constraints that a treaty would impose and the costs Israel would have to pay: handing over the Sinai, the Golan, and the West Bank, which "were perceived as the ultimate guarantees of its security."[10] Moshe Dayan, Yitzhak Rabin, and their contemporary Zionist general and statesman Yigal Allon all warned at various times against trading defensible borders and IDF autonomy for uncertain military guarantees. Eventually, however, those Israeli-left politicians who were ready to contemplate significant territorial concessions returned to the idea of a formal American guarantee. The Shimon Peres government, pursuing a peace agreement with Syria, in April 1986, retabled the idea of a defense treaty.[11] Elections that year and the beginning of the Netanyahu government froze the initiative. But then, at the July 2000 Camp David summit, Labor prime minister Ehud Barak—again ready for significant territorial compromise—also presented a detailed plan for a defense treaty with the United States. As then Clinton aide Bruce Riedel has recalled, Barak proposed that the United States and Israel conclude a formal mutual defense agreement including a commitment by the US to come to the assistance of Israel in the event of attack in the future, enshrined in a treaty to be ratified by the Congress and the Knesset. This treaty would be fully like the American treaty relationship with its NATO allies, and thus include a nuclear umbrella commitment by the US, i.e., an American promise to respond to a nuclear attack on Israel with American nuclear forces.[12]

Israelis have continued to debate the idea off and on. Dore Gold, a Likud intellectual, warned in 1995 that the formal defense treaty could be a trap, luring a complacent Israel into dangerous security concessions and inviting renewed American pressure against Israel's deterrence policy.[13] But three years later, the Israeli Institute for National Security Studies asked Yair Evron, a prominent political scientist of the realist school, to look at the question. His measured response was, on balance, supportive. It was also prescient. Not only would a treaty enhance Israel's own deterrent capability, he wrote, but it would also provide important insurance against a possible change in U.S. commitment, which even in 1998, he argued, could not be discounted. Evron also dismissed the arguments regarding Israeli self-reliance, as outmoded in a changing international order.[14] Today other Israelis will complain that a defense treaty with America cannot protect against the more diffuse security threats they face: knife attacks by Palestinians, the rise of ISIS in neighboring countries and the terrifying prospect of its black flags in Israel proper, falling regimes and growing anarchy across the Middle East. But this complaint would reflect a dangerous, albeit understandable, confusion in Israeli strategic discourse. Israeli leaders have been practically yelling at Washington that their overwhelming threat comes from a state: Iran. A defense treaty would be the best possible reinsurance against that threat. Organized terrorism is a threat that Israel, proudly, is very good at countering. General violence by knife-wielding Palestinians is a prospect that only wise politics, including a negotiated settlement, can stave off.

A grand bargain could take other forms, in addition or as alternatives to the treaty suggested above. Right-wing European politicians including former prime ministers Silvio Berlusconi of Italy and José Maria Aznar of Spain have advocated Israeli membership in the European Union. They were not taken seriously, and rightly so; Aznar said that Israel should be admitted "without preconditions," a preposterous idea. But it is worth reflecting on how badly European governments would like to see an end to the Israeli–Palestinian conflict, and how much they might be willing to pay for it.[15] Other European and American politicians have advocated NATO membership—again, a difficult prospect to imagine when Israel has undefined borders, but perhaps not so preposterous on the basis of a peace agreement. And there might be scope for a more progressive version of the Jordanian option. Although the Hashemite Kingdom severed its connection to the West Bank in 1987, and hasn't looked back, a confederation between the kingdom and an independent Palestine, perhaps even including some association with Israel, could be thinkable on the basis of a truly bold Israeli vision.

There are precedents for such bargains. Profound constitutional changes in Turkey were impelled by the prospect of EU accession, a prize that was hugely desirable to Turkish elites. Up to the point that the EU began to negotiate seriously the possibility of Turkish membership, Turkey's politics were dominated by the military, civil liberties were severely limited, minority rights were disregarded, and political and economic reforms were hobbled by the resistance of entrenched interests. Many observers in the early 1990s held out very little hope for progress as violent conflict permeated Turkish life and Turkey's larger role as a NATO member dwindled with the collapse of the Soviet Union. The point is that the prize was so grand that it thoroughly reshaped Turkish perceptions and incentives.[16] The way was paved for comprehensive reform. With the benefit of hindsight we now know that Turkey was unlikely to be admitted to the EU, whether for cultural reasons or because EU enlargement had reached its destabilizing limits. But at that moment disappointment still lay in the future.

Turkey, it must be said, has not turned out brilliantly. The hybrid mix of Kemalist democracy and military rule has been replaced by an elected Islamist government with authoritarian tendencies—precisely what the Kemalists said they feared all along. However, Turkey is unquestionably more democratic than in the days of hard and soft military coups. The precedent, moreover, speaks in Israel's favor. Whatever the undemocratic trends that we fear, and have criticized in these pages, Israel, much more than Turkey, has been a genuine and vibrant democracy, with a liberal heritage and culture. It has venerable democratic traditions that can be strengthened. Our proposed grand bargain should appeal to and empower the liberal and secular aspirations of Tel Aviv, over the more conservative and religious forces in Jerusalem. But not entirely. America's presentation of such a choice to the Israelis would, if taken seriously, roil Israeli society. But the purpose is to avoid, not precipitate, civil conflict (although removal of settlers probably will entail some violence in any event). To be successful the grand bargain would have to appeal to conservatives as well.

There is hope that it might, because it would be an offer that would be difficult for sensible people to refuse. There will be Israelis who are beyond the offer's reach. Part of Israeli society is determined to hold on to the West Bank, considers the settlements in theological terms as part of salvation history, and in the most extreme version believes that the murder of a prime minister was morally preferable to breaking a compact with God. These Israelis will not be impressed by a treaty requiring concessions that, in their view, disrupt the moral order of the universe. Other Israelis are convinced that United States is unreliable under any circumstances, that Israel's threat environment precludes territorial compromise, and that Israel's future lies in tacit alliances with Gulf monarchies and Asian powers. But the Israeli right is not monolithic and not all of its key players would subscribe to any of these propositions. The bargain should appeal to the kind of right-wing ministers—including Yuval Steinitz, Benny Begin (son of Menachem), and even Moshe Ya'alon—who in 2012 ended up blocking the plan to bomb Iran's nuclear facilities.[17] They did so, it appears evident, at least partly out of concern for wrecking the alliance with America.

It may not work. Israelis may believe they have the benefits of alliance already, without the encumbrances. And yet the current government has loudly and repeatedly cast doubt on Washington's promise to prevent Iran from building nuclear weapons. If ministers do not believe in American protection, perhaps they should get it in writing.

It may not work also because the internal political challenge would be too difficult for Israel to master. An Israel–Palestine agreement would necessitate the relocation of more than 100,000 settlers.[18] This relocation effort will be unimaginably hard. Many settlers are in the West Bank because they are ideologically committed to Jewish ownership of the land, but they also live there in quotidian ways that amount to more than a political statement or religious expression. There will be passive and active resistance to relocation, including resort to violence against Israeli authorities and against Arabs whom the settlers will see as benefiting from their tragedy. The integrity of the IDF will be tested by calls for mutiny. And there will be the question of destination: Where will all these people live? In close proximity to Israeli Arabs? And how will they influence the political direction of the country and therefore the implementation of Israeli obligations under the terms of a peace agreement and Israel's defense treaty with the United States? These are deep questions, and they raise an even deeper question: Is it too late?

There is also the danger that Jerusalem will manage to pocket the offer of alliance without delivering on Israel's side of the grand bargain. The character of American politics, together with the genuine difficulty of reaching accommodation with the Palestinians, makes this one-sided result possible. The administration that negotiated such a treaty would need to be firm in its demands, and ready to walk away. At the end of the day, however, we do not worry about this prospect, because we believe that the United States is practically committed to Israel's defense anyway. The downside of formal negotiations is not very steep. The upside would be a process to define mutual obligations, not just America's commitment to Israel.

A purely strategic alliance—one without moral or emotional content—can function well until the strategic ground shifts. This has happened in America's strategic partnerships with both Pakistan and Saudi Arabia; the relationships endure, but they are rocky. The American link to Israel was always more like its European alliances, with both strategic and moral roots (and a considerable American entanglement in the domestic politics of individual European countries as well as Israel). In the European case, the moral dimension had great strategic effect. The transatlantic alliance proved winning over a long Cold War in precisely the way that George Kennan predicted at the Cold War's beginning. In 1947 he wrote, "If western Europe . . . could be made the home of a vigorous, prosperous and forward-looking civilization—the Communist regime in eastern Europe would never be able to stand the comparison."[19]

Israel in its region has not exerted the same moral magnetism, for reasons associated with its birth before 1949 and its expansion in 1967. But from the outset there has been moral magnetism between Israel and America. Both the strategic and emotional dimensions have been profound and enduring. It is these that are now threatened. A grand bargain should aim to restore both. Treaty alliances are, by definition, strategic commitments.

America will always maintain that defending democracies is an important national interest, and if this grand bargain helps strengthen Israel's democracy, it will help secure a common future.

The plausible alternative should not be ignored: a dysfunctional couple in a loveless marriage, moving inexorably in separate ways.

Acknowledgments

Many have helped this book along the way. It would not have been possible without the generous support of the Robert and Ardis James Foundation and Richard (Rick) E. Grove Jr. Both Bob James and Rick Grove were also thoughtful interlocutors on the large questions raised by our project.

The book comes out of a two-and-a-half-year research project that engaged a number of talented research assistants. Asaf Zilberfarb of Dartmouth College provided crucial support throughout the project, guiding us through Hebrew sources and providing his own informed insights into Israeli politics. Others came in at various stages from Allin's home base at the International Institute for Studies (IISS) and from among his students at the Johns Hopkins University School of Advanced International Studies (SAIS): Zach Abels, Giacomo Baldini, Stephan Crosse, John Drennan, Paulina Izewicz, Holly Martin, Guilia Parzani, Luigi Scazzieri, Madeleine Schnur, and Caitlin Vito. Our research also involved many hours of interviews with current and former U.S. and Israeli officials; we are grateful for their time and their insights.

A number of colleagues have reviewed chapters or the whole manuscript at various stages, or offered analytical guidance on specific questions, including participants in workshops at the IISS Global Strategic Review, the Harvard Kennedy School, Dartmouth College, and the Institute for National Security Studies in Tel Aviv; we thank Christoph Allin, Bernard Avishai, Peter Beinart, Aluf Benn, Shlomo Brom, Steven Brooks, John Carey, Dan Ben-David, Toby Dodge, Mark Fitzpatrick, Philip Gordon, Rick Grove, Matthew Harries, Mark Heller, Efraim Inbar, Daniel Kurtzer, Eli Levite, Martin Malia, Aaron David Miller, Steven Miller, Asaf Orion, Barry Posen, Ben Rhode, Gary Samore, James Steinberg, Jonathan Stevenson, Steven Walt, William Wohlforth, and Amos Yadlin.

The authors have enjoyed the support of other institutional colleagues: Simon's at Dartmouth College; Allin's at the IISS in London and Johns Hopkins SAIS in both Bologna and Washington, D.C. Allin additionally is grateful for the creative benefits of the now customary hospitality of David P. Calleo and Avis Bohlen at Casa Fangati on the island of Elba, the best place in the world to write portions of a book.

Portions of Chapters 1, 2, and 5 are adapted from essays by Allin and Simon posted on *Politics and Strategy,* the *Survival Editors' Blog* at the IISS, or published in *Survival: Global Politics and Strategy; Strategic Survey* (IISS); from Steven Simon and Daniel Benjamin, "Don't Create a New Al Qaeda," *New York Times,* January 6, 2014; and from Dana Allin, "Obama and the Middle East: The Politics, Strategies and Difficulties of American Restraint," in *Middle Eastern Security, the US Pivot and the Rise of ISIS,* ed. Toby Dodge and Emile Hokayem (Abingdon: Routledge for the IISS, 2014).

Clive Priddle, our editor at PublicAffairs, gave wise advice and a scrupulous eye to the shaping of the manuscript; Michael Carlisle of Inkwell Management weighed in at a crucial stage for thinking how this argument would work as a book.

Finally, it must be acknowledged that this, our second coauthored book, required, once again, the forbearance and ever-patient love and counsel of our immediate families: Virginia, on one side of the Atlantic; Elisabeth, Christoph, and Sophie, on the other. We are immensely grateful.

Notes

Introduction

1. Peter Beinart, "The Failure of the American Jewish Establishment," *New York Review of Books*, June 10, 2010, http://www.nybooks.com/articles/2010/06/10 /failure-american-jewish-establishment/; and Beinart, *The Crisis of Zionism* (New York: Times Books, 2012).

2. See, for example, Bernard Avishai, "Israel's New Political Center," *New Yorker*, March 16, 2015, http://www.newyorker.com/news/news-desk/israels-new -political-center.

3. The swelling of these communities has been encouraged by government benefits lavished on the Haredi sector.

4. Steven T. Rosenthal, *Irreconcilable Differences? The Waning of the American Jewish Love Affair with Israel* (Boston: Brandeis University Press, 2001).

Chapter 1

1. Michael Oren and David Rothkopf, "'A' Jewish State vs. 'The' Jewish State," *Foreign Policy*, May 15, 2015, http://foreignpolicy.com/2014/05/15/a-jewish-state-vs -the-jewish-state/.

2. Committee Study of the Central Intelligence Agency's Detention and Interrogation Program, Senate Select Committee on Intelligence, U.S. Government Printing Office, 2014, http://www.feinstein.senate.gov/public/index.cfm/senate -intelligence-committee-study-on-cia-detention-and-interrogation-program; see also Dana Priest and William M. Arkin, *Top Secret America: The Rise of the New American Security State* (New York: Little, Brown and Company, 2011).

3. Peter Grose, *Israel in the Mind of America* (New York: Alfred A. Knopf, 1983), p. 195.

4. Ibid., p. 159.

5. The lobby has also generally been careful to frame its cause in terms of moral values and American interests.

6. Native Americans suffered genocidal oppression, but they were not, of course, immigrants.

7. Grose, *Israel in the Mind of America*, pp. 73–74.

8. John B. Judis, *Genesis: Truman, American Jews, and the Origins of the Arab-Israeli Conflict* (New York: Farrar, Straus, and Giroux, 2015), p. 145.

9. Ibid., p. 155.

10. Simon Sebag Montefiore, *Jerusalem: The Biography* (London: Weidenfeld & Nicolson, 2011), p. 425.

11. Louis D. Brandeis, "The Jewish Problem: How to Solve It," speech to the Conference of Eastern Council of Reform Rabbis, April 25, 1915, http://louisville .edu/law/library/special-collections/the-louis-d.-brandeis-collection/the-jewish -problem-how-to-solve-it-by-louis-d.-brandeis.

12. Grose, *Israel in the Mind of America*, pp. 62–65.

13. Ibid., p. 67.

14. Montefiore, *Jerusalem*, p. 428.

15. Grose, *Israel in the Mind of America*, pp. 82–91.

16. U.S. Department of State, *Papers Relating to the Foreign Relations of the United States: The Lansing Papers, 1914–1920* (FRUS), Vol. 2, p. 71, http://digicoll .library.wisc.edu/cgi-bin/FRUS/FRUS-idx?type=goto&id=FRUS.FRUS19141920v2 &isize=M&submit=Go+to+page&page=71.

17. Though there had been strong and consistent official American protests against Russian persecutions of Jews.

18. Warren Bass, *Support Any Friend: Kennedy's Middle East and the Making of the US-Israel Alliance* (New York: Oxford University Press, 2003), p. 21.

19. Grose, *Israel in the Mind of America*, p. 146.

20. Ibid., p. 134.

21. There was little doubt that FDR, presiding over a nation at war, would win that election, but Dewey was Republican standard bearer again in 1948. That contest was famously expected to be a difficult one for Harry Truman.

22. Noah Feldman, *Scorpions: The Battles and Triumphs of FDR's Great Supreme Court Justices* (New York: 12 Hachette, 2010), p. 246.

23. Grose, *Israel in the Mind of America*, pp. 138–139.

24. U.S. Department of State, *Foreign Relations of the United States Diplomatic Papers, 1943: The Near East and Africa (1943)*, p. 790, http://digicoll.library.wisc.edu /cgi-bin/FRUS/FRUS-idx?type=turn&entity=FRUS.FRUS1943v04.p0802&id =FRUS.FRUS1943v04&isize=M.

25. Grose, *Israel in the Mind of America*, pp. 152–158.

26. On Truman's casual anti-Semitic remarks, see Judis, *Genesis*, p. 193. On his radical domestic agenda, see "Harry S. Truman: Domestic Affairs," The Miller Center of the University of Virginia, http://millercenter.org/president/biography /truman-domestic-affairs.

27. Judis, *Genesis*, pp. 4, 210. Our discussion of Truman's ambivalent Zionism, as well as the more general Zionist enthusiasm of mid-century American liberals, owes much to Judis's important book.

28. Grose, *Israel in the Mind of America*, pp. 167–176.

29. Tony Judt, *Postwar: A History of Europe Since 1945* (London: William Heinemann, 2005), pp. 803–831.

30. Department of State Bulletin, September 30, 1945, 13, pp. 456–463. Preliminary Report (Harrison) to President Truman on Displaced Persons in Germany and Austria, in J. C. Hurewitz, *The Middle East and North Africa in World Politics: A Documentary Record* (New Haven, CT: Yale University Press, 1979), pp. 812–819.

31. Ibid.

32. Benny Morris, *1948: The First Arab-Israeli War* (New Haven, CT: Yale University Press, 2008), pp. 31–34.

33. Dean Acheson, *Present at the Creation: My Years in the State Department* (New York: W. W. Norton & Company, 1987), p. 172; Dennis Ross, *Doomed to Succeed: The U.S.-Israel Relationship from Truman to Obama* (New York: Farrar, Straus, and Giraux, 2015), p. 10.

34. William Roger Louis, *Ends of British Imperialism: The Scramble for Empire, Suez, and Decolonization* (London: I. B. Tauris, 2006), p. 443.

35. Ross, *Doomed to Succeed*, pp. 13, 14.

36. FRUS, 1948, Vol. 1, Part 2, General; The United Nations, Document 4, Report by the Policy Planning Staff [Washington], February 24, 1948, https://history .state.gov/historicaldocuments/frus1948v01p2/d4.

37. To be clear, it was not just the State Department. As Dennis Ross recounts critically, many if not most of the national security Wise Men were opposed to the partition of Palestine and U.S. recognition of Israel. Ross catalogues this opposition in *Doomed to Succeed*, pp. 20–26.

38. Warren Bass, *Support Any Friend*, p. 31.

39. Ibid., p. 33.

40. Avi Shlaim, "The Debate About 1948," *International Journal of Middle East Studies* 27, no. 3 (August 1995): 393.

41. Avi Shlaim, "Israel and the Arab Coalition in 1948," in *The War for Palestine: Rewriting the History of 1948*, ed. Eugene L. Rogan and Avi Shlaim (New York: Cambridge University Press, 2007), pp. 80–81; see also Judis, *Genesis,* pp. 32–34.

42. Morris, *1948*, pp. 267–269.

43. Judis, *Genesis*, p. 326.

44. For an example and good summary of the archival research, see Benny Morris, "Revisiting the Palestinian Exodus of 1948," in Rogan and Shlaim, eds., *The War for Palestine*, pp. 37–59.

45. Montefiore, *Jerusalem*, p. 477.

46. Ibid., pp. 471–473.

47. Morris, *1948*, pp. 120–121.

48. Ari Shavit, "Lydda, 1948: A City, a Massacre and the Middle East Today," *New Yorker*, October 21, 2013, http://www.newyorker.com/magazine/2013/10/21/lydda-1948.

49. Ibid.

50. United Nations, Progress Report of the United Nations Mediator on Palestine Submitted to the Secretary-General for Transmission to the Members of the United Nations, Part 1, Section V, Paragraph 6, http://domino.un.org/unispal.nsf /9a798adbf322aff38525617b006d88d7/ab14d4aafc4e1bb985256204004f55fa, cited in Judis, *Genesis,* p. 330.

51. *The Acting Secretary of State to Certain Diplomatic and Consular Offices*, FRUS, 1948, Vol. 5, Part 2, The Near East, South Asia, and Africa, Document 593, https://history.state.gov/historicaldocuments/frus1948v05p2/d593, cited in Judis, *Genesis*, pp. 330–331.

52. *The President to Mr. Mark Ethridge, at Jerusalem* (April 29, 1949), FRUS, 1949, Vol. 6, The Near East, South Asia, and Africa, Document 612, https://history .state.gov/historicaldocuments/frus1949v06/d612, cited in Judis, *Genesis*, p. 343.

53. *The Acting Secretary of State to the Embassy in Israel*, Washington, May 28, 1949, FRUS, 1949, Vol. 6, The Near East, South Asia, and Africa, Document, 700, https://history.state.gov/historicaldocuments/frus1949v06/d700, cited in Judis, *Genesis*, pp. 344–345.

54. Shavit, "Lydda, 1948."

55. Judis, *Genesis*, p. 347.

56. One can imagine an alternative history in which the Palestinian refugees were integrated and contributed to the development of new homelands in Lebanon, Syria, Jordan, and, perhaps, other Arab states to which they might have been invited. But those Arab states (with the partial exception of Jordan) found them to be politically more useful in what became permanent refugee camps.

57. Judis, *Genesis*, p. 352.

58. Bass, *Support Any Friend*, p. 15.

59. This is a central thesis of Bass in *Support Any Friend*.

60. Patton was in charge of the postwar Displaced Persons camps, and he was furious about the report that Earl Harrison had sent to Truman. "Harrison and his ilk believe that the Displaced Person is a human being, which he is not, and

this applies particularly to the Jews who are lower than animals," Patton wrote in 1945 in his journal. Eric Lichtblau, "Surviving the Nazis, Only to Be Jailed by America," *New York Times*, February 7, 2015, http://www.nytimes.com/2015/02/08 /sunday-review/surviving-the-nazis-only-to-be-jailed-by-america.html?_r=0.

61. Ross, *Doomed to Succeed*, p. 8.

62. Bass, *Support Any Friend*, p. 33.

63. Ibid., p. 39.

64. Ibid., pp. 40–41.

65. Ibid., pp. 41, 42.

66. Henry Kissinger, *Diplomacy* (New York: Simon & Schuster, 1994), p. 531.

67. Bass, *Support Any Friend*, p. 41.

68. Michael B. Oren, *Ally: My Journey Across the American-Israeli Divide* (New York: Random House, 2015), pp. 23–24.

69. John F. Kennedy, "Imperialism—The Enemy of Freedom," Congressional Resolution 153 (July 2, 1957). Available at: www.jfklink.xom/speeches/jfk/congress /jfk020757_imperialism.html. By "carefully," we mean that Kennedy prefaced his speech by saying that "Soviet imperialism" and "Western imperialism" were "not to be equated"; he then proceeded to equate them.

70. Bass, *Support Any Friend*, p. 7.

71. Ibid., pp. 186–238.

72. Gordon M. Goldstein, *Lessons in Disaster: McGeorge Bundy and the Path to War in Vietnam* (New York: Henry Holt and Company, 2008), p. 41.

73. For a good sense of the Vietnam War's importance in U.S. deliberations on the June 1967 Arab–Israeli crisis, see William Quant's remarks in conference proceedings assembled in Richard B. Parker, ed., *The Six-Day War: A Retrospective* (Gainesville: University Press of Florida, 1996), pp. 204–213.

74. Johnson quoted in Michael B. Oren, *Six Days of War* (New York: Presidio Press, 2003), p. 26.

75. Tom Segev, *1967: Israel, the War, and the Year That Transformed the Middle East* (New York: Metropolitan Books, 2007), p. 127.

76. Ibid.

77. Ibid., p. 129.

78. Samuel C. Heilman, *Portrait of American Jews: The Last Half of the 20th Century*, The Samuel and Althea Stroum Lectures in Jewish Studies (Seattle: University of Washington Press, 1995), p. 58.

79. Shazar, quoted in Judith Klinghoffer, *Vietnam, Jews, and the Middle East: Unintended Consequences* (New York: St. Martin's Press, 1999), p. 57.

80. "Memorandum of Conversation," Washington, August 2, 1966, FRUS, 1964–1968, Volume XVIII, Arab-Israeli Dispute, 1964–67, Document 314, https:// history.state.gov/historicaldocuments/frus1964-68v18/d314.

81. Segev, *1967*, pp. 43–50, 151–160, 230–268.

82. Malcolm H. Kerr, *The Arab Cold War: Gamal Abd Al-Nasir and His Rivals, 1958–1970* (London: Published for the Royal Institute of International Affairs by Oxford University Press, 1971), p. 114.

83. United Nations General Assembly, Official Records, June 19, 1967, http://radioart.org/abba-eban/1967_speech_transcript.pdf.

84. Segev, *1967*, p. 186.

85. Ibid., p. 183.

86. Oren, *Six Days of War*, p. 35.

87. Ibid., p. 36.

88. Asher Susser, *On Both Banks of the Jordan: A Political Biography of Wasfi Al-Tall* (Newberry Park, UK: Frank Cass, 1994), p. 55.

89. Martin Gilbert, *The Routledge Atlas of the Arab-Israeli Conflict* (Abingdon, UK: Routledge, 2008), p. 69.

90. Conor Cruise O'Brien, *The Siege: The Story of Israel and Zionism* (London: Paladin Grafton Books, 1988), p. 413.

91. Ibid., p. 416.

92. Steven L. Spiegel, *The Other Arab Israeli Conflict: Making America's Middle East Policy* (Chicago: University of Chicago Press, 1985), p. 143; FRUS, *1964–1968*, Volume XIX, Arab–Israeli Crisis and War, 1967, https://history.state.gov/historicaldocuments/frus1964-68v19.

93. O'Brien, *The Siege*, p. 490.

94. Doris Kearns Goodwin, *Lyndon Johnson and the American Dream* (New York: St. Martin's Press, 1991), pp. 251–252.

95. Robert F. Kennedy, "Jews Have a Fine Fighting Force: Make Up for Lack of Arms with Undying Spirit, Unparalleled Courage—Impress the World," *Boston Post*, June 4, 1948, http://www.robertkennedyandisrael.blogspot.co.uk/2008/06/kennedy-in-palestine-part-two.html.

96. "Sirhan Felt Betrayed by Kennedy," *New York Times*, February 20, 1989, http://www.nytimes.com/1989/02/20/us/sirhan-felt-betrayed-by-kennedy.html.

Chapter 2

1. Regarding *Munich*'s closing image, Spielberg told an interviewer, "I don't think you can look at the Palestinian desire for a homeland in the same way you can look at [al Qaeda's] desire for an Islamic world and their attack on the Twin Towers. You can't speak of them in the same breath. But terrorism informs terrorism, and certainly the planners of the 9/11 attacks had to be aware of Munich when they plotted their arrival on the world stage. So if there's any linkage at all it's the way terrorism is demonstrated before the cameras." Andrew Anthony,

"The Eye of the Storm," *The Observer*, January 22, 2006, http://www.theguardian.com/film/2006/jan/22/awardsandprizes.oscars2006.

2. For a summary, see Michelle Goldberg, "Steven Spielberg's Controversial New Film: The War on Munich," *Spiegel International*, December 20, 2005, http://www.spiegel.de/international/steven-spielberg-s-controversial-new-film-the-war-on-munich-a-391525.html.

3. George Lardner Jr. and Michael Dobbs, "New Tapes Reveal Depth of Nixon's Anti-Semitism," *Washington Post*, October 6, 1999, p. A31.

4. Scott Shane, "Parsing the Nixon and Kissinger Pas de Deux, *New York Times*, April 17, 2007, http://www.nytimes.com/2007/04/17/books/17dall.html?_r=0&pagewanted=print.

5. Lardner and Dobbs, "New Tapes," p. A31.

6. Timothy Noah, "Nixon's Jew Count: the Whole Story!" *Slate*, September 26, 2007, http://www.slate.com/articles/news_and_politics/chatterbox/2007/09/nixons_jew_count_the_whole_story.html.

7. Robert Dallek, *Nixon and Kissinger: Partners in Power* (New York: Penguin Books, 2007), pp. 93, 170–171.

8. Henry Kissinger, *Years of Upheaval* (Boston: Little, Brown, 1982), pp. 202–203.

9. George Packer, "The Fall of Conservatism," *New Yorker*, May 26, 2008, http://www.newyorker.com/magazine/2008/05/26/the-fall-of-conservatism.

10. Rick Perlstein, *Nixonland: The Rise of a President and the Fracturing of America* (New York: Scribner, 2009).

11. Nixon's policies included wage and price controls, significant environmental legislation including the creation of the Environmental Protection Agency, détente with the Soviets, and proposals for national health insurance and even a guaranteed annual income.

12. Dallek, *Nixon and Kissinger*, p. 171.

13. This discussion of the Nixon administration and the Arab–Israeli conflict is laid out at greater length in Dana H. Allin, *Cold War Illusions, America, Europe and Soviet Power, 1969–1984* (New York: St. Martin's Press, 1994), Chapter 2.

14. William B. Quandt, *Decade of Decisions: American Policy Toward the Arab-Israeli Conflict, 1967–1976* (Berkeley: University of California Press, 1977), pp. 72–104.

15. Nadav Safran, *Israel: The Embattled Ally* (Cambridge, MA: Harvard University Press, 1981), p. 418.

16. Conor Cruise O'Brien, *The Siege: The Story of Israel and Zionism* (London: Paladin Grafton Books, 1988), p. 496.

17. Kissinger, *Years of Upheaval*, p. 460.

18. Ibid., pp. 492–493.

19. Dallek, *Nixon and Kissinger*, pp. 520–533.

20. For example, George F. Kennan, who in 1966 testimony on Vietnam to the Senate Foreign Relations Committee stated, "There is more respect to be won . . . by a resolute and courageous liquidation of unsound positions than in the most stubborn pursuit of extravagant or unsound objectives." Cited in Seyom Brown, *Faces of Power: Constancy and Change in United States Foreign Policy from Truman to Obama* (New York: Columbia University Press, 2015), p. 193.

21. Roy Licklider, "Oil and World Politics," in *Encyclopedia of U.S. Foreign Relations*, Vol. 3, ed. Bruce W. Jentleson, Thomas G. Paterson, and Nicholas X. Rizopoulos (New York: Oxford University Press, 1997), pp. 313–315.

22. Alfred Grosser, *The Western Alliance: European-American Relations Since 1945* (New York: Vintage Books, 1982), p. 274.

23. Kissinger, *Years of Upheaval*, pp. 897–898.

24. Roy Licklider, "Oil and World Politics."

25. An excellent and mainly sympathetic account of the origins and evolution of neoconservatism is provided by Francis Fukuyama, who had identified himself as neoconservative but renounced the label because of what he saw as its "Leninist" departures in the George W. Bush administration; see Fukuyama's *After the Neocons: America at the Crossroads* (London: Profile Books, 2006), pp. 12–65.

26. Paul Berman, "The Passion of Joschka Fischer," *New Republic*, August 27, 2001, https://newrepublic.com/article/78957/the-passion-joschka-fischer.

27. John J. Goldman, "Passengers Beaten, Sprayed with Mace: Jet Takeover Was Brutal, Freed Stewardesses Say," *Los Angeles Times*, June 17, 1985, http://articles.latimes.com/1985-06-17/news/mn-12571_1_stewardesses.

28. The conclusion of UN General Assembly Resolution 3379 states that "Zionism is a form of racism and racial discrimination."

29. For an extended historical critique of the "Reagan won the Cold War" argument, see Allin, *Cold War Illusions.*

30. John Harper, review of Marvin Kalb and Deborah Kalb, *Haunting Legacy: Vietnam and the American Presidency from Ford to Obama* in *Survival* 53, no. 6 (December 2011–January 2012): 209.

31. Israel was given "Major Non-NATO Ally" status under Title 10, U.S. Code, Sec. 2350a (Nunn Amendment of 1987) along with Egypt, Japan, Australia, and the Republic of Korea.

32. Alberto Bin, Richard Hill, and Archer Jones, *Desert Storm: A Forgotten War* (Westport, CT: Praeger, 1998), p. 47.

33. "Address to the United Nations General Assembly by President George H. W. Bush," October 1, 1990, http://www.state.gov/p/io/potusunga/207268.htm.

34. Thomas L. Friedman, "Baker Rebukes Israel on Peace Terms," *New York Times*, June 14, 1990, http://www.nytimes.com/1990/06/14/world/baker-rebukes-israel-on-peace-terms.html.

35. L. Sandy Maisel and Ira Forman, eds., *Jews in American Politics* (Lanham, MD: Rowman & Littlefield, 2001), p. 153, cited in *Jewish Virtual Library*, https://www.jewishvirtuallibrary.org/jsource/US-Israel/jewvote.html.

36. Aaron David Miller, *The Much Too Promised Land: America's Elusive Search for Arab-Israeli Peace* (New York: Bantam, 2009), p. 273.

37. Dennis Ross, *The Missing Peace: The Inside Story of the Fight for Middle East Peace* (New York: Farrar, Straus, and Giroux, 2004), p. 449.

38. James D. Besser, "News Analysis: Netanyahu Cozies Up to Falwell, Gingrich," Jweekly.com, January 23, 1998, http://www.jweekly.com/article/full/7416/news-analysis-netanyahu-cozies-up-to-falwell-gingrich/; Robert L. Jackson, "Falwell Selling Tape That Attacks Clinton: Accusations Include One That Alleges Complicity by the President in 'Countless' Murders. The Charge Is Unsupported," *Los Angeles Times*, May 14, 1994, http://articles.latimes.com/1994-05-14/news/mn-57626_1_clinton-presidency.

39. Ron Pundak, "From Oslo to Taba: What Went Wrong," *Survival* 43, no. 3 (Autumn 2001): 31–45; Robert Malley, "Camp David: The Tragedy of Errors," *New York Review of Books* 48, no. 13 (August 9, 2001), http://www.nybooks.com/articles/2001/08/09/camp-david-the-tragedy-of-errors/; Dennis Ross, Gidi Grinstein, Hussein Agha, and Robert Malley, "Camp David: An Exchange," *New York Review of Books* 48, no. 14 (August 23, 2001), http://www.nybooks.com/articles/2001/09/20/camp-david-an-exchange/; Ehud Barak and Benny Morris, "Camp David and After," *New York Review of Books* 49, no. 11 (June 27, 2002), http://www.nybooks.com/articles/2002/06/13/camp-david-and-after-an-exchange-1-an-interview-wi/.

40. Miller, *The Much Too Promised Land*, pp. 335–336.

41. See Jeffrey M. Jones, "Americans Show Increased Support for Israel Following Terrorist Attacks," Gallup Organization, September 29, 2001.

42. Thomas L. Friedman, "Suicidal Lies," *New York Times,* March 31, 2002. European critics have long argued that Americans are inconsistent on the question of terrorism. For many years, there was an open spigot of private American funds to the Irish Republican Army. Moreover, while American commentators have long criticized European governments, such as France's, for their history of occasional pragmatic accommodation with terrorist groups, it was the Reagan administration that sent weapons to Iran in an attempt to secure the release of hostages held by Iranian-backed terrorists in Lebanon.

43. Samuel G. Freedman, "Six Days After 9/11, Another Anniversary Worth Honoring," *New York Times*, September 7, 2012, http://www.nytimes.com/2012/09/08/us/on-religion-six-days-after-9-11-another-anniversary-worth-honoring.html?_r=0.

44. "Is Torture Ever Justified?" *The Economist*, September 20, 2007, http://www.economist.com/node/9832909; Amy Lorentzen, "Romney Backs Interrogation,

Patriot Act," *Washington Post*, July 30, 2007, http://www.washingtonpost.com/wp
-dyn/content/article/2007/07/20/AR2007072001071.html.

45. The best witness to these developments might be former Bush speech-writer
Michael Gerson who, after recalling Bush's efforts after 9/11 to avoid stigmatizing
Islam, noted that: "During the last two presidential nomination cycles, Republican
candidates, at various points, have proposed requiring a loyalty oath for Muslims
to serve in government; ruled out Muslims serving in their Cabinet; called sharia
law 'a mortal threat to the survival of freedom in the United States'; raised alarms
about the 'creeping attempt' to 'ease [sharia] law and the Muslim faith into our
government'; warned of 'no go' zones where sharia law rules; described Muslim
immigration as 'colonization' and warned that immigrants 'want to come and
conquer us'; said there were only a 'handful' of 'reasonable, moderate followers of
Islam'; described Islam as 'a religion that promotes the most murderous mayhem on
the planet.'" See Gerson, "Republicans' Fringe Tone on Islam Shows a Sharp
Turn Since 9/11," *Washington Post*, September 10, 2015, https://www.washingtonpost
.com/opinions/republicans-fringe-tone-on-islam-shows-a-sharp-turn-since-911
/2015/09/10/5a1d6d80-57d9-11e5-8bb1-b488d231bba2_story.html. (This was published
before Republican presidential candidate Donald Trump called for banning Muslims from entering the United States—and saw his polling position improve.) See
also, C. A. Bail, "The Fringe Effect: Civil Society Organizations and the Evolution of Media Discourse About Islam Since the September 11th Attacks," *American Sociological Review* 77 (2012): 855–879; David A. Fahrenthold and Michelle
Boorstein, "Peter King's Muslim Hearings: A Key Moment in an Angry Conversation," *Washington Post*, March 9, 2011, http://www.washingtonpost.com/wp-dyn
/content/article/2011/03/09/AR2011030902061.html?sid=ST2011031002070; David W.
Brown, "Gingrich Denounces Ground Zero Mosque," *The Atlantic*, July 22, 2010,
http://www.theatlantic.com/politics/archive/2010/07/gingrich-denounces
-ground-zero-mosque/60244/.

46. CNBC Transcript of *Hardball with Chris Matthews* interview, May 1, 2002.
For a comment, see Peter Beinart, "Bad Move: Does the Christian Right Understand Zionism?" *New Republic*, May 20 2002.

47. "Campaign 2008—Candidates: Mike Huckabee," Council on Foreign Relations, http://www.cfr.org/staff/b13301#7; "Palestinians Are an Invented People,
Says Newt Gingrich," *The Guardian*, September 10, 2011, http://www.theguardian
.com/world/2011/dec/10/palestinians-invented-people-newt-gingrich.

48. Jimmy Carter, "Address Before a Joint Session of Congress," September 18,
1978, http://www.presidency.ucsb.edu/ws/?pid=29799.

49. Lawrence Wright, *Thirteen Days in September: Carter, Begin, and Sadat at
Camp David* (New York: Alfred A. Knopf), pp. 3–6.

50. Ibid., p. 285. On Carter's religious devotion as driving his determination at Camp David, see also Wright's interview by Terry Gross on her radio program *Fresh Air*, September 16, 2014, http://wunc.org/post/13-days-high-emotion-led-egypt-israel-peace.

51. Bill Scher, "When Reagan Dared to Say 'God Bless America,'" *Politico*, July 17, 2015, http://www.politico.com/magazine/story/2015/07/reagan-god-bless-america-120286.

52. For informed students of American culture and hairstyles, it is necessary to clarify something: This was a seventh–twelfth grade high school, and the beatings were administered when Allin was in seventh grade, 1970–1971. Five years later, many rural male students had long hair (and Allin's was shorter by that time).

53. Paul Miller, "Evangelicals, Israel and US Foreign Policy," *Survival: Global Politics and Strategy* 56, no. 1 (February–March 2014): 7–26.

54. Ibid., p. 13. Miller cites Hal Lindsey, *The Late Great Planet Earth* (Grand Rapids, MI: Zondervan, 1970), p. 43. It is worth noting that the pastor of Jimmy Carter's Plains Baptist Church, Royal Holloway, preached the same doctrine in the years that Carter grew up there; "the Jews would soon return to Palestine and bring on the return of Christ and the rapture of true Christians into Heaven." Wright, *Thirteen Days in September*, p. 16.

55. John Lloyd, "Rowing Alone," *Financial Times*, August 3, 2002; "Among Wealthy Nations—US stands Alone in Its Embrace of Religion," Pew Research Center, December 19, 2002, people-press.org/reports/display.php3?ReportID=167.

56. Daniel Benjamin and Steven Simon, *The Age of Sacred Terror: Radical Islam's War Against America* (New York: Random House Trade Paperback, 2003), pp. 425–432.

57. In an interview with ABC News before Camp David, Begin expressed confidence that his determination to hold onto the West Bank would not cause a problem with Washington because, "President Carter knows the Bible by heart, so he knows to whom this land by right belongs." "Begin: Israel Won't Give Up 'Liberated' Lands," *St. Petersburg Times*, May 23, 1977, p. 1, https://news.google.com/newspapers?nid=888&dat=19770523&id=46wpAAAAIBAJ&sjid=m1oDAAAAIBAJ&pg=3682,5807581&hl=en.

58. Benjamin and Simon, *The Age of Sacred Terror*, pp. 423–424.

59. James Fromson and Steven Simon, "ISIS: The Dubious Paradise of Apocalypse Now," *Survival: Global Politics and Strategy* 57, no. 3 (June–July 2015): 7–56.

60. Benjamin and Simon, *The Age of Sacred Terror*, p. 428.

61. In Chapter 7 we will consider the future implications of the growing number of Israeli Jews who believe their religious faith precludes territorial compromise with the Arabs.

62. Robert Kagan, "Power and Weakness," *Policy Review*, June/July 2002.

63. On the historical traditions, see Robert Kagan, *Dangerous Nation: America and the World, 1600–1898* (London: Atlantic Books, 2006).

64. Barak Obama, Strasbourg Town Hall Speech, Strasbourg, France (April 3, 2009), http://www.whitehouse.gov/blog/2009/04/03/a-town-hall-strasbourg.

65. Peter Beinart, "The End of American Exceptionalism," *National Journal*, February 3, 2014, http://www.nationaljournal.com/magazine/the-end-of-american-exceptionalism-20140203.

66. Mitt Romney, New Hampshire Primary Victory Speech, Concord, NH (January 10, 2012).

67. "He's taking us down a path towards Europe. He wants us to see a bigger and bigger government, with a healthcare system run by the government. He wants to see people paying more and more in taxes." Mitt Romney, Father's Day Brunch Speech, Cleveland, OH (June 28, 2012). In another speech Romney claimed that Obama "wants to fundamentally transform America," and added, "I kind of like America. I'm not looking for it to be fundamentally transformed. I don't want it to become like Europe." New Hampshire Primary Debate, Concord, NH (January 7, 2012).

68. Though the intensity, not to mention the monotony, of the American right's most recent anti-Europe campaigns is surpassingly strange, not least because it is hardly obvious that it has much political resonance. Most Americans have favorable and even warm views of Europe. Joshua Keeting, "Do Americans Really Hate Europe That Much?" *Foreign Policy*, January 11, 2012, http://passport.foreignpolicy.com/posts/2012/01/11/do_americans_really_hate_europe_that_much.

69. Darren Samuelsohn, "Guiliani: Obama Doesn't Love America," *Politico*, February 18, 2015, http://www.politico.com/story/2015/02/rudy-giuliani-president-obama-doesnt-love-america-115309.html#ixzz3eMoTekbY.

70. "Barack Obama's Speech on Race," *New York Times*, March 18, 2008, http://www.nytimes.com/2008/03/18/us/politics/18text-obama.html?_r=0.

71. "Remarks by the President at Cairo University," The White House, Office of the Press Secretary, June 4, 2009, https://www.whitehouse.gov/the-press-office/remarks-president-cairo-university-6-04-09.

72. Ryan Lizza, "Battle Plans: How Obama Won," *New Yorker*, November 17, 2008, http://www.newyorker.com/magazine/2008/11/17/battle-plans.

Chapter 3

1. Peter Beinart, *The Crisis of Zionism* (New York: Times Books/Henry Holt and Company, 2012), pp. 78–79.

2. On the controversy, see Leida Snow, "'Selma' Distorts History by Airbrushing Out Jewish Contributions to Civil Rights," *Forward*, January 5, 2015, http://forward.com/culture/212000/selma-distorts-history-by-airbrushing-out-jewish-c/; William Bole, "'Selma' Is True to the Story It Needs to Tell," *Tikkun*, January 19, 2015, http://www.tikkun.org/tikkundaily/2015/01/19/selma-is-true-to-the-story-it-needs-to-tell/.

3. Beinart, *The Crisis of Zionism*, pp. 89–91.

4. David Squires, "Rev. Geremiah Wright Says 'Jews' Are Keeping Him from President Obama," *Daily Press* (Newport News, Virginia), June 10, 2009, http://www.dailypress.com/news/dp-local_wright_0610jun10-story.html.

5. Michael Hirsh, "Clinton to Arafat: It's All Your Fault," *Newsweek*, June 27, 2001, http://europe.newsweek.com/clinton-arafat-its-all-your-fault-153779.

6. Elliot Abrams, *Tested by Zion: The Bush Administration and the Israeli-Palestinian Conflict* (New York: Cambridge University Press), p. 132.

7. "PIJ Policy Paper: Israeli Settlements and the Two State Solution," *Palestine-Israel Journal*, August 2019, p.1, http://www.pij.org/pijpapers/settlements_pijpaper.pdf.

8. Yinon Cohen and Neve Gordon, "The Demographic Success of the West Bank Settlements," December 2012, http://www.columbia.edu/~yc2444/pages/Demographic%20Success%20of%20the%20West%20Bank%20Settlers.html.

9. Ibid.

10. Ronald Reagan, "Address to the Nation on United States Policy for Peace in the Middle East," September 1, 1982, http://www.reagan.utexas.edu/archives/speeches/1982/90182d.htm.

11. Harry Zi Hurwitz, *Begin: His Life, Words and Deeds* (Jerusalem: Geffen, 2004), p. 185.

12. "The Mitchell Report," November 29, 2001, *BBC News: Key Documents*, http://news.bbc.co.uk/1/hi/in_depth/middle_east/2001/israel_and_the_palestinians/key_documents/1632064.stm.

13. "A Performance-Based Roadmap to a Permanent Two-State Solution to the Israeli-Palestinian Conflict," *BBC News*, April 30, 2003, http://news.bbc.co.uk/1/hi/world/middle_east/2989783.stm.

14. Daniel Kurtzer, "Real Talk on Israeli Settlements," *Foreign Affairs*, January 13, 2016, https://www.foreignaffairs.com/articles/israel/2016-01-13/real-talk-israeli-settlements.

15. "Letter from President Bush to Prime Minister Sharon," April 14, 2004, http://georgewbush-whitehouse.archives.gov/news/releases/2004/04/20040414-3.html.

16. Mike Allen and Glenn Kessler, "Bush Goal: Palestinian State by 2009," *Washington Post*, November 13, 2004, http://www.washingtonpost.com/wp-dyn/articles/A46469-2004Nov12.html.

17. Abrams, *Tested by Zion*, p. 245.

18. Ibid., p. 259.

19. Alex Altman, "Middle East Envoy George Mitchell," *Time*, January 22, 2009, http://content.time.com/time/world/article/0,8599,1873532,00.html.

20. John Heilemann, "The Tsuris," *New York*, September 18, 2011, http://nymag.com/news/politics/israel-2011-9/.

21. See Yehuda Ben-Meir, "The Struggle over Freezing of Settlements," in *Strategic Assessment for Israel 2010*, ed. Shlomo Brom and Anat Kurz (Tel Aviv: The Institute for National Security Studies, 2010), p. 15. http://www.inss.org.il/uploadImages/systemFiles/%D7%94%D7%A2%D7%A8%D7%9B%D7%94%202010%20%D7%9E%D7%9C%D7%90492929173.pdf.

22. Glenn Kessler and Howard Schneider, "U.S. Presses Israel to End Expansion of Settlements; Bush Pact Complicates Issue," *Washington Post*, May 24, 2009, http://www.washingtonpost.com/wp-dyn/content/article/2009/05/23/AR2009052301536.html; Ron Kampeas, "At White House, U.S. Jews Offer Little Resistance to Obama Policy on Settlements," *Jewish Telegraphic Agency*, July 14, 2009, http://www.jta.org/2009/07/14/news-opinion/politics/at-white-house-u-s-jews-offer-little-resistance-to-obama-policy-on-settlements.

23. "Remarks by President Obama and Israeli Prime Minister Netanyahu in Press Availability," The White House, Office of the Press Secretary, May 18, 2009, https://www.whitehouse.gov/the-press-office/remarks-president-obama-and-israeli-prime-minister-netanyahu-press-availability.

24. Simon McGregor-Wood, "Israel Pressured by Obama's Tough Stand on Settlements," May 28, 2009, http://abcnews.go.com/International/story?id=7694664&page=1&singlePage=true.

25. Ibid.

26. Ibid.

27. Laura Rozen, "In Letters, Obama Asked Arab States for Confidence-Building Measures Toward Israel," *Foreign Policy*, July 26, 2009, http://foreignpolicy.com/2009/07/26/in-letters-obama-asked-arab-states-for-confidence-building-measures-toward-israel/; Michael Slackman, "Arab States Cool to Obama Pleas for Peace Gesture," *New York Times*, June 2, 2009, http://www.nytimes.com/2009/06/03/world/middleeast/03saudi.html?_r=0.

28. Laura Rozen, "Revisiting Obama's Riyadh Meeting," *Foreign Policy*, July 17, 2009, https://foreignpolicy.com/2009/07/17/revisiting-obamas-riyadh-meeting/; Slackman, "Arab States Cool to Obama Pleas for Peace Gesture."

29. Laura Rozen, "Revisiting Obama's Riyadh Meeting."

30. Aaron David Miller, "Israel's Lawyer," *Washington Post*, May 23, 2005, http://www.washingtonpost.com/wp-dyn/content/article/2005/05/22/AR2005052200883.html.

31. Daniel C. Kurtzer, Scott B. Lasensky, William B. Quandt, Steven L. Spiegel, and Shibley Telhami, *The Peace Puzzle: America's Quest for Arab–Israeli Peace, 1989–2011* (Ithaca, NY: Cornell University Press, 2012), pp. 252–253; Heather Sharp, "Goldstone Fallout Plagues Abbas," *BBC News*, October 9, 2009, http://news.bbc.co.uk/1/hi/world/middle_east/8297698.stm.

32. Ethan Bronner, "As Biden Visits, Israel Unveils Plan for New Settlements," *New York Times*, March 9, 2010, http://www.nytimes.com/2010/03/10/world/middleeast/10biden.html.

33. Akiva Eldar, "U.S. Gave Israel Green Light for East Jerusalem Construction," *Haaretz*, March 12, 2010, http://www.haaretz.com/u-s-gave-israel-green-light-for-east-jerusalem-construction-1.266426.

34. Dennis Ross, *Doomed to Succeed: The U.S.-Israel Relationship from Truman to Obama* (New York: Farrar, Straus, and Giroux, 2015), p. 373.

35. Ross, *Doomed to Succeed*, pp. 376–378; Barak Ravid and Natasha Mozgovaya, "U.S. Offers Israel Warplanes in Return for New Settlement Freeze," *Haaretz*, November 13, 2010, http://www.haaretz.com/israel-news/u-s-offers-israel-warplanes-in-return-for-new-settlement-freeze-1.324496.

36. Amir Tibon, "The Secret Back Channel That Doomed the Israel-Palestine Negotiations," *New Republic*, November 26, 2014, https://new`republic.com/article/120413/secret-negotiations-between-yitzhak-molho-abbas-representative; Barak David, "Identity of Secret Mediator in Israeli-Palestinians Talks Revealed," *Haaretz*, November 27, 2014, http://www.haaretz.com/israel-news/.premium-1.62897; this chapter's account of the London process is based on these reports and on author interviews, Washington, DC.

37. "Remarks by the President on the Middle East and North Africa," The White House, Office of the Press Secretary, May 19, 2011, https://www.whitehouse.gov/the-press-office/2011/05/19/remarks-president-middle-east-and-north-africa.

38. Dilip Hiro, *Inside the Middle East* (Abingdon, UK: Routledge, 1982), p. 219.

39. Reagan, "Address to the Nation on United States Policy for Peace in the Middle East," September 1, 1982, www.reagan.utexas.edu/archives/speeches/1982/90182d.htm.

40. Bill Clinton, "Remarks at an Israel Policy Forum Dinner in New York City," January 7, 2001, in Public Papers of the Presidents of the United States: William J. Clinton, pp. 2842–2843, http://www.archives.gov/federal-register/publications/presidential-papers.html.

41. "Exchange of Letters between PM Sharon and President Bush," April 14, 2004, Israel Ministry of Foreign Affairs, http://www.mfa.gov.il/mfa/foreignpolicy/peace/mfadocuments/pages/exchange%20of%20letters%20sharon-bush%2014-apr-2004.aspx; for Bush's 2002 statement, see "Bush's Mideast speech," *BBC News*, June 24, 2002, http://news.bbc.co.uk/1/hi/world/middle_east/2064021.stm.

42. "Remarks by the President at the AIPAC Policy Conference 2011," The White House, Office of the Press Secretary, May 22, 2011, https://www.whitehouse.gov/the -press-office/2011/05/22/remarks-president-aipac-policy-conference-2011.

43. Ross, *Doomed to Succeed*, p. 376.

44. Benjamin Netanyahu, "Address to US Congress, May 2011," http://www.cfr .org/israel/netanyahus-address-us-congress-may-2011/p25073.

45. Jeffrey Goldberg, "The Crisis in U.S.-Israel Relations Is Officially Here," *The Atlantic*, October 28, 2014, http://www.theatlantic.com/international/archive/2014 /10/the-crisis-in-us-israel-relations-is-officially-here/382031/.

Chapter 4

1. Steven Lee Myers, "Israeli Leader Makes Case Against Iran on U.S. TV," *New York Times*, September 16, 2012, http://www.nytimes.com/2012/09/17/world /middleeast/netanyahu-says-iran-is-20-yards-from-nuclear-bomb.html.

2. Peggy Noonan, "Monday Morning," *Peggy Noonan's Blog*, November 5, 2012, http://blogs.wsj.com/peggynoonan/2012/11/05/monday-morning/; "George Will Predicts Romney Win's Big, 321–217, *Real Clear Politics Video*, November 4, 2012, http://www.realclearpolitics.com/video/2012/11/04/george_will_predicts _romney_wins_big_321-217.html; Jan Crawford, "Adviser: Romney 'Shellshocked' by Loss," cbsnews.com, November 8, 2012, http://www.cbsnews.com/news/adviser -romney-shellshocked-by-loss/.

3. Dennis Ross, *Doomed to Succeed: The U.S.-Israel Relationship From Truman to Obama* (New York: Farrar, Straus and Giraux, 2015), pp. 379–380.

4. Simon left the White House at the beginning of Obama's second term.

5. Jeffrey Goldberg, "Obama: Israel Doesn't Know What Its Best Interests Are," *Bloomberg View*, January 14, 2013, http://www.bloombergview.com/articles /2013-01-14/what-obama-thinks-israelis-don-t-understand-.

6. "Remarks of President Barack Obama to the People of Israel," The White House, Office of the Press Secretary, March 21, 2013, https://www.whitehouse.gov /the-press-office/2013/03/21/remarks-president-barack-obama-people-israel.

7. Tovah Lazaroff, "US embassy Keeps Ariel U. Out of Obama Visit," *Jerusalem Post*, March 14, 2013, http://www.jpost.com/Diplomacy-and-Politics/US-embassy -keeps-Ariel-U-out-of-Obama-visit.

8. "New Secretary of State Kerry Speaks to Netanyahu, Abbas About Peace," Reuters, February 3, 2013, http://www.reuters.com/article/us-israel-palestinians -usa-idUSBRE9120EG20130203.

9. Raphael Ahren, "Netanyahu 'Determined' to Move Forward with Peace Process," *Times of Israel*, April 9, 2013, http://www.timesofisrael.com/netanyahu -determined-to-move-forward-with-peace-process/.

10. Confidential author interviews with White House and State Department officials, Washington, DC, 2015.

11. This account of Kerry's peace mission is based in significant measure on Ben Birnbaum and Amir Tibon, "The Explosive, Inside Story of How John Kerry Built and Israel-Palestine Peace Plan—and Watched It Crumble," *New Republic*, July 20, 2015, https://newrepublic.com/article/118751/how-israel-palestine-peace -deal-died. Their meticulous reporting is supplemented by author interviews conducted in summer 2015 with key participants in the diplomacy and policy process at the White House and State Department.

12. Birnbaum and Tibon, "The Explosive, Inside Story."

13. Ibid.

14. Elad Benari, "Kerry: There's Progress, but I Can't Tell You About It," *Arutz Sheva*, June 12, 2013, http://www.israelnationalnews.com/News/News.aspx/174858# .Vp97wSuqmy5.

15. Dan Williams, "Israel Minister Apologizes to Kerry over Scorn for Peace Drive," Reuters, January 14, 2014, http://www.reuters.com/article/us-palestinians -israel-kerry-idUSBREA0D0IY20140114.

16. Ibid.

17. Birnbaum and Tibon, "The Explosive, Inside Story."

18. Confidential author interviews with White House and State Department officials, Washington, DC, 2015.

19. Birnbaum and Tibon, "The Explosive, Inside Story."

20. Mark Landler, "Mideast Frustration, the Sequel," *New York Times*, April, 8 2014, http://www.nytimes.com/2014/04/09/world/middleeast/israeli-settlement -plan-derailed-peace-talks-kerry-says.html.

21. Jeffrey Goldberg, "The Four Questions: Martin Indyk on the Failure of Peacemaking," *The Atlantic*, January 27, 2009, http://www.theatlantic.com /international/archive/2009/01/the-four-questions-martin-indyk-on-the-failure -of-peacemaking/9441/.

22. See Birnbaum and Tibon, "The Explosive, Inside Story" where Erekat expresses himself in nearly identical terms to John Kerry: "He [Netanyahu] is refusing to negotiate on a map or even say 1967," a frustrated Erekat complained to John Kerry in one conversation.

23. Roger Cohen, "Lo, the Mideast Moves," *New York Times*, March 29, 2010, http://www.nytimes.com/2010/03/30/opinion/30iht-edcohen.html?_r=0.

24. Peter Beinart, *The Crisis of Zionism* (New York: Times Books, 2012), p. 3.

25. "Full Text of Netanyahu's Foreign Policy Speech at Bar Ilan," *Haaretz*, June 14, 2009, http://www.haaretz.com/news/full-text-of-netanyahu-s-foreign -policy-speech-at-bar-ilan-1.277922.

26. Jodi Rudorenjan, "Sticking Point in Peace Talks: Recognition of a Jewish State," *New York Times*, January 1, 2014, http://www.nytimes.com/2014/01/02 /world/middleeast/sticking-point-in-peace-talks-recognition-of-a-jewish-state .html?hp&_r=0; for a very thoughtful critique, see Bernard Avishai, "The Jewish State in Question," *New Yorker*, January 2, 2014, http://www.newyorker.com/news /news-desk/the-jewish-state-in-question.

27. Justin Lane, "We Don't Want to 'Flood' Israel with Palestinian Refugees: Abbas," Reuters, February 16, 2014, http://www.reuters.com/article/us-palestinians -israel-idUSBREA1F0OE20140216.

28. Peter Beinart, "Enraged by Netanyahu's Rhetoric, White House Officials Believe Israeli-U.S. Relations Fundamentally Changed," *Haaretz*, March 19, 2015, http://www.haaretz.com/israel-news/.premium-1.647859.

29. Indyk interviewed by David Rothkopf, "The U.S.-Israel Relationship Arrives at a Moment of Reckoning," ForeignPolicy.com, August 26, 2014, http://foreignpolicy .com/2014/08/26/the-u-s-israel-relationship-arrives-at-a-moment-of-reckoning/.

30. Steven L. Spiegel, "What Should America's Strategy Be in the Middle East?" *UCLA Today*, December 12, 2006, http://newsroom.ucla.edu/stories/steven-spiegel _middle-east.

31. Scott Wilson, "Obama Searches for Middle East Peace," *Washington Post*, July 14, 2012, https://www.washingtonpost.com/politics/obama-searches-for-middle -east-peace/2012/07/14/gJQAQQiKlW_story.html.

32. Author interviews, White House and State Department, summer 2015.

33. Josh Marshall, "Does Obama Have the 'Special Feeling?'" TalkingPoints-Memo.com, August 12, 2015, http://talkingpointsmemo.com/edblog/does-obama -have-the-special-feeling.

34. Yezid Sayigh, "Inducing a Failed State in Palestine," *Survival* 49, no. 3 (Autumn 2007): 14–15.

35. Joshua Keating, "Twitter Is Changing How the Media Covers the Israeli-Palestinian Conflict," *Slate*, July 21, 2014, http://www.slate.com/blogs/the_world_ /2014/07/21/twitter_is_changing_how_the_media_covers_the_israeli_palestinian _conflict.html.

36. Barak Ravid, "U.S. to Israel on Kerry Criticism: 'Not the Way Allies Treat Each Other,'" *Haaretz*, July 29, 2014, http://www.haaretz.com/israel-news/.premium -1.607748.

Chapter 5

1. David D. Kirkpatrick and Heba Afify, "Protest of Thousands in Cairo Turns Violent," *New York Times*, September 9, 2011, http://www.nytimes.com/2011/09/10 /world/middleeast/10egypt.html?_r=0; "Egyptian Protesters Break into Israeli

Embassy Building," *BBC News*, September 10, 2011, http://www.bbc.co.uk/news /world-middle-east-14862159.

2. Adrian Blomfield, "Egypt's Military Rulers Ignored Pleas from US as Mob Attacked Israeli Embassy," *The Telegraph*, September 11, 2011, http://www.telegraph .co.uk/news/worldnews/africaandindianocean/egypt/8756111/Egypts-military -rulers-ignored-pleas-from-US-as-mob-attacked-Israeli-embassy.html; Michael Oren, *Ally: My Journey Across the American-Israeli Divide* (New York: Random House, 2015), pp. 240–241.

3. Barak Ravid, "Netanyahu: Cairo Embassy Attack Was Assault on Israel-Egypt Peace," *Haaretz*, September 11, 2011, http://www.haaretz.com/news/diplomacy-defense /netanyahu-cairo-embassy-attack-was-assault-on-israel-egypt-peace-1.383760.

4. Dennis Ross, *Doomed to Succeed: The U.S.-Israel Relationship from Truman to Obama* (New York: Farrar, Straus, and Giroux, 2015), p. 353.

5. Ari Shavit, "Obama's Betrayal: As Goes Mubarak, So Goes U.S. Might," *Haaretz*, January 31, 2011, http://www.haaretz.com/print-edition/news/obama-s -betrayal-as-goes-mubarak-so-goes-u-s-might-1.340244.

6. Douglas Hamilton, "Israel Shocked by Obama's 'Betrayal' of Mubarak," Reuters, January 31, 2011, http://www.reuters.com/article/us-egypt-israel-usa -idUSTRE70U53720110131.

7. Condoleezza Rice, "Remarks at the American University in Cairo," June 20, 2005, http://2001-2009.state.gov/secretary/rm/2005/48328.htm.

8. The U.S. Congress made it difficult to stick to such a position, however, by conditioning assistance to Egypt on compliance with civil rights norms and on the new government's as yet untested capacity for self-restraint.

9. At the working level, the Israeli government has a fine-grained picture of the U.S. government and how it operates. Most observers take this for granted vis-à-vis Congress, where the Israeli government navigates the corridors of power very effectively. With the help of AIPAC, which funds fact-finding trips to Israel for members of Congress and enjoys good working relationships with most members on both sides of the aisle, Israelis enjoy superb access and have a good feel for dynamics on the Hill. But with the exception perhaps of a handful of NATO allies, Israelis have the best grasp of what goes on in the executive branch as well. This stems, in part, from a history of cooperation, especially in the security realm, and in part from the assiduous effort that Israeli officials make to keep their finger on the pulse of the executive branch. Thus, during the first month or so of a new NSC official's assignment, a couple of dozen senior military officers, intelligence officials, and diplomats descend on the Old Executive Office Building to impart the Israeli government's perspective on a range of topics, and to get a sense of the new official in charge of coordinating regional foreign and defense policy in Washington. These are useful meetings for both sides.

10. In response, to all of this, the obvious question was, what does one do in such a beleaguered situation? For example, might there be measures Israel could take to strengthen Jordan's ruler politically, by taking an initiative in the Palestinian arena? Or consider ways in which Israel might approach a Muslim Brotherhood–led government should one be elected? These were probing questions, meant to elicit out-of-the-box thinking and not to extract answers in the form of specific, bold initiatives that would in any case be well above the pay grade of these officials. The answers, like the worldview that produced them, were strikingly uniform. There was simply nothing to be done. In a situation this unstable and with outcomes so unpredictable and so likely to be adverse, the answer had to be the strategic equivalent of a deep crouch. There was one intriguing exception to this understandable panorama of fear and resolve. One of the visitors in that period, an intelligence officer who had just been promoted to a senior rank and to a position that carried serious responsibilities, answered by shrugging his shoulders and saying, "What to do . . . ? . . . Make deals!" The next time he showed up at the White House in his new capacity, however, his entrepreneurial zeal was no longer on display.

11. Y. Harkabi, *Arab Attitudes to Israel* (Piscataway, NJ: Transaction Publishers, 1974).

12. Kareem Fahim, "Egypt, Dealing a Blow to the Muslim Brotherhood, Deems It a Terrorist Group," *New York Times*, December 25, 2013, http://www.nytimes.com/2013/12/26/world/middleeast/egypt-calls-muslim-brotherhood-a-terrorist-group.html.

13. Merna Thomas, "Muslim Brotherhood Leader Arrested in Egypt," *New York Times*, November 20, 2014, http://www.nytimes.com/2014/11/21/world/middleeast/muslim-brotherhood-leader-arrested-in-egypt.html.

14. "Egyptian Brotherhood Leader Handed Sixth Life Prison Sentence—Judicial Sources," Reuters, August 22, 2015, http://uk.reuters.com/article/2015/08/22/uk-egypt-verdict-idUKKCN0QR0A120150822.

15. Mohammed M. Hafez, *Why Muslims Rebel: Repression and Resistance in the Islamic World* (Boulder, CO: Lynne Rienner Publishers, 2004); Ted Robert Gurr, *Why Men Rebel* (Abingdon, UK: Routledge, 2012).

16. "Transcript: Obama's Speech Against the Iraq War," delivered in Chicago, October 2, 2002, http://www.npr.org/templates/story/story.php?storyId=99591469.

17. Bob Woodward, "McChrystal: More Forces or 'Mission Failure,'" *Washington Post*, September 21, 2009, http://www.washingtonpost.com/wp-dyn/content/article/2009/09/20/AR2009092002920.html.

18. Barack Obama, "Remarks by the President in Address to the Nation on the Way Forward in Afghanistan and Pakistan," West Point, NY, December 1, 2009, http://www.whitehouse.gov/the-press-office/remarks-president-address-nation-way-forward-afghanistan-and-pakistan.

19. Barack Obama, "Remarks by the President at the Acceptance of the Nobel Peace Prize," Oslo, Norway, December 10, 2009, http://www.whitehouse.gov/the-press-office/remarks-president-acceptance-nobel-peace-prize.

20. Ryan Lizza, "The Consequentialist: How the Arab Spring Remade Obama's Foreign Policy," *New Yorker*, May 2, 2011, http://www.newyorker.com/magazine/2011/05/02/the-consequentialist.

21. Obama, "Remarks by the President at the Acceptance of the Nobel Peace Prize."

22. Obama interview with Franklin Foer and Chris Hughes, "Barack Obama Is Not Pleased," *New Republic*, January 27, 2013, https://newrepublic.com/article/112190/obama-interview-2013-sit-down-president.

23. Jay Solomon, "U.S., Israel Monitor Suspected Syrian WMD," *Wall Street Journal*, August 27, 2011, http://www.wsj.com/articles/SB10001424053111904009304576532652538547620; R. Jeffrey Smith, "Suiting Up: What the United States Is Doing to Prepare for Chemical War in Syria," *Foreign Policy*, January 17, 2013, http://foreignpolicy.com/2013/01/17/suiting-up/.

24. Ross, *Doomed to Succeed*, pp. 357, 358.

25. "Remarks by the President to the White House Press Corps," The White House, Office of the Press Secretary, August 20, 2012, https://www.whitehouse.gov/the-press-office/2012/08/20/remarks-president-white-house-press-corps.

26. Paul F. Walker, "Syrian Chemical Weapons Destruction: Taking Stock and Looking Ahead," *Arms Control Today*, December 2014, http://www.armscontrol.org/ACT/2014_12/Features/Syrian-Chemical-Weapons-Destruction-Taking-Stock-And-Looking-Ahead.

27. Ross, *Doomed to Succeed*, p. 359.

28. Ibid.

29. Mohammed Bin Nawaf Bin Abdulaziz al Saud, "Saudi Arabia Will Go It Alone," *New York Times*, December 17, 2013, http://www.nytimes.com/2013/12/18/opinion/saudi-arabia-will-go-it-alone.html?.

30. Gordon M. Goldstein, *Lessons in Disaster* (New York: Times Books, 2008), pp. 40–41.

31. The countervailing case has always rested on the fact that when LBJ did expand the war, he was listening to the advisers he had inherited from his slain predecessor. But historian Lyle Goldstein has documented the five occasions in 1961 alone when Kennedy resisted the urgent counsel of those same advisers: They said the introduction of American ground troops into Vietnam was necessary to avert disaster there, but Kennedy refused. Counterfactual history has its limits, of course, but in a certain sense it is also unavoidable. It is the implicit comparative basis for any assessment of the actual history. In this case, it is useful to imagine what the consequences might have been had JFK lived and kept us out of Vietnam. Georgetown historian Michael Kazin did so in a 2013 article in *The*

New Republic. Writing for the fiftieth anniversary of Kennedy's assassination, Kazin argued that the consequences of such restraint would hardly have been trouble-free. "[T]he Vietcong and North Vietnamese would probably have triumphed under his watch; hawks in both parties would never have forgiven him." Michael Kazin, "We Don't Need Another JFK: Fifty Years Later, Kennedy's Legend Makes Life at the White House Harder for Democrats," *New Republic*, November 20, 2013, http://www.newrepublic.com/article/115655/jfks-assassination -made-governing-harder. Kazin's broader point is that John F. Kennedy's imagined and mythologized second term has set a pernicious standard among American liberals for heroic presidential leadership, one that bears little comparison to the frustrating realities of actually governing. But there is also a very specific lesson regarding many decision points of military intervention. Even in the case of Vietnam, where hindsight strongly suggests that strategic restraint would have been the far wiser and far less costly policy, some political and moral consequences of such restraint would have been ugly. Which is not to say that restraint would have been wrong. It would almost certainly have been right, with fewer Vietnamese and Americans killed, less treasure exhausted, and U.S. morale and credibility sooner recovered. Still, the Kennedy presidency would have been tarnished, in his own time and thereafter, by the chaotic loss of Vietnam.

32. David J. Kramer, "US Foreign Policy Comes Home to Roost with Russia's Action in Ukraine," *Washington Post*, March 1, 2014, https://www.washingtonpost .com/opinions/us-foreign-comes-home-to-roost-with-russias-action-in-ukraine /2014/03/01/10be38bc-a18d-11e3-b8d8-94577ff66b28_story.html.

33. Editorial Board, "President Obama's Foreign Policy Is Based on a Fantasy," *Washington Post*, March 2, 2014, https://www.washingtonpost.com/opinions /president-obamas-foreign-policy-is-based-on-fantasy/2014/03/02/c7854436 -a238-11e3-a5fa-55f0c77bf39c_story.html.

34. "Senator McCain Remarks at AIPAC Conference," C-Span.org, March 3, 2014, http://www.c-span.org/video/?318071-1/sen-john-mccain-addresses-aipac-conference.

35. Peter Beinart, "The U.S. Doesn't Need to Prove Itself in Ukraine," *Atlantic*, May 5, 2014, http://www.theatlantic.com/international/archive/2014/05/us-credibility -fallacy-ukraine-russia-syria-china/361695/2/; Daryl G. Press, *Calculating Credibility: How Leaders Assess Military Threats* (Ithaca, NY: Cornell University Press, 2005).

Chapter 6

1. Richard V. Allen, "Reagan's Secure Line," *New York Times*, June 6, 2010, http://www.nytimes.com/2010/06/07/opinion/07allen.html.

2. Robert M. Gates, *Duty: Memoirs of a Secretary of War* (London: W. H. Allen, 2014), pp. 171–176.

3. Richard K. Betts, "The Osirak Fallacy," *National Interest*, Spring 2006, http://nationalinterest.org/article/the-osirak-fallacy-1093.

4. Gates, *Duty*, p. 177.

5. Gardiner quoted in James Fallows, "The Nuclear Power Beside Iraq," *Atlantic*, May 2006, http://www.theatlantic.com/magazine/archive/2006/05/the-nuclear-power-beside-iraq/304819/. Gardiner himself was speaking specifically to the last problem of rhetoric limiting American options.

6. Robert M. Gates, *Duty*, p. 182.

7. Ibid., pp. 192–193.

8. Ibid., p. 192.

9. Iran: Nuclear Intentions and Capabilities, NIE, November 2007, http://www.dni.gov/files/documents/Newsroom/Reports%20and%20Pubs/20071203_release.pdf.

10. Dana H. Allin and Steven Simon, *The Sixth Crisis: Iran, Israel, America, and the Rumors of War* (New York: Oxford University Press, 2010), p. 21.

11. This was certainly Gates's view; see *Duty*, p. 190.

12. Mark Fitzpatrick, personal communication with author, March 2, 2012.

13. "Barack Obama's Inaugural Address," *New York Times*, January 20, 2009, http://www.nytimes.com/2009/01/20/us/politics/20text-obama.html?_r=0.

14. "Iran Leader Urges Destruction of 'Cancerous' Israel," CNN.com, December 15, 2000, http://archives.cnn.com/2000/World/meast/12/15/mideast.iran; Yossi Melman, "Ahmadinejad: Israel Is 'Rotten Tree That Will Be Annihilated," *Haaretz*, April 16, 2006, http://www.haaretz.com/ahmadinejad-israel-is-rotten-tree-that-will-be-annihilated-1.185329; "Iran's Leader Reiterates Threat Against Israel," *Washington Post*, April 15, 2006, http://www.washingtonpost.com/wp-dyn/content/article/2006/04/14/AR2006041401471.html; Nazila Fathi, "Iran's President Says Israel Must Be 'Wiped Off the Map,'" *New York Times*, October 26, 2005, http://www.nytimes.com/2005/10/26/international/middleeast/26cnd-iran.html; see also, Karim Sadjapour, *Reading Khamenei: The World View of Iran's Most Powerful Leader* (Washington DC: Carnegie Endowment for International Peace, 2008).

15. Ethan Bronner, "Just How Far Did They Go, Those Words Against Israel?" *New York Times*, June 11, 2006, http://www.nytimes.com/2006/06/11/weekinreview/11bronner.html.

16. Death tolls are not always easy to estimate. Charles Kurzman of the University of North Carolina has analyzed census data in both countries which, he suggests, cast doubt on claims of more than a million deaths. "Death Tolls of the Iran-Iraq War," October 31, 2013, http://kurzman.unc.edu/death-tolls-of-the-iran-iraq-war/.

17. Department of State Cable from George P. Shultz to the United States Embassy in Sudan, "Briefing Notes for Rumsfeld Visit to Baghdad," March 24, 1984, http://www.gwu.edu/~nsarchiv/NSAEBB/NSAEBB82/iraq48.pdf; see also Christopher Marquis, "Rumsfeld Made Iraq Overture in '84 Despite Chemical

Raids," *New York Times*, December 23, 2003, http://www.nytimes.com/2003/12/23/world/struggle-for-iraq-documents-rumsfeld-made-iraq-overture-84-despite-chemical.html.

18. Ray Takeyh, *Guardians of the Revolution: Iran and the World in the Age of the Ayatollahs* (New York: Oxford University Press, 2009), p. 105.

19. Ibid., p. 212.

20. Trita Parsi, *Treacherous Alliance: The Secret Dealings of Israel, Iran, and the U.S.* (New Haven, CT: Yale University Press, 2008), pp. 243–249. The content and authenticity of the Iranian bid was confirmed by Guldiman in a communication with author.

21. Dennis Ross, *Doomed to Succeed: The U.S.-Israel Relationship from Truman to Obama* (New York: Farrar, Straus, and Giroux, 2015), p. 367.

22. Michael Crowley, "Plan B for Iran: If the Nuclear Negotiations Go Bad, the US Has a Backup: Obama Can Drop the MOP, the World's Largest Non-Nuclear Bomb," *Foreign Policy*, June 24, 2015, http://www.politico.com/magazine/story/2015/06/plan-b-for-iran-119344?o=2.

23. Authors' meeting with Ariel Levite, Tel Aviv, July 2009.

24. Authors' meeting with Shlomo Brom, Tel Aviv, July 2009.

25. Authors' interview with James Dobbins, Arlington, VA, July 2009.

26. Jeffrey Goldberg, "Obama to Iran and Israel: 'As President of the United States, I Don't Bluff,'" *Atlantic*, March 2, 2012, http://www.theatlantic.com/international/archive/2012/03/obama-to-iran-and-israel-as-president-of-the-united-states-i-dont-bluff/253875/.

27. "Remarks by the President at AIPAC Policy Conference," The White House, Office of the Press Secretary, March 4, 2012, https://www.whitehouse.gov/the-press-office/2012/03/04/remarks-president-aipac-policy-conference-0.

28. Ross, *Doomed to Succeed*, p. 369.

29. Adam Entous, "Spy vs. Spy: Inside the Fraying U.S.-Israel Ties," *Wall Street Journal*, October 22, 2015, http://www.wsj.com/articles/spy-vs-spy-inside-the-fraying-u-s-israel-ties-1445562074.

30. Ross, *Doomed to Succeed*, p. 369.

31. Indira A. R. Lakshmanan, "'If You Can't Do This Deal . . . Go Back to Tehran': The Inside Story of the Obama Administration's Iran Diplomacy," *Politico Magazine*, September 25, 2015, http://www.politico.com/magazine/story/2015/09/iran-deal-inside-story-213187.

32. Ibid.

33. Adam Entous, "Spy vs. Spy."

34. Ibid.

35. U.S. officials believed that Israelis including Israel's ambassador Ron Dermer used secret information, gleaned from its espionage against American targets, to

lobby the U.S. Congress against the emerging nuclear deal. Adam Entous, "Israel Spied on Iran Nuclear Talks with U.S.: Ally's Snooping Upset White House Because Information Was Used to Lobby Congress to Try to Sink a Deal," *Wall Street Journal*, March 23, 2015, http://www.wsj.com/articles/israel-spied-on-iran-talks-1427164201.

36. Graham Allison, "9 Reasons to Support the Iran Deal," *The Atlantic*, August 4, 2015, http://www.theatlantic.com/international/archive/2015/08/iran-nuclear-deal -reasons-support/400466/.

37. Stuart Winer, "Netanyahu: Iran Wants to 'Take Over the World,'" *Times of Israel*, July 7, 2015, http://www.timesofisrael.com/netanyahu-iran-wants-to-take -over-the-world/.

38. Karoun Demirjian and Carol Morello, "How AIPAC Lost the Iran Deal Fight," *Washington Post*, September 3, 2015, https://www.washingtonpost.com /news/powerpost/wp/2015/09/03/how-aipac-lost-the-iran-deal-fight/.

39. Adam Entous, "Inside Israel's Bid to Derail Iran Pact," *Wall Street Journal*, September 3, 2015, http://www.wsj.com/articles/inside-israels-bid-to-derail-iran -pact-1441329584.

40. Barak Ravid, "Iranian General Killed in Reported Israeli Strike on Hezbollah in Syria," *Haaretz*, January 19, 2015, http://www.haaretz.com/israel-news/1.637874.

41. Omar explained, according to the sources, that if he was known to have prayed there, his followers would want to erect a mosque on the site. Simon Sebag Montefiore, *Jerusalem: The Biography* (London: Weidenfeld & Nicolson, 2011), pp. 173–177.

42. Ibid.

43. As Peter Beinart observed, channelling Walter Russell Mead's famous categories, these heinous acts revived America's "Jacksonian" instincts—"the peculiar combination of jingoism and isolationism forged on the American frontier." Beinart, "Pursuing ISIS to the Gates of Hell," *The Atlantic*, September 4, 2014, http://www.theatlantic.com/international/archive/2014/09/why-americas-pursuing -isis-to-the-gates-of-hell/379622/?single_page=true.

44. Wesley Lowery, "Biden to Islamic State: We Will Follow You 'To the Gates of Hell,'" *Washington Post*, September 3, 2014, http://www.washingtonpost.com /blogs/post-politics/wp/2014/09/03/biden-to-islamic-state-we-will-follow-you-to -the-gates-of-hell/.

45. National Security Strategy, February 2015, www.whitehouse.gov/sites/default /files/docs/2015_national_security_strategy_2.pdf. President Obama defended the doctrine in his January 20, 2015, State of the Union Address. "When we make rash decisions, reacting to the headlines instead of using our heads; when the first response to a challenge is to send in our military—then we risk getting drawn into unnecessary conflicts, and neglect the broader strategy we need for a safer, more prosperous world. That's what our enemies want us to do." http://www.whitehouse.gov/the -press-office/2015/01/20/remarks-president-state-union-address-january-20-2015.

46. Conversation with author. See also Peter Beinart, "Face It: U.S. and Israel Don't Have the Same Interests," *Haaretz*, July 15, 2015, http://www.haaretz.com /opinion/.premium-1.666211.

47. General David Petraeus was among many who warned that the United States could not find itself acting as "the air force of Shia militias or a Shia on Sunni Arab fight." http://www.nbcnews.com/storyline/iraq-turmoil/david-petraeus-u -s-cant-be-air-force-iraqs-militias-n135311.

48. The rebalancing rhetoric, first invoked by Secretary of State Hillary Clinton (she used the word "pivot") and President Barack Obama in the autumn of 2011 but actually a continuation of their predecessors' policies, can have both good and bad consequences. On the positive side, it is a statement of some obvious realities: U.S. resources are limited, strategy means setting priorities, the region with half the world's population is of huge importance (economic and otherwise) to America, and wisdom in managing relations with China could be the single most important factor in avoiding great-power war in the twenty-first century. It is also, as a Pentagon interlocutor reminded one of us, a necessary signal for the purposes of bureaucratic policy-setting within a massive U.S. Defense Department that contains competing armed services and eternal problems of profligacy and inertia. The bad consequences flow from the fact that simple statements of strategic purpose can be understood differently by different foreign audiences. So, for example, at the 2013 Shangri-La conference, then Defense Secretary Chuck Hagel insisted that the "rebalancing should not . . . be misinterpreted. The US has allies, interests and responsibilities around the globe. The Asia-Pacific rebalance is not a retreat from other regions of the world." Such statements have not prevented anxious Gulf Arab countries from adding an exaggerated interpretation of the rebalance to their accumulated anxieties about the future U.S. presence in the Gulf—even though that presence is, and will almost certainly remain, immense.

49. "Russia and the West: A New Cold War," April 15, 2015, https://www.iiss.org /en/events/events/archive/2015-f463/april-09d7/a-new-cold-war-6a8f.

50. "Saudi Arabia Warns of Shift Away from US Over Syria, Iran," *Reuters*, October 22, 2013, http://www.voanews.com/content/reu-saudi-arabia-us-relations -syria-iran/1774995.html.

51. Eric Schmitt and Tim Arango, "Billions from U.S. Fail to Sustain Foreign Forces," *New York Times*, October 3, 2015, http://www.nytimes.com/2015/10/04 /world/middleeast/uss-billions-fail-to-sustain-foreign-forces.html?_r=0.

52. Fareed Zakaria, "In Syria, Whose Side Is the United States On?" *Washington Post*, October 1, 2015, https://www.washingtonpost.com/opinions/in-syria-whose -side-is-the-united-states-on/2015/10/01/27163ec4-6875-11e5-9ef3-fde182507eac _story.html.

53. Warren Bass, *Support Any Friend: Kennedy's Middle East and the Making of the U.S.-Israel Alliance* (New York: Oxford University Press, 2003), pp. 186–238; Avner Cohen, *Israel and the Bomb* (New York: Columbia University Press, 1998); Amir Oren, "How Israel's Dimona Nuclear Reactor Was Concealed from the U.S.," *Haaretz*, April 15, 2015.

54. Adam Entous, "Gaza Crisis: Israel Outflanks the White House on Strategy," *Wall Street Journal*, August, 14, 2014, http://www.wsj.com/article_email/u-s-sway -over-israel-on-gaza-at-a-low-1407979365-lMyQjAxMTA2MDIwNTEyNDUyWj.

Chapter 7

1. "Statement to the Knesset by Prime Minister Begin upon the Presentation of His Government," June 20, 1977, Israel Ministry of Foreign Affairs, http://www.mfa.gov.il/mfa/foreignpolicy/mfadocuments/yearbook3/pages/1%20 statement%20to%20the%20%20knesset%20by%20prime%20minister%20begi .aspx.

2. Ze'ev Schiff and Ehud Ya'ari, *Israel's Lebanon War* (New York: Simon & Schuster, 1984), p. 221.

3. Ibid, p. 228.

4. For a broad historical account, see Guy Ben-Porat, Yagil Levy, Shlomo Mizrahi, Arye Naor, and Erez Tzfadia, *Israel Since 1980* (Cambridge: Cambridge University Press, 2008).

5. Aaron David Miller, "What Would Have Happened if Yitzhak Rabin Had Lived?" *Foreign Policy*, November 3, 2015, https://foreignpolicy.com/2015/11/03 /what-would-have-happened-if-yitzhak-rabin-had-lived-israel-palestine -peace/.

6. Genesis 1:28.

7. Asher Arian, Tamar Hermann, Yuval Lebel, Michael Philippov, Hila Zaban, and Anna Knafelman, *Auditing Israeli Democracy—2010 Democratic Values in Practice* (Jerusalem: Israel Democracy Institute, 2010), p. ix.

8. Dror Etkes and Laura Friedman, "The Ultra-Orthodox Jews in the West Bank," *PeaceNow*, January 23, 2016, http://peacenow.org.il/eng/content/ultra -orthodox-jews-west-bank.

9. Shlomo Swirski and Etty Konor-Atias "Inequality in Central Government Transfers to Municipalities," Adva Center, September 9, 2014, http://adva.org/en /post-slug-1816/.

10. Ibid.

11. Chaim Levinson, "Is Netanyahu Responsible for Rise in Settler Numbers?" *Haaretz*, October 14, 2015, http://www.haaretz.com/news/diplomacy-defense/ .premium-1.680304.

12. Tamar Hermann et al., *The National-Religious Sector in Israel 2014: Main Findings* (Jerusalem: Israel Democracy Institute, 2014), p. 9, http://en.idi.org.il/media/3863902/Madad-Z-English_WEB.pdf.

13. Ibid., p.45.

14. Ibid., p. 8.

15. Ibid., p. 12.

16. "The Role of Hovshei Kipot in the IDF's Tactical Command," *Maarachot* 432 (2010): 53, http://maarachot.idf.il/PDF/FILES/0/112470.pdf.

17. OECD, "PISA 2012 Results in Focus: What 15-Year-Olds Know and What They Can Do with What They Know," http://www.oecd.org/pisa/keyfindings/pisa-2012-results-overview.pdf.

18. Josie Gurney-Read, "OECD League Table: English Pupil 11th in Job Skills Ranking," *The Telegraph*, April 1, 2014, http://www.telegraph.co.uk/education/league tables/10734609/OECD-league-table-English-pupils-11th-in-job-skills-ranking.html.

19. Or Kashti, "Poll: Young Israelis Moving Much Farther to the Right Politically," *Hazaretz*, March 31, 2011, http://www.haaretz.com/print-edition/news/poll-young-israelis-moving-much-farther-to-the-right-politically-1.353187.

20. C. Friedrich-Ebert-Stiftung and Macro Center for Political Economics, "All of the Above: Identity 4. Paradoxes of Young People in Israel (the 3rd Youth Study): Changes in National, Societal, and Personal Attitudes," Herzliya, Israel, March 31, 2011 (excerpts), *Journal of Palestine Studies* 40, no. 4 (Summer 2011): 214–217.

21. Arian, Hermann,Lebel, Philippov, Zaban, and Knafelman, *Auditing Israeli Democracy*, p. v.

22. Dan Ben-David, *The Shoresh Handbook on Israel's Society and Economy* (Jerusalem: Shoresh Institution for Socioeconomic Research, 2015), p. 36, http://shoresh.institute/ShoreshHandbook2015-English.pdf.

23. Ibid., p. 37.

24. Dan Senor and Saul Singer, *Start-Up Nation: The Story of Israel's Economic Miracle* (New York: Warner Books, 2011).

25. It could even be argued that the success enjoyed by Israeli high-tech, especially in the cyber arena, is owing to education and training subsidized or provided for soldiers in elite techno-war military organizations, such as Talpiyot and Unit 8200, whose graduates populate a range of inventive—and profitable—companies.

26. Ben-David, *The Shoresh Handbook on Israel's Society and Economy*, p. 60.

27. Ibid., p. 62.

28. Ibid., p. 64.

29. Chuck Freilich, "AIPAC Had No Choice," *Jerusalem Post*, October 8, 2015.

30. Phil Weiss and Annie Robbins, "Video: Israel's Celebrated Labour Party 'Is the Mother and Father of Racism,' Says Member of Knesset," *Mondoweis*, September 12, 2015, http://mondoweiss.net/2015/09/israels-celebrated-knesset.

31. Donald Horowitz, "Ethnic Power Sharing: Three Big Problems," *Journal of Democracy* 24, no. 2 (April 2014), http://www.journalofdemocracy.org/sites /default/files/Horowitz-25-2.pdf.

32. Michael N. Barnett, "Thinking Beyond the Two-State Solution," *Washington Post,* August 25, 2015, https://www.washingtonpost.com/blogs/monkey-cage /wp/2015/08/25/thinking-beyond-the-two-state-solution/. Already, as Barnett notes, the share of Israeli Jews who place equal value on the state's Jewish and democratic character has fallen from 48 percent in 2010 to 24 percent in 2014. It would also be unwise to expect that the periodic eruptions of violence will reduce Israelis to despair and then to compromise. The fact is that Israelis are pretty happy despite the grinding conflict in which they are entangled. A RAND Corporation study of the cost of the conflict to Israelis and Palestinians anticipated psychological costs that would compound the significant quantifiable costs estimated by the economists on the study team. The actual research confounded this expectation. Rates of depression and anxiety among Jewish Israelis are no better or worse than those in Western Europe. And opinion surveys routinely show that Israelis express much higher levels of life satisfaction and personal happiness than among their regional neighbors. These feelings of psychological well-being coincide with a tremendous pride in being Israeli among almost all sectors of the population. These are not a people beset by self-doubt or on the verge of crisis of confidence. For U.S. policymakers dreaming of powerfully effective appeals to the Israeli people over the heads of misdirected leaders, these facts merit close attention. See Daphna Levinson, Nelly Zilber, Yaacov Lerner, Alexander Grinshpoon, and Itzhak Levav, "Prevalence of Mood and Anxiety Disorders in the Community: Results from the Israel National Health Survey," *Israel Journal of Psychiatry and Related Sciences* 44, no. 2 (2007): 94–103.

33. Karoun Demirjian and Carol Morello, "How AIPAC Lost the Iran Deal Fight," *Washington Post,* September 3, 2015, https://www.washingtonpost.com /news/powerpost/wp/2015/09/03/how-aipac-lost-the-iran-deal-fight/.

34. David Petraeus, "Statement Before the Senate Armed Services Committee," Washington, DC, March 16, 2009, cited in Dennis Ross, *Doomed to Succeed: The U.S.-Israel Relationship from Truman to Obama* (New York: Farrar, Straus, and Giroux, 2015), p. 348.

35. Conversation with authors, Tel Aviv, October 2013.

36. Ross, *Doomed to Succeed,* p. 348.

37. Cited in ibid., p. 74.

38. Ibid., p. 362.

39. James Dobbins, conversation with author, Arlington, VA, November 2014.

40. John B. Judis and Ruy A. Teixeira, *The Emerging Democratic Majority* (New York: Scribner, 2002), p. 2.

41. A case that American political polarization stems mainly from a Republican party moving much further to the right was laid out by Thomas E. Mann and Norman J. Ornstein, *It's Even Worse Than It Looks: How the American Constitutional System Collided with the New Politics of Extremism* (New York: Basic Books, 2012).

42. Peter Beinart, "The Failure of the American Jewish Establishment," *New York Review of Books*, June 10, 2010, http://www.nybooks.com/articles/2010/06/10/failure-american-jewish-establishment/.

43. Steven M. Cohen, "What Is to Be Done? Policy Responses to the Shrinking Jewish Middle." *Berman Jewish Policy Archive*, New York University, June 25, 2014, pp. 3, 4, http://www.bjpa.org/publications/downloadFile.cfm?FileID=21111.

44. Owen Alterman and Cameron S. Brown, "Support for Israel in a Changing America," *Strategic Assessment* 15, no. 4 (January 2013): 11–14.

45. On American Hispanics' attitudes toward Israel, see Alterman and Brown, "Support for Israel in a Changing America," pp. 14, 15.

46. Melani McAlisster, *Epic Encounters: Culture, Media, and U.S. Interests in the Middle East Since 1945* (Oakland: University of California Press, 2005), chapter 4.

47. Conversation with author, Hanover, NH, August 2015.

48. Paul Krugman, "Israel's Gilded Age," *New York Times*, March 16, 2015, http://www.nytimes.com/2015/03/16/opinion/paul-krugman-israels-gilded-age.html.

49. Ibid.

50. Michael Oren, *Ally: My Journey Across the American-Israeli Divide* (New York: Ballentine Books, 2015), pp. 92–99, 267–268. One of Oren's targets, the famously pro-Zionist (but also Netanyahu-critical) writer Leon Wieseltier, dispatched the suggestion rather well: "Speaking only for myself, I have searched my heart and am pretty satisfied that I have not carped about Netanyahu because I want to be asked into the Metropolitan Club." Wieseltier, "On Jewish Dissent," *The Atlantic*, June 28, 2015, http://www.theatlantic.com/international/archive/2015/06/michael-oren-israel-jews/397043/.

51. Oren, *Ally*, p. 233; Jeffrey Goldberg, "A Former Israeli Ambassador Takes Aim at Obama—and American Jewry," *The Atlantic*, June 29, 2015, http://www.theatlantic.com/international/archive/2015/06/michael-oren-interview-obama-israel/396896/.

52. "So what's with all the torn-between-two-Muslim-daddies psychobabble about Obama?" asked *Atlantic* journalist Jeffrey Goldberg in an interview with Oren, before making the obvious point that "Any president who followed George W. Bush would have sought to reset relations with the Muslim world, with Muslim nations, just to try to lower the temperature." Goldberg, "A Former Israeli Ambassador Takes Aim at Obama—and American Jewry."

53. Allison Kaplan Sommer, "Former Netanyahu Aide Calls U.S. Ambassador to Israel 'Jew Boy,'" *Haaretz*, January 19, 2016, http://www.haaretz.com/israel-news /.premium-1.698358.

54. Rebecca Shimoni Stoil, "Kerry Blasts 'Reprehensible Attacks' on Civilians," *Times of Israel*, October 15, 2015, http://www.timesofisrael.com/kerry-blasts -reprehensible-attacks-on-civilians/.

55. Adam Entous, "Spy-vs.-Spy: Inside the Fraying US-Israel Ties," *Wall Street Journal*, October 22, 2015, http://www.wsj.com/articles/spy-vs-spy-inside-the -fraying-u-s-israel-ties-1445562074.

Chapter 8

1. For example, Martin Peretz, longtime publisher of *The New Republic*, called him "neo-fascist . . . a certified gangster . . . the Israeli equivalent of [Austria's] Jörg Haider." Fareed Zakaria, "Zakaria on Avigdor Lieberman and Israel's Arabs," *Newsweek*, February 14, 2009.

2. "Israel Hails India's Abstention at UN Vote on Gaza War Report," i24news, July 5, 2015, http://www.i24news.tv/en/news/international/77241-150705-india -abstains-from-unhcr-vote-sign-of-golden-age-in-relationship-with-israel.

3. Indyk said the attitude reminded him of the period "before the 1973 war, when Israelis felt they were the superpower in the region and so didn't have to worry about support from the United States. And it turned on a dime once Egypt and Syria attacked Israel by surprise on Yom Kippur in 1973, and suddenly Israel found itself totally dependent on the United States. So it may be that the bubble of illusion will burst here too and Israeli politicians on the right will come to understand that for all their bravado, the United States is not just Israel's most important friend but in a real crunch its only reliable friend." http://www.brookings.edu /research/interviews/2014/08/26-us-israel-relationship-indyk-rothkopf.

4. Ze'ev Schiff and Ehud Ya'ari, *Israel's Lebanon War* (New York: Simon & Schuster, 1984), pp. 164–168.

5. Hillary Clinton, "Taking the U.S.-Israel Relationship to the Next 'Level,'" *Jewish Journal*, January 6, 2016, http://www.jewishjournal.com/opinion/article /hillary_clinton_taking_the_u.s._israel_relationship_to_the_next_level.

6. "Oliver Miles: The Key Question; Is Blair a War Criminal?" *Independent*, November 21, 2009, http://www.independent.co.uk/voices/commentators/oliver -miles-the-key-question-ndash-is-blair-a-war-criminal-1825374.html; http://www .independent.co.uk/voices/columnists/richard-ingrams/richard-ingramsrsquos -week-will-zionists-links-to-iraq-invasion-be-brushed-aside-1829896.html.

7. Jeffrey Goldberg, "French Prime Minister: If Jews Flee, the Republic Will Be a Failure," *The Atlantic*, January 10, 2015, http://www.theatlantic.com/international

/archive/2015/01/french-prime-minister-warns-if-jews-flee-the-republic-will-be
-judged-a-failure/384410/.

8. Peter Beinart, *The Crisis of Zionism* (New York: Times Books, 2012), p. 11.

9. Donald Trump, campaigning in late 2015 in the Republican presidential primary campaign, said he would "go after" the family members of Islamist terrorists because those family members "know what's happening." In a CBS News
interview aired on December 6, 2015, in reference to the September 11 hijackers,
he insisted: "At least I would certainly go after the wives who absolutely knew it
was happening, and I guess your definition of what I'd do, I'm going to leave that
to your imagination." (Most of the hijackers were, in fact, unmarried.) For decades Israel has punished family members of terrorists by demolishing their
houses. On Trump, see http://www.cbsnews.com/news/donald-trumps-latest-911
-claim-draws-more-scrutiny.

10. Yair Evron, "An Israel-United States Defense Pact," *Strategic Assessment* 1,
no. 3 (November 1998): 12–15.

11. Ibid., pp. 12, 13.

12. Brucee Riedel, "Camp David—The US-Israeli Bargain," *Bitter Lemons*, Edition
26 (July 15, 2002), http://www.bitterlemons.org/previous/bl150702ed26extra.html.

13. Dore Gold, "Is Mutual Defense Treaty Between Israel, U.S. Needed?—Proceed
with Caution," Jweekly.com, December 22, 1995, http://www.jweekly.com/article
/full/2209/is-mutual-defense-treaty-between-israel-u-s-needed-proceed-with
-caution/.

14. Evron, "An Israel-United States Defense Pact?"

15. Israel, of course, is not in Europe, which is a geographical criterion for membership. But depending on how one reads the map, neither is EU member Cyprus.

16. Senem Aydin and E. Fuat Keyman, "European Integration and the Transformation of Turkish Democracy," *EU-Turkey Working Paper No. 2*, August 2004,
accessed at www.ceps.be.

17. Ehud Barak, a supporter of the aborted bombing campaign, revealed the
cabinet debate in interview tapes that his biographer released, against his wishes,
because of a dispute over rights to the English edition of the biography. http://
www.timesofisrael.com/barak-netanyahu-wanted-to-strike-iran-in-2010-and
-2011-but-colleagues-blocked-him.

18. Unless the peace agreement included workable provisions for the security
of settlers who were offered and accepted Palestinian citizenship under the terms
of the deal. But that too would be an extraordinarily daunting challenge.

19. George F. Kennan, Lecture at Joint Orientation Conference, Pentagon,
November 8, 1948, cited in John Gaddis, *Strategies of Containment: A Critical Ap-
praisal of Postwar American National Security Strategy* (New York: Oxford
University Press, 1982), p. 45.

Index

Credit: Virginia Liberatore

STEVEN N. SIMON served on the National Security Council as a senior director for Middle Eastern and North African affairs. He is coauthor of numerous books including *The Age of Sacred Terror*, winner of the Arthur Ross Book Award, and *The Next Attack*, a finalist for the Lionel Gelber Prize. He is a lecturer at Dartmouth College and lives in Norwich, Vermont.

Credit: IISS

DANA H. ALLIN is a senior fellow at the International Institute for Strategic Studies and editor of *Survival*. He is an adjunct professor at the SAIS Europe center of the Johns Hopkins University School of Advanced International Studies in Bologna, Italy; he also taught for several years at the SAIS campus in Washington, D.C. He is the author or coauthor of five previous books, including *Cold War Illusions*, *Weary Policeman*, and *The Sixth Crisis*. Allin was previously Deputy Director of the Aspen Institute Berlin and a newspaper and financial news journalist. He lives in London.

PublicAffairs is a publishing house founded in 1997. It is a tribute to the standards, values, and flair of three persons who have served as mentors to countless reporters, writers, editors, and book people of all kinds, including me.

I. F. STONE, proprietor of *I. F. Stone's Weekly*, combined a commitment to the First Amendment with entrepreneurial zeal and reporting skill and became one of the great independent journalists in American history. At the age of eighty, Izzy published *The Trial of Socrates*, which was a national bestseller. He wrote the book after he taught himself ancient Greek.

BENJAMIN C. BRADLEE was for nearly thirty years the charismatic editorial leader of *The Washington Post*. It was Ben who gave the *Post* the range and courage to pursue such historic issues as Watergate. He supported his reporters with a tenacity that made them fearless and it is no accident that so many became authors of influential, best-selling books.

ROBERT L. BERNSTEIN, the chief executive of Random House for more than a quarter century, guided one of the nation's premier publishing houses. Bob was personally responsible for many books of political dissent and argument that challenged tyranny around the globe. He is also the founder and longtime chair of Human Rights Watch, one of the most respected human rights organizations in the world.

·   ·   ·

For fifty years, the banner of Public Affairs Press was carried by its owner Morris B. Schnapper, who published Gandhi, Nasser, Toynbee, Truman, and about 1,500 other authors. In 1983, Schnapper was described by *The Washington Post* as "a redoubtable gadfly." His legacy will endure in the books to come.

Peter Osnos, *Founder and Editor-at-Large*